D1710254

The Afternoon Tea Cookbook

Also by Linda Hewitt:

All About Auctions
Chippendale and All the Rest

The Afternoon Tea Cookbook

Linda Hewitt

Illustrations by
Robert G. Hewitt

STEIN AND DAY/Publishers/New York

First published in 1982
Copyright © 1982 by Linda G. Hewitt
All rights reserved
Designed by Louis A. Ditizio
Printed in the United States of America
STEIN AND DAY/*Publishers*
Scarborough House
Briarcliff Manor, N.Y. 10510

Library of Congress Cataloging in Publication Data

Hewitt, Linda,
    The afternoon tea cookbook.

    Includes indexes.
    1. Cookery.   2. Tea.   3. Entertaining.
I. Hewitt, Robert G.   II. Title.
TX652.H48   641.5'3   80-6212
ISBN 0-8128-2801-1   AACR2

For
my Mother

Good cook, good sport,
and
fellow tea lover

CONTENTS

The Afternoon Tea Cookbook

ACKNOWLEDGMENTS

Thanks are due to Pat Bell, Ruth Hannah, and Gene Witherspoon for their inspiration, to Carrie Baker, Ethel Love, and Maggie McLendon, who live in happy memory, and most particularly to my mother, Evelyn McLendon Love, a naturally gifted cook who makes good food a natural part of life. Very special thanks are owed to my editor, Benton Arnovitz, for his timely suggestions.

1

Tea and bread by the fire.

PREFACE

This is a cookbook, that one form of prose Joseph Conrad held to be above suspicion because its sole purpose is the enhancement of life. It is, specifically, a book about tea, "the muse's nectar," about how it became the most popular drink in the world save water, and about tea drinking's evolution into afternoon tea—that small meal, the one all the more satisfying because it is not essential to either the culinary or the social scheme of things.

Like all refinements, afternoon tea is a product of the past. And at its best it incorporates the best of that past—from the beauty and emotional kinship of the Japanese tea ceremony to the delectable cuisine and kindliness of English teatime. This book melds the traditions of both cultures with our American way of doing things, offering practical suggestions for making this special form of hospitality distinctively your own, and sharing over one hundred new and traditional recipes tested and scaled for the smaller guest list.

As you turn these pages, forget the intimidating tea party. Here you will find no reception lines, no be-hatted, be-gloved, daintily mannered

3

women, no ill-at-ease men juggling stale petits fours and fragile teacups. Here there is no pretension and no stuffiness, only a way of entertaining that perfectly suits the American preference for intimacy and for food that is fun both to make and to eat, that allows us to be as elegant or as casual, as lavish or as frugal as we choose.

This is a work on good food, good times, and good feelings, about something that we do because we find it pleasing, with people we choose to see rather than feel we must, and with food and drink that are offered only because they afford the eye and the palate the most agreeable sensations. Here is a reminder that in a world of pressing occupations and causes, we still have personal lives to be led and that we owe it to ourselves and to those around us to live as well as possible. Finally, this is a book about friends, about fellowship, and about the ambience in which they flourish.

PART I

In Which the Past is Prologue

· 1 ·

Tea

The name even *sounds* good: *Camellia sinensis* to botanists. *Chah* in the Cantonese dialect, *tay* in the Amoy, and *Cha* in Japanese. Tea to you and me.

We call it tea because it was the Dutch who sold the English their first tea. Two of their sources for the valuable leaf were the Bantam on Malay, who called it *te* and *teh*, and Formosan traders, who used the Chinese Amoy dialect term *t'e*, pronounced *tay*. It was one variation or another of these terms by which the leaf was known when it reached Holland and was transshipped by the Dutch to other Europeans and to the English. In England it was first known as *tay*, then *tee* and—finally —*tea*.

A pretty plant, it grows wild in odd corners of Asia to the size of a standard apple tree, about thirty feet. It's an evergreen with dark green, lance-shaped leaves and fragrant cream-colored blossoms. As a commercial crop grown in warm, rainy climates on well-drained soil, it is kept pruned to a height of no more than five feet and produces its prized leaves for as long as fifty years. It is propagated from smooth, dark brown seeds one-half inch in diameter.

In the service of these seeds, centuries of explorers explored, emperors endorsed, seafarers sailed, experts experimented, and planters produced. Even now tea retains an exotic quality, a suggestion of the distant. In a time where so much of what we eat and drink comes from no place in particular, tea has very definite origins, and in them we touch worlds older than and far different from our own. Sri Lanka, India, Indonesia, Formosa—between them suppliers of most of the Western world's teas, their very names are romance.

As for "all the tea in China," today most of it is brewed in Chinese pots. For centuries the world's chief supplier and inextricably linked with tea in the mind of the West, China grows only about a third as much tea as it did forty-five years ago, and very little of it is exported.

It was in China that farmers first cultivated tea, in the fourth century A.D. Until then, they had simply cut down wild tea trees and stripped the leaves from the fallen branches. Increasing demand made this happy-go-lucky harvesting impractical, and a primitive but less wasteful way of ensuring a supply of tea leaves began to develop.

In spite of the fact that tea grew wild in other parts of Asia, most notably in Assam on China's southwestern border with India, cultivation remained a Chinese monopoly until the eighth century when a Japanese emperor started handing out free tea samples and encouraging the planting of tea shrubs.

Japan continued to cultivate tea, but it was a thousand years before anyone else would make the attempt. So much time went by because China sold tea to its neighbors when they wanted it and because the West did not learn of the beverage until the sixteenth century. Even after that the distance between Europe and the Orient, and China's efforts to keep the relatively complex tea manufacturing process secret, discouraged would-be imitators. Once tea had become popular in the West, the powerful British trading company that held the monopoly of trade with China knew what a money-maker it had in Chinese tea and used its considerable political and monetary muscle to discourage its commercial cultivation elsewhere.

It was in America, a continent unsuspected when tea became the drink of China and Japan, that a French botanist tried his luck at tea cultivation, setting up his experiment near Charleston, South Carolina, where conditions seemed promising. How he might have fared remains a mystery because his timing was bad—1775, two years after the Boston Tea Party and just at the beginning of the American Revolution—and the experiment was abandoned when he returned to France. In retrospect this aborted attempt in America seems to have been the signal for the start of a race to see where tea would be established next. Made more interesting by the British East India Company's loss of its monopolies in the China and India trade, the race was between two great colonial powers, Britain and Holland, and it involved some gambles that didn't pay off, some that did, and not inconsiderable chicanery mixed with danger.

China, embittered by centuries of exploitation and manipulation by the West, had ordered foreigners not to enter its interior. Defying this edict, a tea expert and adventurer hired by the Dutch government invaded the forbidden zone and spirited away from the tea plantations 7 million seeds and several experienced workers. Infuriated, the Chinese government outlawed the Dutchman and offered a reward for his death. Escaping the mandarins, he sailed his seeds and the Chinese workers to Java in the Dutch East Indies (now Indonesia). The seeds flourished, but the resulting plants produced an unpleasant tasting tea that no one would buy.

In India the British were having no better luck with seeds imported from China. Tea, considered god-given by the Chinese, was not producing in the Western-controlled lands to which it had been carried, leading to a suspicion that perhaps it really was not meant to be taken out of China. But in the end colonial tenacity conquered superstition. As early as 1823 an Englishman had found wild tea plants in the hills of Assam in northeastern India, and somewhat later a successful effort was made to find wild colonies in the jungles of the area, to reclaim them, and to harvest a tea crop. It was from the seeds of these Assam plants that the Indian tea industry grew. By 1838 the first shipments of Indian tea were arriving in London for sale, and the fledgling industry found itself an immediate success, an enviable position that it has maintained.

Meanwhile, in Java, things weren't going well. Javanese tea's bitter taste did not improve, and the 1870s found the industry about to go under. As a last-ditch effort Java planters imitated their successful Indian counterparts and planted some of the Assam seeds. The gamble paid off with spectacular speed, so much so that Sumatra, Java's neighbor to the west, imported seeds and began planting, also successfully.

Ceylon (now Sri Lanka), which floats off India in the Indian Ocean, hadn't been interested in tea. It hadn't any reason to be, for it had a lucrative trade in coffee. But in 1877 a blight wiped out the coffee plants, and desperate British colonists began to plant tea, which proved an almost overnight salvation for their beleaguered plantations.

Formosa (now Taiwan) became a major tea producer when refugees from the Chinese mainland arrived after the Communist Revolution in the late 1940s. It turned out that this beautiful island was ideal terrain for cultivating several of the teas the exiles could no longer obtain from the original sources, and in some instances they produced a tea superior to what they had left behind.

In order, the major producers of tea today are: India, Sri Lanka, China, Japan, Indonesia, the Soviet Union, and Taiwan. Between them, India and Sri Lanka provide over half the tea imported by other nations. Like China, Russia keeps its tea at home. Japan exports a small amount, but imports more than it exports, much of it from Great Britain, still a clearinghouse for tea.

In this century commercial tea production has spread further afield—to the Middle East, to Africa, and to South America—although none of these areas has yet made a significant addition to the world supply. One country to which the industry has not spread, in spite of several attempts in the nineteenth and early twentieth centuries, is the United States; and the cheap labor required for competitive tea manufacture makes its later introduction here unlikely.

A lot of labor is involved. Harvesting of the leaf is still done by hand. For the finest quality tea only the one or two youngest shoots are ordinarily plucked, together with their immature, unopened buds. The goal of plucking, whether of the youngest leaves or of the more mature ones that go into other grades, is to harvest leaves of the same size. This simplifies the process of turning the leaves into tea.

The manufacturing is very important, for all tea comes from the same basic plant. What makes one tea different from another are the growing and harvesting conditions and the manufacturing process to which it is subjected.

To begin with, in China, the leaves were formed into cakes, which were roasted until red-brown, then cooled and crushed. As might be expected in fifteen hundred years, techniques have been refined, and there are now three basic types of tea, depending on the manufacturing process used: black, green, and oolong.

To produce black tea, the leaves are first dried, or withered, to evaporate any moisture and make them pliable for rolling, which is the next step, during which they are crushed to release their juices. The lumps formed during rolling are then broken up, the leaves are spread, and fermentation begins, an interval that allows oxidation to take place.

Picking tea in China.

It is this step that produces the distinctive taste and color that we associate with black teas. The leaves are then fired by a blast of hot, dry air to end the fermentation. Most black teas are made in India, Sri Lanka, China, and Indonesia. Some of the world's most prized teas are blacks, including Darjeeling, Assam, Ceylon, Orange Pekoe, Keemun, and Lapsang Souchong.

Green tea, which is made primarily in Japan, China, and Taiwan, undergoes a somewhat different process. Rather than being dried as is black tea, it is steamed before being rolled. There is no fermentation period, and the leaf remains green after firing. The point of the process is to concentrate the oils and tannins present in the leaf, rather than allow oxidation to alter them. The best known greens are Gunpowder and Imperial.

Oolong tea, made in Taiwan and China, is manufactured by a process that falls between those for blacks and greens. It is withered, but only lightly, then rolled, fermented, fired, fermented again briefly, then fired, and re-fired. The purpose is to produce a tea that has much of the body and flavor associated with blacks, yet with the delicacy and fragrance more usually found in the green teas. As even this capsule description suggests, this is a much trickier process than either of the others. Best known of this type is Formosa Oolong.

After the tea passes through one of these processes it is graded. Before China ceded its leadership role in the world of tea, its tea merchants recognized several thousand different grades. Today's system, though much less comprehensive, is scarcely more comprehensible to the layperson. Black tea is graded only by size of leaf, green tea by age and type of leaf, and oolong strictly on the basis of quality. Grade is therefore not necessarily a guide to quality in blacks and greens, but it is in oolongs.

When the leaves have been graded, what is left is steamed and molded to form bricks, an old method of manufacturing that produces tea in a form still popular in Russia and Tibet. In China, where tea manufacturing began, the ancient method of making cakes using bitter leaf remnants continues along with more modern processes. At the end of the grading process, there remains in the sorting machines only tea fluff, particles sold for commercial caffeine used mostly in making medicines.

As for the graded leaves, they are packed in half or whole tea chests. Once made of exotic woods and lead-lined, today they are made of plywood lined with aluminum foil. A tea chest will hold from eighty to one hundred and thirty pounds, depending on leaf size. The chests go to a tea center for auction unless the crop was contracted for in advance. Most centers are in countries that produce tea, but London remains the most important because of its long-standing domination of the tea market. In effect, London auctions set world tea prices because so much is bought and sold there.

Much as wine buyers must be able to understand the qualities of any vintage, successful tea buyers must be able to "read" the leaf—recognizing its geographical origin, whether it was grown in a dry or wet season, in a shaded or open location, the type of the pluck, and the quality of the manufacturing process. These details determine the quality of the tea, distinguishing a mediocre tea from a superior one and a superior from one that is exceptional.

A few of the finest or most distinctive teas are sold "straight," but most of the teas that consumers buy are blends, created from the three basic types of black, green, and oolong. A blend combines two or more teas to make a beverage incorporating the characteristics of each. A tea merchant catering to a small clientele familiar with the qualities of individual teas might, for example, blend Ceylon and Assam, both blacks, for a particularly robust brew. A mass marketer selling to a large number of casual tea drinkers creates a different sort of blend, the aim not so much to produce a particularly distinctive combination as to allow the company to offer what tastes like the same tea year after year. A clever blend gives a mass-market merchant the flexibility that will allow him to alter the combination without affecting its general quality. This is important to a mass marketer because the price or availability of one or more of the teas that go into the blend may change from season to season, making the component tea or teas difficult or even impossible to obtain. This is why mass-market blends contain as many as twenty different teas. Since no one tea is that crucial to the end result, substitutions are much easier to make without the customer noticing any difference. It is possible, of course, to create an almost endless number of blends.

Most tea-drinking Americans are familiar only with blends because few buy anything but mass-market tea products. The recent success of spiced and scented teas shows how ready the American tea fancier is to try something other than the blend of blacks that has come to dominate this market in the last fifty years. Perhaps green teas, which once accounted for much of the market and are now rarely seen at all in this country, will make a comeback.

So far we have examined only so-called true tea, that is, tea made from the leaf of *camellia sinensis,* but to stop there would be to ignore a large and growing body of teas made worldwide from the leaves or flowers of many other plants. These substances, sometimes called tisanes, have always been made, either because they were preferred or because true tea was not available.

Through history, almost any leaf that would brew in water and wasn't poisonous has been made into a tea that somebody, somewhere, drank as enthusiastically as the connoisseur drank the finest, rarest true teas. American pioneers made tea from dried and ground corn, among other things. In Paraguay and Brazil a drink called Maté derives from wild holly leaves. The roasted leaves of coffee plants are sometimes used in Java. Tea is also made from orchids, strawberry leaves, purple lilac, hawthorn, meadow hay, and myrtle, as well as many other plants.

More and more people, especially in the United States, are turning to herb teas, some because they like the taste or believe herbs to be healthier; others because they cannot tolerate the caffeine in true tea. Some of the more popular herb teas are camomile, rose hip, mint, lemon balm, and sarsaparilla. Also now widely available are some new herb blends, some of them as delicate as a whiff of lavender, others potent enough to make the unsuspecting gasp.

You cannot always tell the tea that you are buying by the name; you cannot even tell whether it's a true tea or a herb. Orange spice tea, for example, may be either a blend of black teas scented with spices and orange, or it may be—to cite the ingredient label of a popular herb tea—a combination of wood betony, orange peel, dandelion, and cloves. The names of true teas may reflect color, grade, geographical origin, or a vivid imagination on the part of the marketer. Pekoe, for instance, refers to a leaf grade of black tea. Darjeeling, on the other hand, which is the name of another black tea, derives from the area where it is grown, a town in the foothills of the Indian Himalayas; while Gunpowder Green reflects both the grade of tea and the color of one of the best of the greens.

More poetic are names given because they took someone's fancy. The Chinese, past masters of tea nomenclature, have at one time or another come up with names so delightful that you wonder if the tea could possibly live up to the expectations aroused—Pure Delight and Pearl Dew, to take only two examples. On a more ambiguous note, the Chinese have also given us Green Water Nymph and Eyelashes of the Swan and—sternly—Iron Goddess of Mercy. American manufacturers of herb teas are growing almost equally imaginative. How could anyone looking for an eye-opening breakfast tea resist Morning Thunder?

Whatever the name on the package, box, tin, or tea bag label, the steam that rises from the cup is sending signals from far away. It's the spirit of pioneer housewives foraging wood and meadow for herbs, of Texas Indians sipping their potent "black drink" around flickering fires centuries ago, of all the people who brewed whatever was at hand for the comfort of their hearts. It's the breath of the mist settling over the foothills of Formosa, of harvesters singing as they pluck tender, young leaves in Sri Lanka, of dockers loading tea chests onto ships in Calcutta and Cochin, Colombo and Trincomalee, Shanghai and Keelung. It is the essence of civilizations so ancient that their origins are lost in time.

· 2 ·

Tea Drinking

No one knows the precise point in prehistoric time when tea leaves found their way into boiling water and someone tasted the resulting brew, smacked his or her lips, and said, "Not bad." Legend has it that it was in China, that the drink's appeal was at once obvious, and that the discovery was made under circumstances that implied royal or even celestial endorsement of tea drinking.

Less romantic souls have suggested that it was really tribesmen in Assam in northeastern India who first brewed tea and shared the secret with the Chinese who strayed across the border.

It is unlikely that we will ever know whether it was a philosophical herbalist of a Chinese emperor or a self-sufficient Indian tribesman who made the first cup of true tea, but we do know what happened next: China took tea to its ample bosom, first as a medicine, then—by the sixth century A.D.—as something to be drunk for pleasure. As with China, so with the rest of the East. Tea followed Chinese trade routes into neighboring lands in the seventh and eighth centuries, and for a long time it was in the Orient that tea stayed, although occasional tales began to drift westward of the Chinese court—its opulence, its customs, and the tea drunk by everyone from peasant to courtier.

As trade developed between East and West, Venice emerged as the clearinghouse for the exotic products of the Orient, and it was a Venetian who in a mid-sixteenth century book of travels repeated the story of a Persian merchant about tea's medicinal qualities. This gave Europeans their first published account of the beverage. It was about this same time that Portugal developed long-range sailing ships, and Venice, which "once held the gorgeous East in fee," found the overland route its traders used becoming obsolete as Portugal captured most of the oriental trade.

Portuguese priests followed Portuguese sailors eastward, and their stories of tea aroused the curiosity of their fellow countrymen and women. Other Europeans continued to hear of tea through seamen hired by the Portuguese to work on the oriental run.

At the beginning of the seventeenth century the Dutch, who had been bankers for the trading ventures of both the Venetians and the Portuguese, decided to eliminate the middleman between them and the East, and they formed the Dutch East India Company. By 1610 they were collecting tea in Java (where it had been shipped from China in Chinese junks), sailing it to the Netherlands, then exporting it to other European nations. The Dutch dominated the early tea trade, accounting for tea's introduction into New Amsterdam in America around the middle of the seventeenth century. That it quickly took hold in the Dutch colony is shown by domestic inventories that include tea utensils; and the quality of the tea ware suggests that the new custom had a social significance similar to what it enjoyed in Holland, where later in the century opulent tea parties became something of a fad. From New Amsterdam, which soon became New York and English, tea drinking spread into the surrounding area, where it slowly achieved popularity.

Tea reached Russia in 1618 when the Chinese embassy gave the Czar several chests of the precious leaves. For a long time its cost kept tea drinking at the court or in the drawing rooms of wealthy nobles, but increased trade between Russia and China began to bring the price down. By the end of the seventeenth century the habit was spreading throughout the country.

While the Russians got their tea direct from the source—albeit over an 11,000-mile route that took sixteen months to travel—tea went to Germany and France by way of Holland. The Germans barely gave it a taste before picking up their beer steins again. In France the new drink created a brief flurry, then most of the French went back to wine and coffee.

It was in England where tea found its most enthusiastic reception in the West. Between first reading of the drink in a 1598 translation of a Dutch navigator's *Travels* and 1689, the year that the British East India Company at last began importing tea directly from China, tea reached England in small quantities and by courtesy of the Dutch. Served as an esoteric, expensive drink in London coffee houses after 1657 and as a novelty at court, it caught on slowly but steadily, and during the eighteenth century the habit was firmly entrenched in England, Scotland, and Ireland.

Seventeenth-century silver teapot, Dutch-American.

In America, where New Amsterdam was but the first of tea's conquests, it was a tax on tea in the third quarter of the eighteenth century that was to act as a catalytic agent in the American revolt against England. The Boston Tea Party in 1773, however, was a double-edged event. While it, and the British reaction to it, demonstrated the importance of tea in the relations between colony and mother country, it also signalled an American change of heart about the beverage. To many

Americans tea drinking now became associated with Tories, the colonists who remained loyal to England.

This taint of traitorousness clung to the drink after the successful conclusion of the Revolution, and tea—while still consumed in considerable amounts—never regained its dominance in the new country. As the United States expanded westward, it was coffee rather than tea that ultimately took on the character of a national drink, and in some circles the teacup became a symbol of a way of life somehow not virile enough to justify American enthusiasm.

While the American Revolution was probably the most important political event that tea helped bring about, it had stirred strong emotions through the centuries, calling forth avid defenders and not a few detractors. Tea's adherents have claimed that it fights fatigue, quickens reactions, relaxes the tense body, stimulates the sluggish mind, and refreshes the jaded spirit. Early Zen masters taught that tea prolonged life by strengthening the heart. More specifically, it has been said to cure headaches and colds, alleviate giddiness, relieve shortness of breath, prevent kidney stones, and help poor eyesight. It is widely believed that it encourages sobriety, not only by acting as a substitute for alcohol but also by removing the desire for it.

Whatever medical researchers may ultimately prove or disprove about tea as a wonder drug, one benefit is indisputable—it makes boiled water palatable. Considering the amount of impure water in the world at any given time and the number of diseases to be caught from drinking it, this significant boon undoubtedly helps to account for the many teas made from herbs and roots and served in areas where true tea is either unavailable or unaffordable. It is for herb teas that the most specific health claims are made, among them that sage tea calms the nerves, that mint tea settles an upset stomach, that pennyroyal wards off colds, that strawberry leaf tea is a good gargle for sore throats, and that catnip tea will induce sleep. That there is at least some basis in fact for these medicinal properties claimed for herb teas is suggested by the experience of Hong Kong hospitals during World War II, when, deprived of drugs by the Japanese occupiers, they made do with Chinese herbs.

Ardent claims for tea have been counterbalanced during different periods by protests. These surfaced with particular vehemence in England in the late eighteenth century when tea was becoming the national drink. It was claimed that tea was addictive and unhealthy for body and soul. More interestingly, and perhaps more to the point, it was condemned for wasting the time of the working class, undermining its morals, and therefore endangering public order. A stern man of affairs pronounced it bad for business, and others said that tea drinking was immoral because it took money needed for food.

In America, in a book entitled *Tea and Coffee* published in 1839, Dr. William Alcott described tea as being as evil as opium, and claimed that if used as other than a medicine it was poisonous and intoxicating. He pointed out that nothing in the Bible justified its use, and then topped the list by asserting that tea drinking led to poor citizenship because it enthralled its addicts.

Good or bad, however, down the centuries a lot has happened because people liked to drink tea. Commercial empires rose and fell, wars were risked and sometimes fought, ship design was changed, previously unnecessary utensils were invented and manufactured, Europeans emigrated to the East to run tea estates, unpopular taxes were imposed, laws

Tea drinking with cake, cheese and crackers and a tea kettle over burner.

were made, and laws were broken—all in the service of tea: the growing, selling, buying, transporting, smuggling, or otherwise capitalizing on its value as "the perfect commodity," always in demand, ever renewable.

Worked through this colorful tapestry as an ever-recurring strand was the unrelenting tension between East and West, the determined, even desperate conflict between tea-rich, tradition-proud, but politically weakened China and tea-hungry England, whose all-but-autonomous agent, the British East India Company, ignored a centuries-old pattern of civilization in its pursuit of tea and silks and in its establishment of one of the greatest mercantile empires in history.

The West's sometimes unfortunate persistence in the face of Chinese reluctance to trade and the great lengths to which later entrepreneurs went to establish commercial tea cultivation outside China may be accounted for by the ever-increasing size of the market and the resulting profits. Today, in spite of colas and other relatively recent innovations, tea remains the most popular drink in the world apart from water itself.

For all its worldwide acceptance, it is perhaps in Japan and in England that tea has been brought to the peak of realization both as drink and custom. Each country is an island kingdom with strong traditions, and both share an almost obsessive concern with tea. In spite of superficial differences as to the type of tea preferred, the setting in which it is drunk, and the manners of those drinking it, there is an underlying strain of similarity—of comfort, of fellowship, of putting aside for a spell the cares of the world under the influence of "Tea, Heav'ns Delight, and Nature's truest Wealth . . . the Muse's Nectar."

· 3 ·

The Japanese Tea Ceremony
and
the Shoguns

Even in modern Japan it would be no exaggeration to say that life flows upon a river of tea. The green tea, *matcha,* preferred by most Japanese is an indispensable part of daily routine in the home, the first thing to be offered any visitor whatever the occasion—ordinary social calls, parties, weddings, even funerals. Tea, known as *cha,* is given to pallbearers as they dig graves, and to guests in inns when they've been shown to their rooms. It is served in Zen temples on certain festival days. It is taken to housewarmings as a gift. It is offered automatically in remote, primitive tea houses and in elegant, urban restaurants. It is drunk in such quantities that Japan, fourth largest producer in the world, uses most of what it grows at home and imports enough additional tea to make it the most important customer of Great Britain's tea brokers.

Tea is a vital part of everyday life in Japan, but this tea drunk routinely must not be confused with that uniquely Japanese ritual, the tea ceremony, or *cha-no-yu.* The one is casual, even relatively hurried, the other a precise observance governed by strict rules. Even the form of tea is different: For everyday drinking, the green, unfermented tea leaves are used; for the tea ceremony, a fine green tea powder. And though it has been claimed that *cha-no-yu* is today more honored in the breach than in correct observance, it has for many centuries exerted a deep influence on Japanese life and tradition that still continues.

Cha-no-yu's cultural dominance is explained by an unusual intermingling of political, religious, and aesthetic considerations. Highly placed persons—from early emperors who drank *cha* for its medicinal qualities to later shoguns who used the ceremony as a means of consolidating and displaying their wealth and power—encouraged the development of an increasingly complicated ritual. The different religious and ethical systems that prevailed in Japan in succession either incorporated the ceremony into their observances or promoted beliefs that prompted their followers to respect it as a means of achieving intellectual and spiritual balance. In particular, the Zen Buddhist view of life as work of art advanced the appreciation of this most exacting and aesthetically aware discipline. "Schools" developed over the centuries, offering different approaches to *cha-no-yu,* the students who were taught by the rules of one perhaps disagreeing strenuously with those taught by another, but all of them assuring the continuation of knowledge and interest.

Even the tea hut had an intellectual basis. The high value placed on personal meditation led first to the erection of small, separate garden structures, then to the addition of specially built rooms, the solitude of which was more conducive to meditation than the main body of the house with its continuing distractions. Since the use of tea was encouraged as an aid to meditation, it was perhaps inevitable that the hut as the place of meditation and *cha* as the drink conducive to meditation should combine and that an elaborate symbolism would evolve around drinking tea in this setting. Once the practice began to spread, it was perhaps inevitable, too, that special utensils would be developed and that, in turn, the design of more beautiful kettles, bowls, trays, scoops, and tea caddies would ensure an ever greater interest in *cha-no-yu* because of the Japanese obsession with beauty.

This love of beauty is undoubtedly fostered by living in a land whose climate offers four distinct seasons, each with its own visual appeal, and whose natural geography ranges from the spectacularly beautiful to the quietly lovely. Certainly an important aspect of *cha-no-yu* is the reflection of the changing seasons in the flower or foliage decorating the tea hut and in the color and form of utensils used in the ceremony itself.

The evolution of *cha-no-yu* was affected, as was the spread of casual tea drinking, by the initial scarcity and subsequent availability of *cha.* Although tea grows well in Japan and is today cultivated both commer-

Late eighteenth-century teahouse. The nijiri-guchi, or guests' entrance, is at left. The small size of the entrance is symbolic—the guest must make an effort to go from the everyday world into the rarified atmosphere of cha-no-yu. To get through such an entrance samurai had to remove their swords and leave them outside.

cially and as individual bushes scattered about farm holdings on land not suitable for other crops, *camellia sinensis* is not native to the country.

As far as anyone knows, the first tea in Japan was brought from China, probably in the late seventh century A.D. It was already the well-known drink of Japan's big mainland neighbor, and as there was considerable cultural interaction between the two nations at this time, it was only natural that tea would find its way across the Sea of Japan along with other Chinese innovations. The Japanese imperial court was strongly influenced by Chinese customs and apparently began drinking tea soon after its introduction into Japan, for in 729 the Emperor Shomu was making gifts of tea to priests who had come to his palace at Nara to read Buddhist scriptures. As he had probably hoped, some of the priests began to plant tea in temple grounds, and later in the century, when the Emperor Kammu moved the capital to Kyoto, a tea garden was incorporated into the design of the new Chinese-style imperial palace.

Still, very few of the plants were actually grown in Japan at this period, and because only a small quantity was coming from China, tea continued to be both scarce and expensive, and was used mostly as a medicine. Deteriorating relations with China, and then an actual break, led to a decreased interest in everything Chinese and the beginning of a movement to create an indigenous Japanese culture. Like other Chinese imports, the custom of tea drinking in Japan suffered, leading to the virtual abandonment of the fledgling tea gardens.

As Japan's relations with China declined, so did its political stability. In a long period of warfare that saw the great landowners, or daimyos, aligning themselves into factions, an aristocratic warrior class known as the samurai evolved, creating a body of professional soldiers that ensured that blood would continue to be spilt until one group or the other triumphed. This finally happened late in the twelfth century, and just as the samurai had helped his clan triumph over that of the Taira, they continued to stand behind Minamoto Yoritomo when he forced the weakened emperor to declare him shogun in 1192.

When it was coined in the eighth century, the title Sei-i-tai Shogun (literally, "the barbarian-subduing generalissimo") was meant to be awarded to the commander of the imperial armies. After Yoritomo, and for almost seven hundred years, the shogun or his regent was the actual ruler of Japan. Although the imperial court at Kyoto was not abolished and emperor succeeded emperor, all real power, as well as the actual administration of the country, lay in the shogunate. Succession was hereditary within the ruling clan until another, more powerful clan asserted its right to the shogunate by defeating the shogun in battle.

The different shoguns influenced religion, education, law, aesthetics—in fact, every aspect of Japanese life—and they were also instrumental in the spread and style of tea drinking, especially in the evolution of the Japanese tea ceremony.

The first shoguns—known as the Kamakura because it was at Kamakura that Yoritomo established his headquarters—were particularly important to the reintroduction of tea in Japan because they promoted Zen Buddhism. In the twelfth century, in spite of the daimyo wars, educated Japanese who opposed the imperial court at Kyoto began once more to notice what was happening in China, and Eisai, a Buddhist monk, went there to study Zen, returning to Kyoto in 1191, the year before Yoritomo was declared shogun. Traditional Buddhist sects in the reactionary capital were hostile to the Zen teachings he brought with him, and he fled to Kamakura, taking along not only his objectionable ideas but also some of the tea seeds he had brought back from China.

By going into northeastern Japan Eisai was positioning himself at the heart of the new shogunate, a wise move since his advocacy of both Zen and tea fell on ears that were ready to hear. In 1214 he wrote the *Kissa yōjō-ki* (Drink Tea to Nourish Life). Written in part because he hoped to save the shogun Sanetomo from alcoholism, the essay praised tea as a harmless stimulant, but it also claimed that the newly reintroduced beverage would cure other ailments, among them boils, bad-water disease, paralysis, listless appetite, and beri-beri. Eisai also taught that tea would prolong life, which was worthy of preservation because man was the noblest creation of heaven. Tea did this by supplying the bitter food required for a healthy heart.

Perhaps even more responsible for *cha*'s growing acceptance was the miracle cure that Eisai effected for a seriously ill, highly placed government official. Upon his recovery the official spoke long and loudly of the virtues of the *cha* that the Buddhist monk had poured down him between intervals of prayer.

Ranking members of the Kamakura shogunate were preconditioned to respond favorably to Eisai's imported ideas and the beverage that accompanied them because to favor anything Chinese was to repudiate the insular imperial court, the shogunate's political opponent. It was not long before Eisai was able to establish a Zen study center with the backing of both the third ruling shogun and the widow of the first.

With its emphasis on the here and now, its implicit endorsement of action, and its teaching that each man must find spiritual meaning within the framework of his own life rather than look for it in the person of a supreme being, Zen buddhism appealed strongly to the new ruling class; and *cha,* as an aid to the meditation required by Zen, gained converts. Monks, who had begun to cultivate tea shrubs as a part of their religious routine, found that demand for the beverage grew rapidly, and more and more shrubs were planted.

Seventeenth-century incense container, or kōgō, in the form of a mandarin duck. Made by Nonomura Ninsei, a potter who was influenced by the tea master Kanamori Sōwa and whose work reflects upper-class taste of his time. Such containers are used to hold incense in the teahouse.

Zen monks found themselves in an interesting position early in the Kamakura shogunate. After a long break in official relations between Japan and China, few Japanese had any knowledge of China. Then China and Korea were conquered by the Mongols in the thirteenth century, and Japan began to feel threatened and turned to the monks because many of them had studied in China. The Zen monks were recruited by the government to act as advisors on the assumption that they had at least some first-hand information about the potential enemy, and the priests parlayed this advisory role into a strong secular position that endured for centuries. This secular influence, along with their operation of the only schools, in turn strengthened their hold on the minds and habits of the ruling class. The ideas that the Zen monks put into those receptive minds helped to spread tea's acceptance even further, and gave tea drinking a new dimension.

At the heart of Zen Buddhism lay the search for *satori,* the realization of perfect clarity. Intense meditation was the means used to achieve this end, the master giving the disciple a *koan,* a kind of cosmic riddle, to ponder until he reached the desired result. This process could take years and involved long hours of solitary contemplation that would at times grow tedious. It isn't surprising that the Chinese and Tibetan practice of drinking tea as part of meditation caught on.

A legend repeated by the monks adds a certain glamour to this pragmatic reason for tea drinking: It was told that Bodhidharma, the sixth-century Indian saint and founder of Zen, went to China to teach. He was given a cave temple by the Chinese emperor, and while meditating here he fell asleep. When he awoke and realized what he had done, his mortification was so great that he cut off his eyelids. They fell to the ground, and on that spot appeared a tea plant, the leaves of which would make a drink to banish sleep. Later, after offending the emperor, Bodhidharma fled China and went to Japan, where he died and was buried. It was later found that his tomb was empty, and strange reports began to circulate of his having been seen hurrying across the mountains, heading home. Zen priests told and retold his story and drank tea before his image.

In the long run it was probably the underlying assumptions of Zen that were most responsible for the gradual development of the religion-related habit that evolved into *cha-no-yu.* Starting with the belief that life should be lived as a creative discipline, Zen encouraged—almost demanded—a search for excellence in all aspects of existence. With the beverage already consumed in near-ritualistic fashion, the next logical step was to work out actual rules for the drinking of *cha,* based in large part on the tea code set down by Lu Yu in China in the late eighth century. His *Ch'a Ching* (Classic of Tea), taught that the tea service symbolized the harmony of the universe and outlined a tea code, including a description of the utensils used in the drink's preparation and consumption.

From China, too, came the method of making the powdered tea used in the Japanese ceremony. The leaves were ground into powder, water was added, and the mixture was stirred with a bamboo whisk, another Chinese contribution. This improved the flavor of the tea. Also encouraging the spread of the fledgling tea ceremony, many Zen priests built temples specifically for its performance and began to collect Chinese utensils. Later they began to collect, and then themselves to perfect calligraphy and painting, so the connection between Zen, aesthetics, and tea became more firmly fixed.

Temmyo kettle, iron, influenced by older Chinese kettles of the tenth to fourteenth centuries. The name refers to the area of Japan where the kettle was manufactured. The water for ceremonial tea is boiled in the kettle.

When the Kamakura shogunate fell to that of the Ashikaga in the fourteenth century, the influence of the Zen Buddhists increased even more, as did that of the Chinese. The growing interaction between Zen Buddhism and affluent Japanese could be seen in a secular elaboration of the tea ceremony that had been begun originally by monks as a part of their religious devotions. A document called *Kissa Ōrai* (Correspondence on Tea Drinking) described a party in which banquet guests retired to the garden for tea entertainment in an arbor designed for moon viewing. On the walls of the arbor hung Chinese paintings and scrolls, and the guests were served ten small bowls each of four different kinds of tea.

An entertainment centering on *tōcha,* a tea game imported from China, had been popular for some time. In fact, in the view of the Ashikaga shogun Takauji it had become too popular, and he banned it. In spite of this *tōcha* flourished. It was a favorite pastime of a new class of samurai, called *basara* because of their obsession with luxury. They had prospered during the civil wars, and *tōcha* let them display their wealth and extravagance as well as their knowledge. These large parties, known as *cha yoriai,* turned into elaborate tea-tasting contests in which silk, furniture, and other expensive prizes were awarded to guests who could correctly identify the geographical origin and other characteristics of as many as twenty or thirty different teas. Because the tea was served in the traditional samurai manner, in which the lord took the first sip and then passed on the cup, the game took a long time, but any tedium was lightened by betting on the outcome.

It was also during this period that an unusual tea gathering called *rinkan* grew popular in some circles. Tea was still supposedly the principal entertainment, but as it was consumed while taking a hot bath, the practice had a happily suggestive quality that condemned it in the eyes of more-ascetic tea fanciers.

People were beginning to form definite opinions about *cha* and the ritual accompanying it: how and where it should be served, who should officiate, and the sort of utensils that should be used. A certain type of architecture came to be associated with the tea ceremony room. Adapted from the *shoin* style, which itself derived from temple architecture, the tea ceremony room began to incorporate standard features: the alcove and side alcove, storage and display shelves, a preparation room, and a principal room where the actual tea drinking took place. In the principal room, known as the *shoin,* tea was served by menservants called *dōbōshū,* who wore monks' attire and used Chinese utensils. The floors of such rooms came to be covered by straw mats known as *tatami.* The size of the tearoom was important, employing a psychology of proportion. As a result, rooms sized for the smaller man of medieval Japan can be uncomfortable for his larger modern counterpart, making him feel crowded and ill-at-ease.

The Ashikaga shogun Yoshimasa built a *shoin* in the late fifteenth century as part of his Kyoto villa. Known as the Silver Pavilion, or Ginkahu-ji, its simple yet sophisticated style was a breakthrough of sorts. The construction and decoration of the pavilion became something of an obsession with Yoshimasa—it was rumored that he had turned to the way of tea to escape an unhappy domestic life—and in his pursuit of valuable ceremony paraphernalia and in the perfection of his own ceremonial tea technique, he was aided by a Zen priest named Murata Shukō. Under Shukō's guidance he assembled a large collection and gave many tea parties. This shogun was so involved with the ceremony that he rewarded his soldiers with tea artifacts rather than arms.

Yoshimasa was an enigma. While bloody feuds raged between warring daimyos, he buried himself in the Ginkahu-ji, either refusing or not wishing to recognize the disintegration of the power of the shogunate in the face of rebellious samurai. Yet it is largely to his interest that Japan owes the ruling aesthetic of the tea ceremony heritage, for it was under his patronage that Shukō developed the specific concept that came to be known as *cha-no-yu.*

A talented, near-legendary man, Shukō was a professional tea master who spent much of his life refining the tea ceremony, then teaching his refinements to followers. This could be a profitable occupation for a man with the talent for the different disciplines required by tea, especially one with a knack for changing the existing ritual in a way that better reflected the mood of his times. Now and later, a successful tea master was one who could innovate within a traditional framework, and who so impressed powerful people that they wished to learn tea from him. This desire to learn was more than superficial, for the Japanese concept of personal discipline has always placed a high value on expertness, that stage of proficiency so advanced that the deed is completely effortless. Whether he emphasized a certain handling of the utensils or a type of decoration or frame of mind, a tea master was supposed to be able to inspire in his students a capacity for just this sort of proficiency.

The innovation that set Shukō apart from earlier masters was that he did not use *dōbōshū* to serve the tea, preferring instead to serve his guests himself. His liking for a more intimate ceremony also led him to design smaller tearooms where only a few people might share the tea experience. The dimensions of his tearoom, four-and-a-half *tatami* mats square, or about fifteen feet, became the basis for later tea rooms. Shukō liked a simple, dignified service and took great pains with the aesthetics of both setting and ceremony. His success is suggested by his own contemporaries' recognition of him as "the father of the tea ceremony" and by the fact that it was in his time that *sūki*, which meant literally a "liking of tea" came also to mean "artistic taste."

Iron kettle, or kama, in the lotus leaf shape. Note the holes on either side of the lid for detachable handles and the aesthetically rough surface.

By the end of the Ashikaga shogunate tea drinking and the customs associated with it had spread considerably beyond the upper classes and the Zen priests who had originally inspired them. Tea was sold by the cup in city stalls and wayside stands. *Tōcha,* the tea game, was found to be as entertaining by the commoners as it had by the samurai and, like the samurai, they were not above betting on who would win. As for the ceremonial serving of tea, the aristocratic vogue was copied in simpler style by an increasing number of people in other classes.

The tea ceremony became an important political and military tool with the coming to power of the Tokugawa at the beginning of the seventeenth century. The tea ceremony's new prominence happened partly because of the increase in both the numbers and the power of the middle class, particularly in the self-governing towns of Sakai and Hakata, ports that dominated Japan's foreign trade, limited at this time to China and Portugal.

Portugal had been allowed to begin trading with Japan in the 1540s, bringing velvet, wool, leather, and glassware from Europe, and silk, cotton, pottery, medicine, sugar, and old coins from China, all of which were traded for Japanese copper, gold, and silver. The Sakai merchants who controlled this commerce and who also profited in the burgeoning trade with China were so successful that they achieved a new respectability, and Oda Nobunaga, a powerful military commander, capitalized on their new power.

Using his daimyo father's holdings as a base, the young Nobunaga conquered several provinces near modern Nagoya. The Japanese emperor was appalled at the increasingly bloody and seemingly endless feuds, and he secretly approached Nobunaga. Acting in the imperial name, Nobunaga took on the warring factions and in 1568, at the age of 34, became dictator of Japan. Since his ancestry prevented him from assuming the shogunate personally, he reinstated the ousted shogun, but it was Nobunaga who was in control.

Because Nobunaga's goal, the unification of Japan, threatened the entrenched positions of the daimyos and the great Buddhist sects who had large private armies of their own, the young ruler had to vanquish his opponents militarily. This took money, weapons, and warriors, and he employed his considerable skills to get them.

From the merchants of Sakai he wanted economic aid and Portuguese arms, and the tea ceremony was one of the tools that he used to get them. The ceremony had become an accepted part of life in the city, and it had already produced two noted tea masters, Takeno Jō-ō and Torii Insetsu, both students of Shukō, the Zen priest who had been Yoshimasa's mentor in the building and outfitting of the Silver Pavilion in Kyoto.

Because of the relatively free intermingling of different classes within its boundaries, the tea ceremony had assumed an essentially democratic character in Sakai. Although the tea gatherings were usually held in private homes, anyone could attend, whether he was priest, noble, warrior, or merchant and whether he knew the host or not. In fact, the ceremony seems to have been a useful means of reconciling the nobility to the growing power and importance of the merchants.

Realizing the important role that tea played in Sakai, Nobunaga cleverly invited the most influential of the city's wealthy merchants, known as *machi-shū*, to tea gatherings where he used the old Ashikaga tea utensils to show that he now exercised the power that had formerly belonged to the shogunate and that, in backing him, they were going with a winner. He also chose tea masters from among the *machi-shū* and publicly honored them, with the result that he got the muskets and money that he wanted.

While the merchants could supply arms and help pay for his military

Sixteenth-century tea caddy, or cha-ire, and tea scoop, or chashaku, on a lacquer tray. The ceramic caddy, for holding the ceremonial tea, is in the bunrin, or apple shape. The tea scoop, used to transfer the tea from the caddy to the tea bowl, is of bamboo and was carved by Gamō Ujisato, a well-known tea master who was also a military commander under the dictators Nobunaga and Hideyoshi. These are among the paraphernalia carried into the guests' presence at the start of ceremonial tea.

exploits, it was the samurai who provided the necessary muscle, and once again Nobunaga used the tea ceremony to gain support. In the continuing civil wars, the samurai—especially those in the higher ranks—found a welcome escape from the danger of their lives in the tranquility of the tearoom. They collected tea paraphernalia and made a hobby of arranging the items in their tearooms. They were understandably flattered when Nobunaga invited generals who had especially pleased him to take part in his own ceremonies. Not only did he use the Ashikaga utensils on these occasions, he sometimes made gifts of them to particular favorites, thus proving his right to do as he chose with Ashikaga possessions and helping to ensure the generals' loyalty because of their pleasure at receiving such enviable gifts. This had the incidental effect of making the ceremony even more popular among samurai because they liked giving tea gatherings where they could show off the prized utensils Nobunaga had given them.

Nobunaga was a complex character, and as his forces successfully routed the armies of his enemies he kept a watchful eye on the foreigners. Changes took place in the country that would have been unlikely under the Ashikaga—perhaps as a result of his ancestry and of his long-fought battles with the reactionary daimyos, Nobunaga had a relatively progressive outlook. Although not hesitating to use his power against those who did not share his vision of Japanese destiny, he was not tied to the past. He demolished Buddhist temples for material to repair the shogun's palace. His foot soldiers were among the first in Japan to be armed with muskets.

Creativity flourished, particularly in the tea ceremony and in architecture, which became less derivative of Chinese influence. Castles, homes, and tea houses began to be built less like imitation temples and more like secular structures. Nobunaga himself was very interested in the arts and was, in fact, dancing a piece from a *no* play when Akechi Mitsuhide, an ambitious Buddhist retainer, attacked the temple where he was staying and forced him to commit suicide.

Nobunaga, 48 when he died, had almost but not quite reached his goal of unification. This was accomplished by his commander-in-chief, Toyotomi Hideyoshi, who defeated Mitsuhide in short order and became *kwampaku,* or civil dictator, in 1585. Hideyoshi, obsessed with war and armies from childhood, was a gifted opportunist who used every means at his command to unify Japan. This included continuing to exploit *cha-no-yu* as a political tool.

Like Nobunaga he wooed the Sakai merchants, the suppliers of the essential European weapons, with impressive tea ceremonies. He also kept Nobunaga's three Sakai-connected tea masters on his payroll, and he used the Ashikaga tea paraphernalia to show that the power of the shogunate had now descended through Nobunaga to him. He used this same tactic with his generals, just as Nobunaga had earlier used it with his military men.

In 1587 Hideyoshi extended this aesthetic form of propaganda to the general population by staging a Great Tea Ceremony at Kitano, Kyoto, to which any and all comers were invited so long as each brought with him his own cup, kettle, and mat. This monster entertainment lasted several days, and guests were offered music, dancing, plays, and a good, long look at the ever-useful Ashikaga tea utensils. The big tea gathering was so popular that it was repeated several times, always with the Ashikaga paraphernalia on display. Finally, after he had built his own castle, Hideyoshi made a practice of displaying the tea utensils to the public on a regular basis.

Hideyoshi seems to have been interested in every area of aesthetics, particularly in *cha-no-yu,* and nowhere was his contradictory nature better illustrated than in his dealings with Sen no Rikyū. Rikyū, a merchant from Sakai, was one of the three tea masters that Hideyoshi had inherited from Nobunaga and kept on as a diplomatic gesture to the merchants of Sakai. Of the three, Rikyū was the most astute, for as soon as he heard of Nobunaga's death, he hurried to Hideyoshi's side while the other two tea masters made overtures to both Hideyoshi and Mitsuhide, the general responsible for Nobunaga's death. Rikyū's act was the beginning of a complex relationship between the dictator who recognized a valuable ally in his political use of the tea ceremony and the tea master who saw an ideal vehicle for enhancing his prestige, thereby ensuring that wider attention would be paid to his own ideas of the proper conduct of the ceremony.

Soon after being named *kwampaku,* Hideyoshi asked the emperor to designate Rikyū a *kōji,* or enlightened recluse. In that role he could legally enter the palace as Hideyoshi's tutor. Rikyū, a pupil of Takeno Jō-ō, who in turn had been a pupil decades before of the great Shukō, had evolved an approach to tea that was uniquely his own. Although he strove always for *wabi,* the effect of tranquility and elegance, he did not sacrifice creativity. He experimented constantly with new forms of the ceremony and invented utensils especially for it. One of his favorite devices was to choose a seemingly insignificant household object—an ordinary flower container, for example—and highlight it in the ceremony to bring out its innate interest and grace. He had a good eye for successful innovation, and the restless Hideyoshi must have prized this quality in him. Also, there was a spiritual element in Rikyū's ceremony that seemed to please the dictator.

In turn, Rikyū must have wanted to placate his star pupil for, in spite of his own feelings that *cha-no-yu* should be simplified and stripped of ostentation, it was Rikyū who helped Hideyoshi plan the Great Tea Ceremony at Kitano in 1587. By this time he had become one of Hideyoshi's closest attendants and exercised considerable power in the dictator's household because he knew so much about its affairs.

Then something happened. It is possible that Rikyū reminded Hideyoshi too much of the arrogant Sakai merchants and so became hateful. It may be that he was caught illegally dealing in tea utensils. It was even suggested by his enemies that he had grown too powerful and had conspired with Hideyoshi's enemies against the dictator. Or it may be simply that Hideyoshi had at last come up against an ego as strong as his own and that Rikyū was not tactful enough to conceal his contempt for the elastic ethics of his dictator-pupil.

Whatever the reason, in 1591 Hideyoshi accused his tutor of treachery and ordered him to return to Sakai and commit *seppuku,* or ceremonial suicide. In the two weeks between the command and his death, Rikyū's many students ostracized him. Most of them were well-placed military men or government officials, and they did not wish to be associated with him in Hideyoshi's mind because they feared for their positions and, considering the haphazard bloodthirstiness of feudal Japan, perhaps their very lives.

Before he died, Rikyū urged his pupils to go to Furuta Oribe, a prize student, to learn tea and to Sansai, another student, for instruction in making tea scoops. Considering how eager everyone was not to be associated with him, to be so mentioned may have been something of a double-edged honor. When the appointed time came, Rikyū retired to his tea house, performed *cha-no-yu* for the last time, then died by his own hand.

No other tea master was allowed to fill the exact role that Rikyū had assumed. This may have been partly because Hideyoshi, who was himself highly gifted in the performance of *cha-no-yu,* did not really need a master, and partly because he did not wish to show any dependence on

Seventeen-century fresh water jar, or mizusashi, designed by Furuta Oribe, tea master to the first Tokugawas. Such vessels are used to carry fresh water from the fountain in the roji to the teahouse.

the *machi-shū* of Sakai. He had decided to concentrate instead on the merchants of Hakata for the same sort of cooperation that had been so unwillingly given by Sakai. A hint of what was to come could have been seen in 1587 when he employed two tea masters from Hakata for the Great Tea Ceremony, and after Rikyū's death he turned more and more to the second town.

Rikyū's death seems to have marked the end of an exceptional episode in the evolution of *cha-no-yu*. Rikyū's insistence on simplicity and purity was a reaction to the increasing richness of the ceremony practiced by the daimyos and their samurai in the sixteenth century. He was so successful that the way of tea tends to be divided into three periods: pre-Rikyū; Rikyū; and post-Rikyū.

Because of his exceptional abilities and because of the enormous prestige he enjoyed as Hideyoshi's personal tea master, Rikyū impressed the coming generation of masters to the extent that they at least attempted to follow the austere rules he had laid down for the ceremony. It was not long, however, before the number of schools, or teaching precepts, multiplied and the ceremony became even more complicated and ornate.

This lay years in the future, however, after Hideyoshi himself died and after the Tokugawa shogunate was installed. There wasn't supposed to be a Tokugawa shogunate, and it may be that Hideyoshi himself helped to make it possible, even inevitable, by his attempts to ensure the succession for his only son, Hideyori.

When Hideyoshi lay dying at the age of 62, Hideyori was only seven years old. Knowing better than anyone else the slim chance the boy would have, unassisted, in reaching adulthood and assuming the dictatorship, Hideyoshi chose five trusted subordinates to act as regents and jointly govern Japan until Hideyori came of age. Having provided for the administration of the country, he next made an attempt to secure his son's safety. He called upon Tokugawa Iyeyasu, the most powerful of the five regents, to protect the boy and to do everything in his power to maintain peace in the land while Hideyori grew up.

Iyeyasu, 56 years old, was an able man, a one-time rival who had reluctantly acknowledged Hideyoshi's superior abilities after Nobunaga's death, but the fourteen years since he and the dictator had come to terms had done nothing to quench his ambition. Once Hideyoshi was dead, it became obvious to the other four regents that he was positioning himself to take over, especially since he had all along been allying himself with powerful families throughout Japan by marrying off his many children like so many chess pawns. The other regents challenged him, but his 80,000 troops defeated their 130,000 at Sekigahara. After trouncing his rivals, he got both their surrenders and their unwilling oaths of loyalty.

Although Iyeyasu was neither as gifted nor as spectacular as his near-contemporaries Nobunaga and Hideyoshi, he was determined, and also very good at getting the most out of whatever material lay at hand. This is shown by his treatment of the Englishman Will Adams—the historic basis for the fascinating story in James Clavell's *Shogun.*

Adams, the pilot on a Dutch ship, was taken prisoner by Iyeyasu not long before the battle of Sekigahara. Iyeyasu was pleased by the Englishman, particularly by the fact that his native country was also having problems with the Spanish and the Portuguese, whom Iyeyasu distrusted because of their unsettling influence on Japanese internal affairs. He was also impressed with Adams' knowledge of navigational instruments and maps, and interested in his opinions on the other world powers. When Iyeyasu defeated the other regents and became dictator, he used Adams as an advisor in foreign affairs and as a source of information on shipbuilding, both important because Iyeyasu was interested in boosting Japan's foreign trade using Japanese ships. Adams must have known what he was doing when it came to designing ships, for some years later one of his craft, with a Japanese crew, showed up in New Spain (now California) ten years before his fellow Englishmen landed at Plymouth Rock.

In return for Adams' help, Iyeyasu was neither ungrateful nor stingy. He gave the Englishman a Japanese wife, an estate, and an income, but he would not let him return to England, suspecting that the shanghaied guest could continue to play a role in his plans.

After the battle of Sekigahara the political situation remained dangerously ambiguous, and civil war seemed certain to break out as it had so often in the preceding centuries. In spite of his great military ability, Iyeyasu did not want war and set in motion a chain of events that not only ended domestic strife for two hundred and fifty years, but also firmly entrenched his family in the shogunate and affected every part of Japanese life, including the tea ceremony.

Although he had his son proclaimed shogun, Iyeyasu retained his dictatorial powers, and he used them to put a lid on the unrest that had simmered off and on for almost three centuries. He did this by reorganizing the political system and officially stratifying the Japanese population, placing everyone in a group that was either directly or indirectly susceptible to control by the shogun.

This social reorganization was based on the assumption that a layered population, each group with its duties, limitations, and rights clearly defined, would be less likely to oppose the shogun's power. To this end Iyeyasu divided Japanese society into three classes: samurai in the service of the Tokugawas, lesser feudal lords, and commoners. The commoners were further divided into farmers, artists and artisans, and merchants, brokers and moneylenders.

Iyeyasu not only put everyone into one or the other of the classes, he froze the status quo that was then created so that it was almost impossible to move from one class to another, even by marriage. While rules were not completely spelled out at the beginning, ultimately they were issued in quite specific terms, directing each class's proper activity. Dress, leisure pursuits, the conduct of life, behavior within and without

Seventeenth-century tea bowl, or chawan, with design of symbolic fish scales and waves. Made by Nonomura Ninsei, one of the most-creative Japanese potters of the early Tokugawa shogunate. In the bowl the tea master combines the powdered green tea and boiling water and aerates them with a bamboo whisk until foamy.

Flower container, or hana-ire, from the Karatsu kilns. Influenced by the designs of tea master Furuta Oribe. Flowers are arranged in the container just before the start of the ceremony and placed in the alcove of the teahouse.

the class, housebuilding, marriage, travel arrangements—almost every detail of existence was codified, particularly in the commoner class where there were set down even such minutiae as the amount of money that a parent could spend on a gift for a child.

While this effectively ended the internal strife that had periodically upended Japanese life, it deprived the fighting samurai of even the hope of a good battle. Their role as warriors had been made largely symbolic, and—supported by a generous guaranteed income derived from the labor of the commoner class—they turned more and more to the other pursuits considered acceptable for aristocrats, including *cha-no-yu*.

Samurai had helped to secularize the tea ceremony many years before. Now what had been a fashionable hobby became something of an obsession with many of this class. The refinements of the tea ceremony continued to be taught by private masters. Although it was still considered beneficial for the master to learn Zen, many of the famous masters were not priests, and the ceremony increasingly distorted the Zen precepts of simplicity and spirituality.

Furuta Oribe, the student who had been singled out by Rikyū before his ceremonial suicide, met Iyeyasu only after Hideyoshi's death. In 1605 he became tea master to Iyeyasu's son, Hidetada, and he showed that he was the true descendant of samurai by deviating from the subdued colorings preferred by his teacher Rikyū. Oribe liked a touch of scarlet and more elaborate shapes for utensils, and Rikyū's "pure" ceremony, undisturbed by even bird song or flower scents, began to seem dull when Oribe provided singing doves and fragrant blossoms to add to the sensory enjoyment of the ritual.

The most basic change in *cha-no-yu* between the time of Rikyū, who had died in 1591, and the years when Oribe was the most influential tea master at the Tokugawa court, 1605-1615, was its appropriation by the samurai class. The rules of Iyeyasu's strictly organized society discouraged democracy in any form, even in the tea ceremony, and no longer did different classes or even different ranks within classes participate together in the ceremony. Soon the simple, almost severe Rikyū style favored by the merchant class began to be overpowered.

In keeping with the flamboyant tastes of his samurai pupils, Oribe produced a grand ceremony, this display extending to such details as the *kobukusa,* the small cloths used in the ritual. It was Oribe who originated the practice of cutting up old damasks and piecing the fragments together to make an opulent patchwork *kobukusa.*

Like Hideyoshi's tea master Rikyū two decades earlier, Oribe found that court service could demand a high price. When Hideyoshi's son, Hideyori, took part in an armed revolt against the Tokugawa shogunate, Oribe was suspected by Iyeyasu of having collaborated with the enemy forces, after which the court tea master committed suicide.

After Oribe *cha-no-yu* continued to grow more worldly and complex. From the simple, life-enhancing ritual refined by Rikyū and his like-minded predecessors, the tea ceremony became for most samurai merely an adornment of life and a proof of success. It began to be used as a means of teaching grace and etiquette; the shogun's concubines spent much of their time practicing the increasingly complicated rules of the ceremony, along with flower arrangement and incense discrimination. Daimyos began to collect old tea utensils, pushing their prices higher and higher, which in turn made them more sought after as an indication of the purchaser's prosperity.

Many tea masters began to conduct their ceremonies to please those who could offer them political preferment rather than from any firmly held beliefs about correct procedure. As they were serving lordly, rather materialistic men, their services tended to follow and then to elaborate on those of Katagiri Sekishū, a seventeenth-century daimyo and magistrate of construction for the Tokugawas, who ultimately became their tea master.

Sekishū, himself an aristocrat, understood contemporary aristocratic taste, and he developed a ceremony that, while based on Rikyū's style, was much more ornate and reflected the rigid social distinctions laid down by Iyeyasu. His influence was spread not only by his position but by two works he wrote on tea: *The Essence of Tea* and *Three Hundred Articles,* the latter giving his own ideas on how the ceremony should be performed and attacking the style of other tea masters.

Sekishū's main opposition came from the Senke, a school of tea that derived from the principles of Sen nō Sōtan, the great Rikyū's grandson. The leaders of this school devoted their lives to the tea ceremony and to giving lessons. Rikyū's influence remained stronger here than in the Sekishū school, but even with the Senke the temper of the times led to *iki,* a style that was ostentatiously aesthetic, even epicurean.

Not all tea masters during the Tokugawa shogunate were place-seekers, and from time to time a master would try to reactivate interest in the ceremony as a simple, intellectual tool. Matsudaira Fumai, an eighteenth-century feudal lord, wrote against the extravagant tea ceremonies that were standard for Tokugawa samurai of his day. His work *Idle Talk* attacked such ceremonies as insensitive and vulgar, and claimed that they destroyed the concept of tea as an aesthetic art. Fumai was something of an antiquarian, collecting tea articles to preserve them as works of art; and he ultimately wrote a serious study of tea utensils in daimyo collections. His belief that the ceremony should become more personal, and less opulent and rule ridden, was laid out in his *Foundation of the Tea Cult,* which emphasized the importance of the host's role in tailoring the ceremony to suit the mood of his guests.

In 1867 the Takugawa shogunate ended. It had been beset for years by external pressures for Japan to become an integral part of the international trading community. Also, many Japanese liked neither the governing social structure nor the isolation that the shoguns had forced on the country. Oddly enough, it was a well-known tea master—Naosuke—who had signed the commercial treaty forced on Japan by the

United States in the 1850s, the first important official link between Japan and the outside world since the beginning of its self-imposed isolation more than two centuries earlier.

With the fall of the last shogun, the regime of the boy-emperor Mutsuhito was the first imperial court in seven hundred years to exercise real power, and the Meiji restoration saw the beginning of great change. Japan underwent in decades the transition from feudalism to industrialism that most countries managed only in centuries. The tea ceremony survived in this new environment, but more as a hobby than as part of any intellectual or religious system.

Upper-class houses still provided a separate space for it. It continued to be taught, sometimes by poverty-stricken gentlewomen who had learned the art in a distant, more prosperous girlhood. It was a favorite pastime of retired men and women who would spend whole afternoons conducting or taking part in tea ceremonies, during which they might simply enjoy being with their friends or might, more ambitiously, write poetry, exchange epigrams, or sketch a given subject together. It was the measure of feminine grace and refinement; a woman who had mastered the tea ceremony was thought to have learned poise and tact. Lafcadio Hearn, the naturalized American author who spent the closing years of the nineteenth century in Japan, wrote of the ceremony as "most exquisite art" and observed that mastery of it called for equal portions of native grace and patience.

There were tea masters, like Okakura Kakuzo, author of *The Book of Tea,* who continued to insist that the ceremony was not properly performed unless it reflected certain ethical ideas as to man's role in relation to the universe. In spite of this, the ceremony became more and more the property of a monied class that—like the Tokugawa samurai—used it to prove their success.

Rules multiplied and became increasingly complicated. In "this politest of arts" instruction came to be concerned even less with the mental aspects of the ceremony and more with the specific performance of its different parts. Because of this, *cha-no-yu* has generally come to lack either the lightness of a social occasion or the significance of a religious or philosophical ritual.

Interestingly, the democratic spirit of Rikyū has revived. There are now big tea gatherings that attract as many as two to three thousand people. *Cha-no-yu* has become a stop on tourist itineraries. Commercial tie-ins to the ceremony are used to sell merchandise.

There are scholars who study the history and philosophy of the ceremony, even though they do not bother to master its mechanical intricacies. Because of this and because the way of tea remains closely identified with Buddhism, it is unlikely that interest in the pure, non-materialist ritual will end completely. Unlikely also is that there will ever again be widespread integration of both the physical and intellectual sides of *cha-no-yu.*

To a traditionalist this is undoubtedly a loss, another victim of the increasing split between mind and matter in twentieth-century industrialized society. Yet there are signs of a spirit that, while it may not replace the old religious ethos of *cha-no-yu,* provides proof that it remains something more than mechanics.

In the writings of such modern tea masters as Sen'ō Tanaka and Sen Soshitsu XV there is an emphasis on intimacy, personal consideration, and subtlety, an acute awareness that within the context of the tea ceremony the man and woman of today can find values that are threatened in the outside world.

If *cha-no-yu* originally represented an extension and elaboration of Zen Buddhism's insistence on the isolated effort of the individual coming to terms with himself in this world, at its best today it may be one of the last civilized ways in which one individual can come to terms with another, can communicate a mutually shared appreciation for the aesthetics and the ethics of a ceremony that incorporates much of the best of Japanese tradition.

Nowhere else is the Japanese regard for beauty and proportion more evident than in *cha-no-yu.* The setting, the ritual and utensils, and the purpose all reflect a concern for harmony and detail. While this produces a setting of undeniable beauty and graceful manners that are pleasing in themselves apart from any deeper meaning, their true purpose is rather to free the mind from any jarring distractions that physical ugliness or unseemly behavior would impose. Thus freed, the mind is stimulated by the loveliness that the eye beholds and is capable of experiencing the emotional or spiritual exaltation that is the aim of *cha-no-yu.*

Because of this, and because of Buddhism's insistence upon cleanliness as a prerequisite for ritual, the preparations that the tea master makes before the arrival of his guests are of special significance.

Before the tearoom there is a garden, or *roji,* a pleasant place with winding walks, a low, massive stone fountain, stone lanterns, arbors, perhaps even a pond. The *roji,* a buffer zone of tranquility between the tea house and the clamor of the outside world, symbolizes the ever-changing nature of life in the wind that stirs its trees, the budding and falling of their leaves, and the light that changes with the time of day, the season of the year. Acceptance of the transitoriness of existence is a precondition for true understanding of *cha-no-yu,* so the *roji* assumes a sacramental significance. Always well-tended, it must be in perfect order on the day of the ceremony. It is swept, pruned, and tidied, then sprinkled with water. The water pipe that supplies the wash basin, or *tsukubai,* is replaced with a new one of green bamboo, as are the chopsticks used for placing twigs and leaves in the debris pit. The arbor where the guests will assemble when they first arrive is prepared for their comfort. As a final touch, the moss and grass that cover the ground are sprinkled again.

Inside the tea hut everything must be spotless. Not only the *shoin* or *sōan* where the guests sit to be served but also the *mizuya,* or preparation room, must be scrubbed and cleaned. Not so much as a trace of dust can remain.

Next the master must choose the utensils to be used from the assortment of bowls, caddies, trays, jars, flower containers, and incense cases in his collection. Tea utensils have been made in Japan for centuries, and there are even older examples from China and Korea. Many famous tea masters, among them Shukō, Jō-ō, Rikyū, Enshū, Sōtan, Sōwa, Sekishū, and Sōzen, either themselves designed or were closely involved with the design of one or more of the traditional tea utensils, and an important collection will contain examples associated with their taste. Some designs and colors are considered suitable for a particular season. The value of the utensil must also be taken into account, as it would be inappropriate to use utensils of too humble value in one ceremony, and equally inappropriate to use objects of too great value in another.

Also to be taken into account is the fact that the discriminating tea master makes a conscious effort not to duplicate styles, exact colors, or geographic origin, for such an oversight—called *tsuku*—indicates carelessness. Where in much of the world great care is taken to ensure that items used in meal or beverage service match to the extent possible, in the tea ceremony this approach would be totally unacceptable. Duplication is permitted only as a deliberate attempt at expressing an attitude toward the ceremony. For example the master may, to show his special regard for the style of a particular master, use two or at most three utensils associated with him. If he feels that a particular color is appropriate for the season and weather, he may use as many as three utensils in different tints of that shade.

The master must also consider the impression that the separate utensils will make when taken into the tearoom and arranged for use. The process that this involves is much like that of an artist contemplating all the disparate colors on his palette before combining them into a finished painting. Each individual color for the artist, each individual item for the tea master, is viewed primarily as to how it may best be used for the creation of the effect that is in the mind's eye.

As with the utensils, the scroll, or *kakemono,* that is to be hung in the alcove is chosen with the particular ceremony in mind. The scroll must be appropriate either to the occasion or to the season. If an example of fine calligraphy, the saying or poem it reproduces must be suitable for the occasion. If a painting, the scroll must reflect the season as well. It will not do, for example, to display a summer scene at a November ceremony or a winter scene in August unless one is deliberately trying to create a mood to counteract the weather outside.

The flowers that sit or are hung in the alcove must be fresh and arranged naturally so that the beauty of the individual flower may be appreciated without the distraction of a formal arrangement. The flower container, or *hana-ire,* must complement the blossoms, so it is selected with the same care as that given to the other utensils.

With the *roji* freshly sprinkled, the utensils ready in the *mizuya,* and the preparations for the special food underway, the master is physically ready for his guests. To be truly prepared, he must have extended this state of readiness to his thoughts. He must take care that his mind is free of all extraneous concerns, must contract it to the point where only the world of *cha-no-yu* exists and through this contraction touch the meaning of the universe by his mastery of this one part of it.

Now he is ready for his guests. For an intimate ceremony, they usually number no more than five, and just as the host has made his preparations, they are expected to have made their own for the event.

While there is no uniform or costume for the ceremony, guests are supposed to be simply dressed without jewelry or other unnecessary adornment. Clean, white socks should be worn over stockings. Perfume should not be used, as it might conflict with the smell of incense in the tearoom. The well-prepared guest will have brought along a folding fan (*sensu*) to convey greetings to the host and other guests, a handkerchief (*tenugui*) with which to wipe the hands at certain points in the ceremony, tissue paper (*kaishi*) to wipe the rim of the tea bowl after drinking from it, and a type of brocaded mat or coaster (*kobukusa*) on which to sit the tea bowl.

Courtesy demands that they arrive at least twenty minutes before the appointed time. If the tearoom is in the house, they are taken to a room especially prepared for their comfort while they wait. If there is a separate tea hut and the *roji* is meant for exploring as well as viewing, they are taken directly to the garden, where they assemble in an arbor near the gate to await their host. Here they will find a carpet on which to sit, an iron kettle warm upon the hibachi, cups of hot water to quench preliminary thirst, and pipes and tobacco for those who wish to smoke. During the ceremony itself, smoking is not allowed.

When his servant informs him that all of the guests have arrived, the host leaves the hut, goes into the inner *roji,* and performs a ritual at the *tsukubai* to show his guests that the basin has been filled and that the ceremony is about to begin.

Going to the gate, or *chūmon,* that separates the inner *roji* from the outer, he is approached by his guests. Bows are exchanged in silence; the host returns to the tearoom; and the guests, commenting in complimentary fashion on the garden and scenery, file through the *chūmon* toward the *tsukubai* where, one at a time, they rinse their mouths and wash their hands. At all times they are careful to follow the artistically arranged stepping stones, for to deviate from this path would be to miss the vistas planned for them by their host as well as to risk damage to the carefully tended moss or grass.

Meanwhile the host has reentered the tearoom, leaving the small guests' entrance, or *nijiri-guchi,* ajar, and the guest of honor leans down to enter the small passage, removing his sandals outside. The other guests follow, the last banging the entrance door shut to signal the host that all are arrived.

Upon entering the tearoom, the guests examine and admire the scroll and flowers before taking their seats. In most tearooms there is a place for the guest of honor adjacent to the host-master's own place, and the other guests seat themselves in whatever seems the most fitting manner. When the host appears from the *mizuya* to greet them, they comment on the loveliness and appropriateness of the scroll and flowers.

Unless the fire was laid as one of the preparation steps, in which case the major utensils used will be on display in the waiting area and the water already hot in the kettle, the only utensil present will be the iron kettle, or *kama*. If the fire has not already been laid, the making of it is the first step of the ceremony and the necessary utensils are now arranged about the fire pit if it is winter or the brazier if it is summer.

These utensils include the *sumitori* (charcoal carrier), the *kōgō* (incense case), the *hibashi* (iron-tipped chopsticks for handling hot coals), the *haiki* (a bowl full of specially dampened ash that can be put on the fire to keep down dust) and a metal spoon to put the ash in the hearth when needed, a trivet, metal rings that serve as detachable handles for the kettle, and a cluster of feathers for sweeping the hearth.

Taking the cluster of feathers, the master sweeps the already clean hearth. He then removes the specially cut charcoal from the *sumitori* and arranges it with great care, for the amount and placement determine how long it will take the kettle to come to a boil.

Offering the kaiseki, or small meal, that usually precedes the serving of ceremonial tea. For centuries many Japanese women have learned the tea ceremony. Notice the calligraphic scroll that is part of the decoration of the teahouse. Calligraphy is one of the many disciplines that tea masters must learn, and they often make their own scrolls.

Once the charcoal is arranged to his satisfaction, the host-master sprinkles incense over it. Only when a master wishes to show special veneration for a scroll is an incense burner, or *kōrō*, actually used in the tearoom, and it is then placed in the alcove. Otherwise, the incense is taken from the *kōgō* and added directly to the fire.

The fire lit and the kettle heating, the master starts the serving of the *kaiseki*. This is a special meal consisting of light, delicate foods appropriate to the season. More of a snack, it is presented on dishes chosen to complement both the food and the other utensils, and its arrangement is such that the decoration of the dish is still visible. The master does not share this food, but he does drink saké with his guests, sometimes sharing a cup with the guest of honor. The guests signal that they have finished the *kaiseki* by replacing their dishes and dropping their chopsticks onto the serving tray with an audible click, after which the host removes the soiled utensils to the pantry.

Preliminaries over, the preparation and serving of the tea itself, known as *temae,* can begin.

To bring in all of the tea utensils at once would be to spoil the pleasurable suspense of the guests as they wait to see what the master has considered suitable for their entertainment. It would also deprive the individual pieces of the attention they deserve. Because of this, the utensils are carried into the room in stages.

First the master brings in the *mizusashi,* or jar of fresh water. This placed so that it is displayed to best advantage for the edification of his guests, the master next brings in the *chawan* (tea bowl), the *chashaku* (tea scoop), the *cha-ire* or *cha-ki* (caddies, respectively, for thick or thin tea), and the *chasen* (bamboo whisk). The last items to be brought in are the *mizukoboshi* (waste-water jar), *futa-oki* (lid rest), and a ladle.

The attitude with which the utensils are carried in and arranged is most important. Pride in skill or possession should play no part in it, rather a gratitude at being able to share objects worthy of admiration. Since their arrangement must take into account not only aesthetics but also ease of use by the tea master, it calls for a deft touch.

The master now takes his place beside the hearth, facing his guests. He wipes the tea scoop and ladle with a silk napkin, puts the kettle lid on its stand, ladles hot water into the tea bowl, immerses the bamboo whisk in it, and empties the water into the waste-water jar. Using a cotton cloth, he wipes the tea bowl and whisk.

Before the ceremony, as part of his preparations, he will have removed green tea leaves from the large storage jar in the *mizuya,* powdered them, and placed them in the tea caddy. Now, using the scoop, he puts the correct amount of powdered tea into the cleaned and warmed tea bowl. The measure varies according to whether thick tea (*koicha*) or thin tea (*usucha*) is desired. Using the ladle, he now pours hot water into the tea bowl, and stirs it with the whisk, the amount and motion of the stirring also varying as to the desired consistency of the tea.

The master's pace throughout should be studied and stately. Any suggestion of erraticism would disrupt the serenity of the mood. Absolute silence on the part of the guests is expected because the guest of honor must be able to concentrate on the master's movements and enter into his frame of mind.

When the tea is a pale, foamy green and the master feels that it is ready, the bowl is placed before the guest of honor with much ceremony. After a ritual refusal on the part of the guest and insistence on the part of the host, the guest accepts the bowl with equal ceremony. Then, lifting it in both hands, the better to savor the warmth and substance of the bowl, the guest takes three sips. He then comments on the excellence of the tea.

As the size of the bowl, the number of guests, and the preference of the master may vary, what happens next may change from one ceremony to another.

If the bowl is small and his sips have emptied it, the guest returns it to the host, who washes the bowl and prepares tea for the next guest. If, however, the bowl is larger and its contents meant to be shared, samurai-style, the guest wipes the rim, rotates the bowl so that when picked up the place from which he drank will not touch the lips of the next guest, then places the bowl before the person next to him, who follows his example. Should the level of water in the kettle grow low during the tea preparation, the master replenishes it from the fresh-water jar.

When the last guest has finished his tea, hissing slightly to signify that he is done, the guest of honor will ask to examine the bowl. The master cleans it and hands it to the guest, who ponders it and makes respectful, knowledgeable comments on its quality. He then passes the bowl to the next guest for his examination and admiration.

If those present are connoisseurs, a lengthy discussion on some aspect of the tea utensils may begin, or there may be comment on the exceptional beauty of some natural phenomenon that the guests viewed in the interlude sometimes allowed between the *kaiseki* and the *temae,* such as a display of stars in the heavens or a flowering cherry blossom tree in the *roji.* The guests may offer epigrams upon a subject of interest to all. The only rules are that the talk be totally divorced from the mundane concerns of business, politics, and the like, that it be knowledgeable, and that guests conduct themselves in a manner fitting to the purpose of the occasion. Loud talking or laughing is frowned upon, as is excessive frivolity.

When the conversation has reached a logical conclusion, the master returns the utensils to the pantry in stages, as he brought them in. First he removes the ladle, lid rest, and waste-water jar, then the tea caddy and bowl, and last the fresh-water jar. When he bows to the guests from the threshold of the *mizuya,* the ceremony is over.

There are many variations on this basic theme. Ceremonies are held at special times of day, such as dawn or at night, that use dramatic lighting to emphasize certain aesthetic aspects of *cha-no-yu.* There are ceremonies in honor of particularly distinguished guests when the master uses only his most-prized utensils, and impromptu ceremonies to take advantage of freshly-fallen snow or a full moon. In the warm weather there are out-of-door ceremonies. There are ceremonies, in fact, for almost every occasion—to celebrate winter and summer, holidays, happy personal events, homecomings, and departures. At the last, there are memorial ceremonies.

However their minor details may differ, a common strain runs through them all. Beauty and ritual are neither cultivated for their own sake nor offered to prove expertise or wealth. They are, rather, intended to encourage the master's guests to enter into a world where physical appropriateness symbolizes the possibility of attaining mental harmony.

However fascinating the intricacies of the ceremony, it is the spirit that matters—the host's meticulous preparations for his guests indicating the sincerity of his consideration for them, the guests' response as much a signal of their appreciation of what he has done as of the beauty of a specific object or motion.

In its highest realization, *cha-no-yu* transcends the limits of connoisseurship and tradition and allows both host and guest to reach a state of mind approaching Nirvana. The dimness of the lighting, the fragrance of incense, and the smoke from the charcoal fire drifting slowly upwards create in the tearoom the sense of a self-contained world. Physical objects serve mainly to define the space and silence of the room, which is absolute save for the sound of the boiling water in the kettle. Outside sounds—a distant temple bell, a snatch of bird song, the wind in the pines—seem to have no beginning and no end, so that sound fades imperceptibly into silence to touch eternity.

It is often claimed that the spirit of the ceremony is so fragile that it is almost impossible to recreate in a world as ungentle as our own. This may be so, for few of us have much patience now with the fragile and the rare, even when we claim to prize them. Yet sometimes it must happen, that precious moment when master and guest realize that they are as one, that together they touch an experience that centuries before purified the minds of monks in lonely Buddhist temples and cleansed the hearts of fearless samurai about to face death, and that in reaching this instant of perfect understanding, they have found a phenomenon out of time.

· 4 ·

The English Aristocracy
and
Afternoon Tea

If life floats on a river of tea in Japan, England is an island awash in an ocean of the hot, fragrant drink. The English wake up to it, work by it, and drink it during leisure hours.

They brew a cup to celebrate good news and to help them get through bad. Shop stewards lead workers off assembly lines to protest changes in their tea break; policemen interrupt their rounds for a cup. Cricket matches break for it, and theater-goers are served it at their seats between acts. Soldiers gulp it in tents while on maneuvers; bishops sip it in the great, drafty halls of episcopal palaces. Farm laborers take theirs in the fields with just as much gusto as the well-to-do who drop in at Fortnum's tea rooms.

Each year an average of ten pounds of tea per person is consumed in the British Isles, making the English, the Scots, the Welsh, and the Irish the world's leading tea drinkers. The fact that world tea prices are set at public auction in London has as much to do with this massive consumption as with London's traditional role as a broker of teas.

So deep and heartfelt is the British affair with the drink that it has been only half-jokingly suggested that they would brew tea at the last trumpet—a reasonable assumption since they drink it to see them through everything else.

As nations of tea drinkers, the British and Japanese have much in common. Both originally got their tea from China—Japan directly in the form of tea seeds brought back by Japanese who had visited the nearby neighbor, Britain indirectly from Dutch traders transshipping processed leaf tea from half a world away. Both Japanese and British artisans copied Chinese utensils to be used as the drink grew in popularity, then began to develop their own techniques and styles for pots, kettles, cups and bowls. The people of both lands evolved special ceremonies around tea: *cha-no-yu* by the Japanese and afternoon tea by the British. Tea is also a strong commercial link between them, for today the Japanese are the most important customer of London's tea brokers.

There are, however, many more differences than similarities in the role played by tea in the two island kingdoms. To begin with, the Japanese grow most of the tea that they consume and are, in fact, the fourth largest producer of tea in the world, while the British must import every leaf. Commercial tea production in Japan is supplemented by individual tea bushes grown by farmers in odd nooks and crannies of their farms, but English householders must pay hard cash to indulge their most ingrained habit.

While individual tastes may vary, in general the tea drinkers of each nation prefer different kinds of tea. In Japan, it is green tea—in leaf form for ordinary drinking and as powder for *cha-no-yu*. In Britain, more people drink the hearty black teas—Darjeeling, Assam, Ceylon, Lapsang Souchong, for example. The Japanese generally take theirs straight, while the British like to add milk and sugar.

Tea is a relative newcomer to Britain, arriving only three hundred and thirty years ago. It first appeared in Japan twelve hundred years ago, died out, then reappeared over eight hundred years ago. In the mid-seventeenth century, even as Japan was withdrawing from the world into its two centuries of isolation, tea was helping to thrust Britain into the forefront of a colonial movement that ultimately saw much of the earth flying the Union Jack. Domestically, in Japan the changes in *cha-no-yu* reflected the contractions in Japanese society brought about by the class freeze Iyeyasu had begun in 1603. In England, also a land-based aristocracy, the spread of tea drinking was one evidence of a society expanding and altering from an agricultural past to a mercantile future.

Afternoon tea is even more firmly established as custom in Britain than *cha-no-yu* in Japan, and it is a much different proposition. For all the elegance that can at times attend it, afternoon tea is essentially a

A village teashop today.

pleasant, casual interlude in the hurry of contemporary life, a few minutes aside from the irritations of existence when one can chat with friends about the latest shows, pending business deals, scandal— anything that comes to mind. If alone, one can read or simply sit and stare blankly at the wall while munching cake. Afternoon tea can be taken at home, in a tea shop, on a train, thirty thousand feet above the ocean in a plane—almost anywhere. It is usually served between 4 and 6 P.M., and the food may be as elaborate or as simple as the host or hostess chooses. At a successful tea, the atmosphere will be cozy and the talk gay, or at least comfortable.

Cha-no-yu, on the other hand, may be served at almost any hour of the day or night and may or may not include food. It is performed as a precise ritual in a carefully designed environment of deliberate austerity. The conversation is limited and as structured as the ceremony, and the end result is supposed to be spiritual or mental elevation.

Cha was accepted in Japan first as a medicine, but its approval as a beverage and the evolution of tea-drinking into *cha-no-yu* had much to do with its association with Zen Buddhism. It was as a medicine also that the use of tea was first advocated in Britain; but no Chinese religious or philosophical systems came along with the tea chests, and the spread of tea as a beverage and the ultimate development of afternoon tea were due to nothing more esoteric than fashion and mercantile promotion.

The Japanese may expect a transcendental experience at *cha-no-yu,* but the British are content with a "jolly nice" time at afternoon tea. The reason for this difference is explained in large part by the way that tea came to Britain.

The Chinese and the Japanese were the principal producers of tea in the sixteenth century, were in fact the only producers of tea in any volume, and only China exported the processed leaf. This export had been confined to neighboring Asian lands on the ancient trade routes, and there had been no direct trade with Europe in any sort of goods, including tea. Then, in 1557, the Portuguese were allowed to establish a trading settlement at Macao, an island peninsula in southeastern China on the estuary of the Canton River. The weakened Ming administration had been tempted by the financial advantage to be gained from trade with the West, but it was uncomfortable about the whole idea and put very strict limits on Portuguese activities.

The Portuguese had developed the long-range ships that made sea-borne trade with the Far East possible, but they did not have adequate personnel to staff them and so turned to seafarers from other European lands to supplement their own sailors. One of them, a Dutchman named Jan Hugh van Lin-Schooten, wrote an account in 1595 of his experiences as a navigator on the Portuguese runs to the East. The Portuguese held the trading concession in Japan at this period, and much of their profit came from taking Chinese goods acquired through Macao to Japanese ports like Sakai and trading them for Japanese metals which they then either exchanged in India for fabrics and woods or carried back to Europe. In his book, along with accounts of numerous other wonders, Lin-Schooten described Japanese tea customs and mentioned the high regard the Japanese had for their rare tea utensils. The 1598 English translation of his *Travels* was the first time that most Englishmen had heard of tea.

Accounts of the profitability of the Portuguese trade with the East had attracted the attention of other European governments, including the English, and in 1600 Queen Elizabeth I chartered the British East India Company, giving it considerable powers as to how that trade might be developed. After the trading company set up its operations at Surat in West India, on the Gulf of Cambay, it attempted forays into Dutch colonial territory in the East Indies. These mercantile raids were unsuccessful, but during them English agents saw the Dutch and the Javanese drinking tea, tried it, and found that they liked it themselves. Unaware that the tea plant grew wild in parts of northeastern India, they continued to obtain the leaf in a roundabout way from the Dutch and the Portuguese even after their retreat to Surat.

In India there were goods to make the British trading venture worthwhile—valuable woods, fabrics, and jute, all sorts of merchandise and raw materials that would be profitable for resale in Europe, but all this paled beside the British East India Company's vision of trade with China. Whatever the rest of the Orient might offer, it was always China that lay on the horizon, tempting the adventurous with a cornucopia of exotic goods, including the little-known tea. The only problem was that China remained ambivalent about trade with the West.

It took the English several decades, an unsuccessful invasion of Chinese waters, a revolution and counter-revolution thousands of miles away in England, and a royal marriage to a tea-drinking Portuguese princess bearing trade concessions at Macao as part of her dowry before the British East India Company's ship *Princess* in 1689 carried from the Chinese port of Amoy the first tea to go directly from China to England.

Meanwhile tea, obtained from Dutch and Portuguese merchants, had become available in England on a limited basis, and the spread of the beverage was accelerated by political developments. After the stringent Puritanism of Oliver Cromwell's military dictatorship ended with the return of Charles II, the English allowed themselves a period of gaiety. Two of the places to which they turned with renewed enthusiasm were the tavern and the coffee house, and these very different establishments figured prominently in the early history of tea in England.

There was, of course, nothing at all new about taverns. In the form of the "win-hous" they went back at least to the time of the Saxons, and each invading army since had found taverns on the scene. To begin with, the wine was made in England, but with the coming of the last set of invaders, the Normans in 1066, more of it began to come from France and then from Spain and Germany as well. Over the years different ales were added to the offerings, and the crust of bread that had once been the only food available began to be supplemented by a greater variety of simple victuals.

By the 1630s a different sort of tavern began to appear. At that time London, although already growing rapidly, still contained a fair amount of open space and taverns like the Spring Garden in Charing Cross combined the traditional appeal of spirits with the excitement of a bowling green and high-stakes gambling.

Spring Garden, so named because it had a waterspring or fountain that was set off by the unwary guest treading upon its hidden mechanism, became so infamous for the fighting and quarrelling of its patrons that it was shut down. When it reopened, the emphasis was as much on romance, a sylvan grove where those wishing privacy in a rustic setting could indulge themselves after they had supped. Not surprisingly, Cromwell closed the place in 1654, but after his death it reopened and the gallants and their ladies once again made their way to the Spring Garden's enclosed Eden to listen to the warbling of the birds and the fluttering of their own hearts.

There were many such places. In 1609, on the site of what is now part of the grounds of Buckingham Palace, James I had a mulberry grove planted. A few years later it was here that a private entrepreneur opened the Mulberry Grove, which quickly became the fashionable tavern, the place where hearts and wagers were won and lost by members of the best set. As diarist John Evelyn wrote in 1654, the Mulberry Grove was "ye only place of refreshment . . . for persons of ye best quality to be exceedingly cheated at." His fellow diarist Samuel Pepys described it as "a silly place . . . (but with) a wilderness somewhat pretty." The patrons obviously forgave the silliness for the privacy afforded by the wilderness.

Behind the Piccadilly Hall, begun in 1658, the year of Cromwell's death, the fields off Windmill Street provided a place for the tavern's patrons to bowl and gamble, play tennis and gamble, and stroll gravel walks and gamble—albeit on a different sort of contest.

But these simple places and others like them in the Pre-Restoration period were soon to be eclipsed by Vauxhall Tavern and Gardens. Laid out in 1660 at the time of the Restoration, Vauxhall reflected perfectly the long-suppressed desire for fun. It was a combination of great park and fairground with many walks, an orchestra, masquerades, fireworks, and bowers where those in the mood for rest or dalliance could seek either in privacy. This was where princes and ambassadors, dukes and great beauties went for a night on the town that could be as respectable or as licentious as their moods dictated.

Not that Vauxhall drove the other pleasure grounds out of business. There were those who preferred the more intimate atmosphere of the smaller gardens. Many Londoners, the poet John Dryden for one, could still be found at places like the Mulberry Garden, idling with their masked mistresses in flower-hung arbors and treating themselves to cheesecake, syllabub, and sweetened wine. After the dinner that they somehow managed to consume on top of all this, there began to appear something new—a dish of tea.

Soon almost all of the gardens were offering the new beverage, and these places where the great and the humble might meet to share music, walks, bowers, bird-song, artificial caves, grottoes, and fireworks (thanks to gunpowder, another import from China) frequently gave pleasure-seeking Londoners their first taste of tea.

Coffee houses were the first establishments actually to sell tea to the public in England. A much more recent arrival than taverns—the first in England opened at Oxford in 1650 and the first in London, the Pasqua Rosee, began only in 1652—coffee houses filled a very different need. Coffee was one of the newly-introduced imports from the far-flung countries that European merchants were exploring for profitable merchandise, and it was a Turkish employee of an English Turkey-merchant who opened the Pasqua Rosee.

What the coffee house did was to provide its patrons with a congenial atmosphere that encouraged the drinking of the still-exotic beverage. To forestall any criticism, at almost the very beginning the houses set forth rules for conduct, and those who didn't obey them were no longer welcome. In fact, good behavior and the ability to pay a penny were the only requirements for admission. To drink a bowl of coffee or—after it was introduced—tea cost another two pence. Steady customers had their regular seats, and at some houses could have their shoes cleaned as they sipped.

Silver teapot, c. 1744, W. Williams, London. Engraved with naval battle between the French and the English in the War of the Austrian Succession.

Garraway's, one of the earliest coffee houses, was the first concern in England to sell tea to the public, praising tea's medicinal virtues and announcing that while tea had recently cost as much as two hundred shillings per pound, the proprietor had bought a large quantity and was prepared to sell it for the reasonable price of sixteen to fifty shillings per pound. The owner further announced that he would be pleased to serve the new drink to "noblemen, physicians, merchants, and gentlemen of quality."

And so tea took its place with the other offerings of the coffee house—coffee, cocoa, sassafras, and sherbet. From the beginning it was more expensive. In 1662 the Turk's Head was selling coffee powder for from four shillings to a little over six shillings per pound and chocolate for two shillings, sixpence, while tea was priced "according to goodness," and ranged anywhere from six shillings to sixty shillings per pound.

One of the reasons for the growing popularity of the coffee houses was that, in a day before offices and efficient communications, they provided a place where business could be transacted. Lloyds of London, to take perhaps the best-known example, started in the seventeenth century in Lloyd's Coffee House, a room where the underwriters and insurers of ships' cargoes met to discuss the day's affairs as they drank coffee or tea and smoked.

While coffee house frequenters had enjoyed tea as early as 1658, however, the general public was not as knowledgeable. Samuel Pepys— who got around—could write in 1660 that he "did send for a cup of tee (a China drink) of which I never had drank before." Tea only gradually became more familiar, and then for the most part within a limited, aristocratic circle. This was partly because Charles II had spent the last four years of his exile in the Netherlands, where tea, while hardly common, was available and much better known than in England. Some of the courtiers who had been exiled with Charles came back home with a taste for the new drink, and the marriage of Charles and Catherine of Braganza in 1662 gave the English a queen who began to make tea drinking fashionable in the highest circles.

Meanwhile, back in India, the British East India Company had begun to expand. Given Bombay by the Portuguese as part of Catherine's marriage settlement, it had also developed trading centers in Bengal and Madras. Its backers in England included some of the most powerful men of the time, and after the Restoration they were able without much difficulty to get Parliament to increase the company's already sizeable powers.

In this set of circumstances lay the seeds of empire. Picture the British East India Company with influential friends at home and with powers abroad approximating those of a sovereign state. Think of all the marvelous merchandise waiting to be bought and traded, traded and sold—the silks, the exotic woods, furs, precious metals, porcelains, dyes . . . the list could go on and on. Looking back and knowing what was about to happen, one can't help wondering when it was that from this long and dazzling list tea began to stand out, when the Company realized that in tea it had found the perfect commodity—one that could be obtained in almost limitless amounts and that could be replenished even as it was used up.

The Company was granted the sole monopoly to import tea into Britain, and in the last three years of the seventeenth century it imported an annual average of twenty thousand pounds. This led to a slight drop in prices, making tea more appealing in the marketplace. It was about this time that grocers in London began selling tea to their wealthier customers, and the potential market had also been increased by the introduction of tea into Scotland and Ireland.

The medicinal virtues with which the beverage had been associated were becoming increasingly submerged in the realization of other, more immediate benefits. In 1699, J. Ovington, chaplain to King William, addressed a delightful essay to the Countess of Granthom on the virtues of tea. He mentions the drink's novelty, its medicinal qualities, and its use as an antidote to drunkenness, but he also says that it is to be used for the "pleasure of gratifying the palate."

It was presumably for this reason that Queen Anne, who came to the throne in 1702, began to drink tea with her breakfast. She was not alone. The chocolate that had been the favorite drink for "milady's budoir" in the seventeenth century began to give way to tea.

At the start of the century tea drinking was confined mainly to the homes of the well-to-do who liked to be a little ahead of the crowd—and to the coffee houses, clubs, and what had now become known as tea gardens.

The reign of Queen Anne was the age of the coffee house. Their numbers increased through the last decades of the seventeenth century, and there were about two thousand of them in the first decade and a half of the eighteenth. There were so many and their followers so faithful that they came to be known for their company, and there was a house for almost everyone, whatever his interest.

Sea captains and merchants with concerns in China, India, and Australia congregated at the Jerusalem. Insurers went to Lloyd's, and stock-jobbers to Garraway's and Jonathan's in Change Alley. Gamblers patronized White's Chocolate House and the Covent Garden chocolate houses. Visiting Scots went to the British, and officers favored the Young Man's. Lawyers talked shop at Nando's and at the Grecian, not far from the Temple Bar, and parsons gravitated to Truby's and Child's, the latter in St. Paul's Churchyard. Wits went to Will's and Button's and Tom's, painters and sculptors to Slaughter's.

In these smoky rooms and corridors, noblemen rubbed elbows with merchants and highwaymen with clergymen. Any man with the penny for admission and twopence for a drink, who was decently dressed and knew how to behave, could go into any of the coffee houses, order a pipe and a paper of tobacco to go with his coffee or tea, then settle down to read the papers or converse with his fellows.

Sad to say, it was probably this indiscriminate democracy that doomed the coffee houses as surely as the high import duties imposed on coffee by the government. As one hundred years before the new mercantile interests had resented the entrenched aristocracy, they themselves now came to resent equally the politically and economically ambitious upstarts who were jockeying for position in the Hanoverian court that succeeded Anne, the last of the Stuart monarchs, in 1714.

Out of the political and social turmoil that surrounded the accession of George I, great-grandson of James I and first of the House of Hanover to sit on the throne of England, came the beginning of the era of the great clubs. Clubs had several advantages over coffee houses: the membership was limited, it was exclusive, it allowed for the pursuit of interests that might have been difficult or unwise to admit in the open atmosphere of a coffee house. Also, clubs were effective retreats from troublesome wives or creditors.

Some of the clubs, like White's, a gaming club, were outgrowths of coffee houses. Others, like the Scriblerus Club founded by Jonathan Swift for the purpose of advancing wit and conversation, were new. Even more than the coffee houses, the clubs tended to attract people who shared one interest, like the Lawyer's Club, where attorneys commented on the cases different members had in hand. Sometimes the members shared some characteristic—like those belonging to the Little Club, for men not over five feet in height. Frequently, they were for the perpetuation of an idiosyncrasy or opinion that caught the fancy of the founding members. In this category fell the Everlasting Club, whose members sat in rotation so that the club was everlastingly in session. Into this category, too, fell the Calves Head Club, founded after the Glorious Revolution had removed the autocratic James II from the throne, whose members met to ridicule the memory of Charles I, the ill-fated Stuart who lost his head at Whitehall in 1649.

Tea was served in the clubs; but since dining was a part of the activities, it was used mainly as an after-dinner beverage to clear the head. In these surroundings it is unlikely that tea could have competed with strong liquor or wine.

It was in the old tavern gardens where tea really began to come into its own. So strongly identified did it become with these places that during this century they became known as tea gardens. Vauxhall remained the premiere establishment, and the new gardens imitated it to the extent that they could.

Not all of the tea gardens were built primarily for the nobility. Jenny's Whim in Knightsbridge, which aimed more to attract a lower class, offered the usual bowling green, alcoves, arbors, and flower beds, as well as a fish pond, a cock pit, and a pond for duck hunting. Its large garden contained a variation on the trick fountain that was a feature of the first tavern gardens. At Jenny's Whim it wasn't a water fountain that would be tripped by the unsuspecting treading upon a spring, but a giant figure—a harlequin or some monstrous animal that would pop up before the surprised stroller. There was a sheet of water facing the tea alcoves, and mermaids floated upon its smooth surface. In the alcoves, patrons—whether the modest clientele for which the place was intended or nobility slumming for the night—could order strawberries and cream, syllabub, cake, cider, perry, ale, wine, and—of course—tea.

Porcelain teapot, mid-eighteenth century, Austrian. Painted with flower design in black and gold.

In 1742 Ranelagh Gardens opened, on the site of the gardens of Ranelagh House, east of Chelsea Hospital. Meant to be a sort of winter Vauxhall, it attempted a means of primitive heating in its central gardens, making them usable during the chill and damp of London's cooler months. Like many of the other gardens, Ranelagh depended heavily on the art of the stage designer for its charm. False perspectives at the end of vistas made them seem larger and grander than they were. There were all sorts of trick lighting and painted effects, and the buildings themselves were the work of Capon, a well-known scene painter. There was a rotunda with a Doric portico and arcade and a gallery, also a Venetian pavilion in the lake to which visitors were rowed in fanciful boats. The tree-lined walks widened to encompass garden huts, each containing a painting and comfortable seating. Concerts and masquerades were offered for the amusement of the guests, along with fireworks. On Sunday evenings there were tea drinkings.

Marylebone Gardens, opened in the late seventeenth century on the grounds of the wicked Rose Tavern, was another famous tea garden, with torches lighting romantic walks and latticed alcoves in which lovers might dally or the chilly might sip ale or tea while they listened to the musicians playing in their bow-fronted, balustraded orchestra stand. And there were special rooms for large balls and suppers, at which tea was offered as a restorative after the gaiety was underway and perhaps too much wine had been drunk or too intense a dalliance entered into.

By the closing decades of the eighteenth century, the entertainments offered by the tea gardens were very ambitious and attracted ever-increasing numbers of people to sample tea and all their other delights. In the 1770s at Marylebone, the visitor might find singers of bawdy songs followed by comedians giving magic lantern shows. Or hear tidbits from Shakespeare proclaimed by popular actors, or perhaps see a short play commissioned especially for the gardens. Or see magicians demonstrating sleight of hand—surely easy in the flickering lights of the torches, with the attention of the patrons as much on their companions as on the magician.

And if all this seemed tiresome, if they waited long enough, visitors could probably catch the orchestra playing Handel's Royal Fireworks Music while a fair representation of an erupting volcano lit the skies above London. This addiction to erupting volcanoes as a highlight of the fireworks show went back to Mount Etna in Sicily, which had blown its top with spectacular results in 1669, presenting fireworks designers with a natural model. And when patrons began to tire of watching Etna explode, they might be offered glittering representations of the nighttime Boulevards of Paris or even the Pyramids of Egypt.

In a day before television, motion pictures, radio or even much in the way of traveling entertainers, in a time when all lighting was provided by the sun, by candles, or by fire, when there was very little to divert the average or even the well-to-do citizen, it is no wonder that the tea gardens flourished. They gave variety to a population hungry for anything new, and their popularity seemed to know no bounds.

In the end, as with the coffee houses, it was probably this popularity that doomed them. As the crowds grew greater, the upper classes deserted the old pleasure haunts. More of the patrons ordered liquor instead of tea or wine, and rowdiness began to be a problem. Attempting to make up for the loss of many of their old customers by drawing larger crowds, the managements began to lower prices and the quality of what was offered. That meant that even fewer of the "better sort" came to stroll the shadowy walks with their bowers and alcoves, romantic retreats that also provided excellent hiding places for thieves and ruffians. What had seemed delicious when enjoyed by a few aristocrats began to appear dangerous when offered to the multitudes.

The last gasp of the tea garden movement was the attempt by a chef named Alexis Soyer to capitalize on the aristocratic crowds expected to flock to London for the Great Exhibition of 1851. It was Soyer's idea that, if he gave them a setting more sumptuous, more spectacular than anything they had seen before, the bon ton would come to his restaurant garden for their tea, wine and coffee, their dinners and between-times delicacies. To this end he leased a famous mansion, Gore House, and spent several months and thousands of pounds transforming it.

Gore House's Georgian modesty disappeared under tons of make-believe as each room and passage was given a decoration supposed to evoke a mood of longing for faraway places and unattainable, inexplicable experiences. There was a blue calico room covered in spangles, a pink calico room with an odd door lifted bodily from a dungeon, complete with studded nails and fetters. The back drawing room had become the "Night of Stars," with a cloudy ceiling and blue gauze hangings dotted with stars. One room was a Chinese pagoda, another an Italian cottage overlooking Lake Como. Most bizarre was the room made to look like an ice cavern, complete with stalactites and a stuffed wolf snarling at diners from the fireplace.

The reticent Georgian gardens were buried under thousands of roses. Overlooking them were the Alhambra Terrace and the Venetian Bridge. In the grounds was built a great baronial hall with vaulted ceiling, intended for the sorts of massive suppers and tea parties that the aristocracy had given at Vauxhall and Ranelagh. Like its predecessors, Soyer's Symposium offered walks where the bashful might enjoy each other in privacy. Unlike its predecessors, it couldn't persuade them to come and sample its delights, not even in the heady year of 1851, and poor Soyer lost a considerable fortune in his ill-timed attempt.

The times were changing. Ranelagh had closed in 1803. Vauxhall held on until 1859, then its buildings were demolished, its bowers torn down, its shady walks plowed up to provide building ground for a church and an art school—symbolic of the Victorian obsession with religion in concrete form and improving self-instruction at the expense of the old, lighter amusements.

The old-time coffee houses were only a memory by the time Vauxhall shut its gates for the last time. Most had been long closed, and the remainder had become taverns, so altered in character that they wouldn't have been recognized by the wits who went to Will's and the parsons who puttered into Truby's in the distant days of Queen Anne.

A lot had changed since that time one hundred and fifty years before when only the rich and fashionable drank tea. In some ways 1700 marked the turning point for tea, for after that time its price began to drop, it became more widely available, and it was accepted by an ever-growing public.

In the last year of the seventeenth century, the British East India Company had imported something like twenty thousand pounds of tea. In the years between 1700 and 1708, its annual tea imports averaged sixty thousand pounds and the price of the best Bohea tea was about twenty-six shillings a pound.

Considering other costs, this meant that tea remained relatively expensive, yet its use continued to increase. The government realized that a considerable revenue might be raised by taxing the newly popular drink, and began to levy duties on its importation, easy to collect because only the British East India Company was allowed to bring it in.

Undeterred, the public bought it in greater amounts, lowering its price still further, and in 1712 Bohea was down to only eighteen shillings a pound. In the 1720s the Company's annual imports went over the one million pound mark, and by 1727 Bohea was down to thirteen shillings a pound, by 1732 down to eleven shillings. Tea was now widely available throughout the British Isles, and well-to-do country people in the remotest hamlets ordered the leaf from their London grocers. The price continued to drop, and in 1762 the Company imported four million pounds.

These official importation figures and prices are to some extent misleading because the duty was high enough to make smuggling profitable. Some estimates put the smuggling figures as high as seven million pounds of tea in 1766, up to eight or nine million by 1784, which meant that about three times as much tea was being drunk in Britain as the official figures indicate. The tax on tea was so unpopular that smuggling was not considered much of a crime, and it became a considerable industry employing thousands of people throughout the country. It was only when the taxes on tea were repealed in 1784 and a much lower rate substituted that smugglers turned most of their attention to other, more profitable goods. In 1785, the first year after the reduced duties, official imports of tea reached almost eleven million pounds, and five years later they totalled over fifteen million.

This increase was not without cost. To ensure its position in India, seat of its trading empire in the East, the British East India Company—now known as John Company—and the British government had spent much of the eighteenth century driving out the other European nations who had established themselves there, and had then subjugated the weak Indian government so that by 1757 the British were the rulers of India. An even more unpleasant confrontation took place between Britain and China in the next century when the British went to war to force the Chinese government to allow the legal importation of Indian opium into the country to pay for the Chinese tea and silks that John Company could sell so profitably in Britain. Those drinking the tea in England little suspected the desperate confrontations taking place half a world away.

That tea appealed to the English, indeed fulfilled some need, is clear from its wide acceptance. From a drink favored by a handful of aristocrats and Londoners at the turn of the eighteenth century, it had quickly made its way through other classes. By the middle of the century the middle classes began to view tea drinking as a family affair, and the more prosperous sometimes had their pictures painted around the tea table. By the closing decades of the century, tea had replaced beer as the principal beverage in the laborer's home, and those who couldn't afford tea, which could be bought for two shillings, sixpence a pound, substituted roasted and ground rye.

At the Gooseberry Fair in Spa Fields, Islington, in London, stalls selling gooseberry-fool alternated with tea booths where a bowl could be had for threepence. On a more elevated social plane, at the fashionable spa of Bath, it was the habit of people of means to meet in the public rooms in the evening to chat, drink tea, and play at cards.

In spite of the fact that tea had the advantage of being nonintoxicating at a time when drunkenness was a problem, that its price decreased steadily through the century, and that claims continued to be made for its medicinal virtues, this spread of tea drinking excited a considerable amount of adverse comment. William Cobbett, he of the endless *Rural Rides,* complained of "the slavery of the tea and coffee and other slop-kettle," adding later that tea drinking destroyed health, weakened the frame, encouraged laziness, and debauched youth. He further insisted that patronizing the tea-table was "no bad preparatory school for the brothel."

Jonas Hanway, another eighteenth century commentator on what he saw as the evil of the age, went Cobbett one better, maintaining that tea would make women lose their bloom, their sleep, their teeth, and their digestion—not to mention their sense. As for men, no citizens of a "wise, active and warlike nation" like England would want to imitate "the most effeminate people on the face of the Earth—the Chinese, who are at the same time the greatest sippers of tea."

It would have been interesting to hear Mr. Hanway taken on by Dr. Samuel Johnson, who "swallowed his tea in oceans" and didn't like to have his cups counted. Or to listen to Mr. Hanway try to counter the sarcastic wit of playwright Richard Brinsley Sheridan, who liked a dot of brandy or rum in his breakfast tea. As for the Duke of Wellington, who thought the troops would be better off with more tea and less spirits, Mr. Hanway might have "met his Waterloo" if he had contradicted the hero of the age.

Just when tea, served any time, became the special drink associated with afternoon refreshment is uncertain, but the custom of serving the kinds of food now associated with afternoon tea goes back to the mid-seventeenth century coffee houses and tea gardens. Along with their coffee, tea, and chocolate, patrons were also served biscuits and jelly; and almost from their beginnings the tea gardens were known for offering food that was exceptionally dainty. The White Conduit House, for example, was famous for its hot rolls, and Jenny's Whim served special cakes along with its beverages.

The sandwich, the other mainstay of today's tea table, was supposedly invented during this century by an English aristocrat. According to legend, it was Edward Montagu, the Earl of Sandwich, who was responsible. An addict of the gaming table, he demanded something that he could eat without leaving his game, and his servant produced meat between two slices of bread. The new preparation became known by the title of the man who introduced it to upper class English society, and the sandwich was born.

In private homes the early eighteenth-century tea party was a purveyor of talk rather than food. It was probably in this era that the tea party got a reputation as principally a place for gossip, for discussing— as a contemporary observer disparagingly asserted—"Religion and Cuckoldom, Commodes and Sermons, Politicks and Gallantry, Receipts of Cookery and Scandal, Coquetry and Preserving, Jilting and Laundry." According to this jaundiced male, ladies required a draught or two of scandal in order to digest every sip of tea.

Just when cakes as well as chat began to be offered with tea can only be guessed at, but the reason for the general spread of sweets is easily discovered. Like tea, both white and brown sugar became common in England during the eighteenth century. It was used for sweetening coffee and tea, and for the first time it was cheap enough to be used liberally in food preparation as well, opening a new area of cookery to people who had not been able to afford it before and encouraging the better-to-do to use sugar to a much greater extent. This led to the widespread appearance of all sorts of cakes and confections. Since tea use was increasing at the same time, and since the tea gardens and coffee houses had set a fashion for serving food of this sort with tea, their appearance together on private tea tables was only a matter of time.

Another development that encouraged the taking of tea as a special occasion was the emergence of a large variety of attractive utensils meant especially for tea drinking.

To begin with, teapots had been imported along with tea—small, rather squat Chinese pots of unglazed red earthenware. As utilitarian items the Chinese pots served very well, having a body in which the tea could be brewed, a handle that didn't conduct heat from the boiling water, a spout through which the tea could be poured without spilling it, a top opening through which the pot could be filled and emptied, and a lid to cover the opening. The earthenware retained heat well, and in form and appearance the pots had a certain rustic charm, with a naturalistic handle and spout resembling tree limbs and a raised decoration of flowers on the earth-red ground on the body of the pot.

In terms of fashion, the first Chinese pots had two drawbacks: They were so small that one had to be provided for each tea drinker and they were common. It was not long before English silversmiths were making teapots for those who wanted and could afford something different, and English potters began to produce earthenware teapots. By 1698 two Dutchmen living in England, the Eler brothers, had produced pots much like the Chinese red earthenware examples and were selling them in London for as little as twelve shillings. About the same time in Nottinghamshire, potters were making pots of brown, glazed stoneware with incised decorations. In the early 1700s the British East India Company began to import Chinese porcelains, but they were very expensive.

This left a market for inventive English potters to satisfy: tea drinkers who could afford neither the silver teapots nor the oriental porcelains, yet who weren't satisfied with the simple earthenware pots in dark

Pottery teapot, mid-eighteenth century, Thomas Whieldon, Staffordshire, England. In form of an elephant with a trio of Chinese men for a finial, the serpent for a handle, and the elephant's trunk for the spout. Decorated with colored glazes.

colors. To fill this need the potters began to make pots and other dishes of white, salt-glazed stoneware decorated with embossed designs. When it became clear that the people preferred the bright hues and often-whimsical designs of the oriental porcelains, the potters began to offer teapots in a bewildering array of shapes and colors. Tea drinkers could pour their steaming brew from pots shaped like camels, shells, fruits, vegetables, even houses, painted in brilliant enamel colors. Teapots of ordinary shapes sported painted decorations of flowers, people, birds, feathers, animals, and fanciful landscapes.

John Astbury, one of the most determined experimenters, added calcined flints to clay in an attempt to whiten it still further. His teapots had colored bodies on which was stamped a relief of trailing vines in white clay, all of it covered with a thin lead glaze. With a white handle, spout, and lid finial, Astbury's pots were a distinctive addition to the tea wares available in the first half of the eighteenth century.

Experimentation and innovation were the rule of the day, and along with improving the quality and appeal of their earthenwares, English potters spent decades trying to duplicate the oriental and European porcelains being bought by the upper end of the tea-drinking public. By mid-century the porcelain factory at Chelsea was turning out some exquisitely painted examples that, while they did not look very much like the oriental porcelains, had their own charm. Porcelain was also made during the century at Bristol, Plymouth, Worcester, Derby, Bow, Longton Hall, Swansea, Nantgawr, and Swinton.

Complete dinner services were made at most of the factories, and the teapot and bowl or cup had given way to tea sets. A typical gold-anchor-marked Chelsea porcelain tea set of the highest quality in the 1760s contained a teapot with cover and stand, a sucrier and cover (covered sugar bowl), a slop bowl, a cream jug, a saucer-shaped plate, six tea bowls and saucers, and six coffee cups and saucers. Painted in puce on a white ground, each piece of this particular set was decorated with a different Italianate ruin, reflecting the influence of the Palladian movement that had revolutionized English architecture in the century. With such attractive utensils to be used in serving tea, tea drinkers naturally enjoyed creating occasions for showing off their personal tea sets.

The experimentation that produced all these different sorts of porcelains and pottery led to a competition that was so intense that the courts got involved in the extension and cancellation of patents for manufacturing processes, and apprentices swore to keep their masters' trade secrets when they were taken on. Some craftsmen refused to work with anyone else around, so afraid were they that their special techniques would be discovered and copied. Many of the porcelains and earthenwares that we use today were developed by these busy English potters over two hundred years ago.

In addition to producing his well-known figural teapots, Thomas Whieldon experimented with marbled ware, producing teapots that had brown- and green-streaked and mottled glazes. Josiah Wedgwood became Whieldon's partner for a time and began to manufacture Jasper ware—the unglazed blue, green, black, pink, yellow and lilac stoneware decorated with classical subjects in white relief that we associate with Wedgwood today.

Popular as his Jasper ware was, it was with his Queen's Ware that Wedgwood scored his most impressive coup. This was a highly glazed, cream-colored earthenware that Queen Charlotte, wife of George III, ordered from the potter and subsequently allowed him to designate as her ware. The royal family liked the simple, graceful shapes and the texture so well that they ordered several other services from Wedgwood. This ware was widely imitated by other potters, and variations continue to be produced today.

There were a lot of potters around to imitate Wedgwood or anyone else who came up with a good idea. The largest body of them congregated in Staffordshire in an area still known as "The Potteries." Wood, Wedgwood, Adams, Turner, Whieldon, Spode, Davenport, and Minton were only a few of the manufacturers who located in Staffordshire in this century—their names still familiar to lovers of fine English wares, in many cases their successors still in business.

Soon it was not enough to produce quality teapots, for buyers began to demand novelty. Lustreware, for example, was pottery glazed to resemble silver for a fraction of the price asked for the real thing, and lustreware teapots became the rage. Then, in the 1780s the porcelain factory at Swinton made a lidless teapot, an odd utensil filled from the bottom by means of a tapering spiral tube that ran from the hole in the base almost to the top of the pot. As there was no way to remove used tea leaves from this contrivance, the tea must have been brewed in another pot and then poured into the spiral tube, after which the mystery pot could be set on its bottom and used in the normal way while guests wondered how it had been managed.

Odd kinds of decoration began to be applied to teapots—incongruous motifs, odd sayings or portrait medallions of unlikely people. William Greatbatch of Fenton produced many articles of good quality in the late eighteenth century, but one of his most popular items was a teapot on which was printed, in black, the history of the Prodigal Son. Whether lighthearted tea drinkers were improved by scanning this tale while chatting over the teacups is unknown.

As the century entered its final decades, the growing fashion for transfer decoration on teapots and dishes found its most perennially popular pattern in the English version of an oriental scene now known as *Blue Willow*. Anglicized copies of other oriental patterns followed, and in 1780 John Turner of Caughley, Salop, was making a pattern called *Nankin*. In 1782 a popular tea set, *Broseley*, was fashioned after *Nankin*.

Ceramic teapot, c. 1775, English. Rectangular shape of the pot is copied from the Chinese, but the handle and spout are in the English crabstock form. Decorated with a painting of Chinese figures in a garden.

Turner was but one of many potters who capitalized on the continuing association of all things Chinese with tea. The blue-on-white coloring that became popular at this time was soon being used for the famous Staffordshire Blue wares that, far from copying oriental scenes, showed

English landscapes and very English motifs and, somewhat later, American scenes and events. Some of the handsomest teapots in both decoration and shape, and some of the most typically English, date from the first decades of the nineteenth century before mass-production methods had coarsened the wares.

The increasing availability and variety of tea wares and other utensils led to a great deal of collecting, a hobby among the aristocracy since the time of Catherine of Braganza. When Dutch William and his English wife Mary came to England to claim the throne in the late seventeenth century, they inspired another round of collecting by the fine examples of Delft ware that they brought with them. Defoe, early in the eighteenth century, toured the British isles, and his written account of his travels describes china piled high on tops of furniture, arranged on chimney pieces, and set on shelves specially built to hold it. Throughout the century, many people of taste and means, as well as those who wanted to appear so, collected all sorts of porcelains, particularly jars and tea paraphernalia.

In his poem, *Isabella,* Sir Charles Hanbury Williams wrote:

> To please the noble Dame, the Courtly Squire
> Produced a Teapot made in Staffordshire.

It is to a particularly noble dame, Anna, Duchess of Bedford, that the credit is sometimes given for beginning the custom of afternoon tea. She was visiting Belvior Castle—the elegant pile recently used in the movie as the home of Little Lord Fauntleroy's proud grandfather. As in many great country houses of the day, there was no lunch as such, just a late breakfast followed many hours later by dinner. This custom had evolved because most of the house party spent its days in the hunting field during the season. Anna wasn't keen on hunting, and she began to break the hungry afternoons by serving tea and cake in her rooms at Belvior. She liked the little meal so much that she continued the practice in London and so set a fashion in town.

Whoever was responsible for the first serving of afternoon tea as we know it now, it was well established by the early 1800s. In *Our Village,* a series of charming sketches of village life in Hampshire in the early years of the century, Mary Russell Mitford wrote of a selfish old bachelor who visited her family, had lunch, and puttered around until time for tea. Then "The moment tea was over, without the slightest apology or attempt at conversation, he drew his chair to the fire, set his feet on the fender, and fell fast asleep in the most comfortable and orderly manner possible."

This picture of tea as a pleasant and even relaxing time is ironic because with the coming of Victoria, the serving of afternoon tea, like so much else in that contradictory monarch's reign, took on an air of grandness and ceremony far removed from the notion that tea was a time to be spent in comfort by one's own fireside.

Tea wares, whether silver, porcelain, or pottery, grew heavier and more ornate in keeping with the grandiose taste of an age that felt if a little decoration was good, a lot was better. As the wares grew heavier, so did the atmosphere. Tea parties became very structured. There appeared large numbers of primers, manuals, handbooks, and guides telling middle-class Victorian hostesses in precise detail exactly how every step of afternoon tea should be handled.

Pottery teapot, c. 1825, Ralph Hall, Staffordshire, England. A piece of the famous Staffordshire Blue, decorated with a transfer print of an English scene.

They specified the proper time: 5 P.M. for formal "at homes" in the dining room; 4, 4:30 or 5 P.M. for relatively informal drawing-room tea. They outlined the method. For a small tea, the footman was to take the tea tray into the housekeeper's room, along with the silver teapot and teakettle, the sugar basin, the cream jug, and teaspoons. The housekeeper or cook was to make the tea, fill the hot-water kettle with boiling water, put sugar in the basin and cream in the jug, then arrange the teacups on the tray along with the teaspoons and a plate of thin bread and butter or cake.

Aided by the butler, if the household was too poor to have a second footman, the first footman carried his heavy burden into the drawing room and set it before his mistress on a low table. The preferred taste dictated that these tables be small and covered with their usual cloths of velvet. If the tables were usually uncovered, they were left bare for tea as well. No plates were provided and, usually, no napkins.

A big tea was much more elaborate. More food was offered, and in addition to tea, particularly if men were to be present, sherry, claret, or champagne cup was available.

If the hostess liked entertaining in the afternoon, she might make a habit of having a regular day for tea parties, say every third Tuesday between 4 and 7 P.M. These were sometimes big affairs with music and impressive food presentation. If the weather was fine and the hostess's home boasted sizeable grounds, tea might be served in the garden, where tents and marquees would be scattered around. At these big affairs servants poured the tea and passed the food. (This was the age of servants; even modest households boasted one or two.)

By the 1870s and 1880s afternoon tea in these houses of London's prosperous middle classes had become almost as ritualistic as *cha-no-yu,* even though the desired result was not mental and emotional uplift but a bevy of guests convinced that the hostess knew what was what and had the wherewithal to arrange it. From its relatively modest and intimate beginnings, afternoon tea had begun to assume the character of a large-scale entertainment.

It was only toward the end of the century that the meal began to grow less formal again, particularly in the very best houses in London, where teatime was an acceptable occasion for romance during the social season. It is interesting that, in an era when behavior was circumscribed by all sorts of rules and restrictions, the business of tea and flirtation was so gracefully managed.

Husbands went out to tea, if not to their clubs then to take refreshment with someone else's wife. Meanwhile, it was considered perfectly respectable for the left-at-home wives to assemble their own guest lists for tea. If the list was gradually and discreetly pared to a particular gentleman and certain proprieties were observed, the lady's reputation was not sullied. To begin with, there must be no suggestion that a visit of any length was contemplated by the lucky gentleman. Because of this, he could not leave his hat, gloves, and stick in the hall, but must carry them into the drawing room and lay them on the floor as if he planned to stay only a moment. That done, the Victorian mania for privacy made the hostess's firm closing of the drawing room door nothing to comment on, and a closed door was never entered by a well-trained servant unless he or she had been called for.

With a husband entertaining himself elsewhere, the door closed, the servants safely on the other side of it, and the large sofas of the period scattered invitingly about the room, it was perhaps inevitable that more than cucumber sandwiches was sampled during the afternoon hour sacred to the hissing urn.

As the Victorian age drew to a close and the fun-loving Edwardians began more and more to set the tone for the best society, afternoon tea also became less structured in the great country houses, those "Stately Homes of England" hymned first by Felicia Hemans and then by Noël Coward. House parties had been a regular feature of social life since the advent of fast coaches and, especially, the spread of the railway network in the nineteenth century. By the turn of the century, it was an obligatory part of the season to leave town on occasional weekends and repair to the country for a change in scene.

House parties tended to be large by today's standards—no problem because the houses that were the destination might have as many as forty or fifty bedrooms and staff numbering in the dozens. The guests would leave London, not in the newly available motor cars, but in a train that was stopped by signal at a tiny wayside station serving the host's estate. The horse-drawn carriages that would have been waiting a few years earlier would in all likelihood have been replaced by Rolls-Royces, Swifts, Stars, Argylls, Panhards, Napiers, Talbots, Daimlers, Mercedes—or any of the other better motor cars that had caught the host's fancy. While the maids and valets of the party supervised the loading of heaps of luggage onto omnibuses or carts, the guests would be arranged in the staff-driven cars for the ride to the estate.

There might be a drive through a village belonging to the estate, then a brief stretch of open country before the house's lodge gates came into view, the gatekeeper and his family bowing and curtsying as the cars advanced slowly into the park. Through the host's woods, past his pheasant enclosures and herds of fallow deer, the cars would wind their way around the kitchen gardens, hothouses, stable buildings, and possibly even a tiny church. There might be acres of lawns, then—at last—the house, where the host and hostess, backed up by an army of servants, would be waiting for the party.

The weekend's activities would be centered around the house and the surrounding neighborhood from the time the guests arrived on Saturday until they left on Monday morning. The grounds would be strolled, the stables visited. There might be another drive through the village. On Sunday morning there was church to attend, then a big lunch to digest. On Sunday afternoon the energetic might take out a horse or try their hand at golf on the lawns.

By teatime the party would be tired from all the wholesome activities and fresh air. It was just as well that the pomp and circumstance of mid-Victorian teas was no more, but the more casual proceedings in vogue by this time could have their own pitfalls in this setting. The relaxation in protocol might make for an easier hour, but it also led to something of a letdown in conversational standards. The witty epigrams of a few decades earlier now tended to give way to long and tedious discussions of the pedigrees of animals whose flanks the guests had reluctantly patted earlier in the stables. If the scones were as soggy as the talk and the tea as lukewarm as the party's enthusiasm, teatime was a sentence to be served as quickly as possible, the dullest point of the party. If, on the other hand, the cucumber sandwiches were paper-thin, the crumpets buttery hot, the cakes delicate, the tea strong and practically boiling, and the talk more witty than worthwhile, it was only with reluctance that the guests would get up from deep chairs before the fire and make their way to the distant bedrooms for an obligatory rest before dressing for dinner.

There was no teatime dalliance here. Illicit romance was banished to the later hours and made possible not by the shut door of the town but by the hostess's tactful room placement and by the common practice of not inviting husbands and wives together.

Teatime in the grand country houses had by this era become just another part of the comfortable life that the occupiers of such places considered their due, and their lives were comfortable indeed. Nathaniel Hawthorne was American consul in Liverpool in the 1850s, and after visits to various country seats he made the observation that the English aristocracy possessed one talent above all others—the ability to create congenial private worlds.

Once a landed nineteenth-century Englishman went through the lodge gates of his estates, the road that he traveled was his, laid out to his liking, winding its way through scenery that belonged to him, passing the cottages of people employed by him, circumventing the stables that housed his horses. The cows that grazed in the distance were his cows, the deer that cropped his meadows were his deer, the birds that rested in his trees were his birds, the hounds in his kennels his hounds.

The house that was the centerpiece of the estate was either built by his ancestors and altered by him at his whim or was entirely to his design. Finances allowing—and money went a long way in those days—he might have a castle in the medieval style, an Indian pavilion, a serene Queen Anne façade, or an oversized facsimile of a grand Italian villa. Or, if he were rich enough and his architect eclectic enough, he might have all of them in one house so that Moorish arches sat atop a Romanesque body with a Mansard roof and Neoclassical interiors. He could furnish his house with anything he chose—relics of a profitable sojourn in the East, leftovers from his Elizabethan and Jacobean forebears, chaste pieces of Queen Anne, or fine Louis XIV articles bought from French aristocrats during the Revolution. He could leave his age-begrimed ancestors hanging on the walls in their heavy, gilt frames, or retire them to the attics and put up his hunting trophies in their places.

When he sat on his terrace, sipping his tea, all that he saw was his, adorned and maintained in the way that he decreed. Putting down his cup and going for a walk in his grounds, he might wander for miles without seeing even a distant vantage point that didn't belong to him, might never encounter anyone who didn't work for him or wasn't dependent on the trade of his household.

Within the boundaries of his estate, he was literally lord of all that he surveyed, and he arranged for himself and his family a life where privilege meant comfort. Beauty and order surrounded them; their stomachs were never empty, their throats never dry. Afternoon tea fit nicely into this world. In its more formal phase and in the easier atmosphere that had evolved by the turn of the century, the silver pot of steaming tea and silver chargers piled high with cakes, sandwiches, breads, and confections were a welcome break in the long afternoons between lunch and dinner, particularly in the winter when dark drew in early and the great, impressive halls favored by the Victorians and the Edwardians were reduced by shadows to cozy inglenooks beside the huge fireplaces.

In the fictional Manderlay so evocatively brought to life by Daphne Du Maurier in *Rebecca,* the waste that often accompanied tea in a great house is suggested. The nervous second Mrs. de Winter is momentarily distracted from the brooding atmosphere of Manderlay by the sumptuousness of the afternoon teas. Heaps of scones, mounds of marmalade, crumpets awash in butter, cakes of all sorts, and enough tea to float the British Navy appear in the library each afternoon whether anyone is there to eat them or not.

In the end Manderlay went up in smoke; but had it survived, the odds are very good that, fifty years later, it would no longer be the sole domain of the de Winters. There were hundreds and hundreds of country houses scattered around England, Scotland, and Wales at the end of the nineteenth century, some enormous, some relatively small. Yet most of even

Tea at a Stately Home of England.

the small ones would be considered large today; and almost all of them had some claim to architectural, historical, or local importance. Whether their grounds were measured in tens or tens-of-thousands of acres, they reproduced to a great extent the enviable private world that Hawthorne saw. His observation that such perfection seemed out of place in this too-imperfect world and his doubts that it could last have been justified, for today the private worlds have mostly vanished, conquered by a combination of high death duties, agricultural depressions, energy costs, the servant problem, and changing ideas about the comfortable life.

Compared to the still-considerable number of houses that continue in the middle of their private worlds, there are many more that, while escaping the fate of being turned into offices, hospitals, hotels, or institutions, have become that most valuable of tourist commodities— the historic house. Whether charges of the National Trust, the property of public authorities or private foundations, or still privately owned, they have essentially become museums open to a public that pays to roam their statue-lined corridors and admire their book-filled libraries, be impressed by the centuries of portraits hanging on their walls, and go—at last—to their tearooms to refresh themselves before taking on the all-too-prevalent game park, costume museum, old car exhibit, and antique shop.

Most of the historic houses offer tea on the premises, some in the houses themselves. At Wimpole Hall and Parnham House you can sip a cup and eat your cake in the old dining room. At Hardwick Hall, Kedleston Hall, Felbrigg Hall, Boughton House, Ickworth, Oakes Park, and Parham, you take tea in the old kitchens. Holkham Hall, that marvel of the Palladian age, will serve you tea on the terrace, so you can look over the extensive estate where some of the most-important agricultural experiments of the last few centuries were carried out.

At Badminton House, Dyrham Park, Wrest Park, Mount Edgcumbe, Belton House, Burghley House, and Newby Hall, the orangeries have been converted into tearooms, at Glynde Place the coach house. The stables are where you linger over your cup at Chicheley Hall, Raby Castle, Marble Hill House, Weston Park, Brympton d'Evercy, Temple Newsam, and Althorp, family home of Lady Diana Spencer, the Princess of Wales. At The Vyne and Chastleton House it's the old brewhouse where the tea is poured. Tapeley Park and Great Comp produce the steaming cup in the dairy, while Cotehele House, Trerice, and Bickleigh

Castle send you to the barn for your afternoon repast. At Knebworth House there's a real tithe barn to tower over you while you take a break.

Some of the historic houses take special pride in their homemade teas, among them Langton Hall, Rockingham Castle, Quenby Hall, Attingham Park, Hanch Hall, Dalemain, Levens Hall, Ednaston Manor, Breamore House, Eyhorne Manor, Saltwood Castle, and Hoghton Tower.

There are hundreds more where you can roam premises once lived in by names from history books and maintained by fortunes large even by today's standards. For the hour or day that you choose to visit, these private worlds become yours to enjoy without the bother of worrying about dry rot or taxes. Where an aristocratic few once sat on sun-dappled lawns, took their scones from old Spode plates, and sipped green tea from Chinese cups, the visitor can drink hot, strong brew from thick, white earthenware mugs before wandering down to the stable block to look at vintage cars where horses used to be.

It isn't quite the same, of course, sharing the orangery or kitchen tearoom with a dozen other people instead of sipping tea alone in the library or listening to the idle conversation of fellow tourists rather than sinking into the hush of a vast house maintained for one's own benefit. You haven't just come in from playing on the tennis lawns that lie beyond the kitchen garden or from handing your horse over to the groom at the stable; and when you finish your tea, you won't be going up to your bedroom to relax before dinner, but only to the discreetly disguised car park to collect your MG or Maxi and go on to your next stop. Those aren't your great-aunts and great-great-uncles lining the walls of the corridor that led to the tearoom, and it wasn't your family's servants who used the quaint utensils displayed on the kitchen shelves. Chances are that you wouldn't want them to be, for few of us would want to return to the economic and social realities that supported such a world.

And yet . . . and yet there are echoes here of what the best of it must have been like, sunlight slanting through the window of time to strike a faded tapestry, bringing it to life again, suggesting the value of seeking the beautiful and of adopting the nuances that provide pleasant shadings for the harsh outline of existence. This world, though not our world, can teach us something about the art of living, about grace and charm and the ability to recognize that we can—that we should—bring taste and conviviality into our own lives. And few things make one more receptive to instruction than a cup of well-brewed tea and a well-baked scone.

While afternoon tea was evolving into an art in these stately purlieus and was being used by middle-class Victorian hostesses to prove their social prowess, it was discovered by the general public as well. The first A.B.C. shop opened in 1880 at London Bridge, serving tea and snacks mainly to typists employed in the area. Fourteen years later the first Lyons Tea Shop opened in Piccadilly and began to serve good tea and cake to anyone who wanted a reasonably priced tea in a hurry. The demand was so great that both stores became the flagship concerns for successful chains.

The improvement in rail services and, after the turn of the century, the spread of the motorcar led to a large increase in the number of people taking holidays away from home, and those who stayed at home were getting into the habit of eating out occasionally. All this boded well for the spread of the tearoom. It was a rare hamlet that did not boast at least one attractive house with a discreet sign in a front window proclaiming, "Teas," and one especially pretty village had over twenty.

With the explosion in travel in the twenty-one years between the First and Second World Wars, probably thousands of redundant vicarages, disused stables, and otherwise unrentable shop premises were transformed into well-appointed tea shops complete with fresh napery, flower-sprigged china, old oak furniture, and masses of antique copper and brasses. All over the land sprang up the Wisteria Tree and the Wishing Well, the Singing Kettle and the Whistling Pot, the Primrose Cafe and the Rose Cottage. No respectable cathedral close was without its tearoom; no castle worthy of a guidebook failed to have one beside its gatehouse. Tearooms overlooked seaside promenades, abbey ruins, and mountain passes. They were crammed cheek-by-jowl with antique shops and souvenir stands in well-known beauty spots, or stood on remote moors with only wild ponies to notice their rose-hung charms.

Changing habits and the rationing of tea, sugar, and gasoline during World War II were obstacles that many of the tea shops could not overcome; and since the war even more have closed, victims of competition from fast-food restaurants and catering laws that are particularly crippling to small, marginal food operations. It is a common complaint in the pages of the *Guardian* and the *Times* that it is next to impossible to find a decent tea shop anymore. It is harder, certainly, than it was in the days when thousands of village tea shops dotted the countryside, but it's far from impossible.

The Wisteria Tree still blooms and the Singing Kettle hums across the green and smiling land. There are still signs in farmhouse windows offering "Homemade Teas." In London there is still Fortnum and Mason's Tearooms with page after page of cakes and breads and sandwiches, not to mention the palm-strewn court of the Ritz where the ceremony would not shame the writers of Victorian etiquette guides.

The smallest country inn and plainest village cafe will usually offer at least bread-and-butter sandwiches and a pot of tea. More-ambitious establishments provide menus with dozens of possibilities ranging from meringues and Florentines to seed cake and Sally Lunn and then on to lobster salad sandwiches. By and large the seeker after tea and sustenance in the late afternoon will be offered a choice of set teas, usually a cream tea, a tea with cakes, or a full tea with cakes and sandwiches.

A cream tea, that most ambrosial of delights, is made up of scones, strawberry preserves, a pot of Devonshire cream (or Somerset cream, Sussex cream, or whatever is handy in that line), and a pot of hot,

An English set tea with bread and butter, Dundee Cake, Scones, Clotted Cream, Preserves, and a gigantic pot of tea.

Afternoon tea with nut cake, sandwiches, pound cake, crumpets, scones, clotted cream, preserves, mints, teapot and hot-water pot.

fragrant tea. A full tea gives the hungry pilgrim two or three kinds of sandwiches, cakes, and bread of some sort as a general rule.

Some tearooms offer what amounts to a buffet—several kinds of cakes, sandwiches, breads, tarts, confections, and pastries—and the guest pays for the items selected. Almost all of the historic-house tearooms use this method of serving.

As for the main feature, the tea itself, everywhere it tends to be served hot enough to scald the unwary tongue and so strong that the extra pot of hot water that is automatically offered is just as automatically used to dilute the potent liquid to a drinkable consistency.

The ambience of most tearooms is equally strong, tending to a kind of cozy cheerfulness that seems to exclude anything unpleasant. There are few moments more satisfying than sitting in an English tearoom as evening closes in, listening to the muted laughter of the party across the room that seems to be having such a good time, watching the waitress deftly arrange plates of sandwiches and cakes around your pot of tea, and letting the smell of hot butter drift slowly into your consciousness.

Without company and old copper the moment can be even better. There is something quintessentially English about tea in an old country inn on an afternoon when light rain streaks the thick window panes, about sinking into a Windsor chair with arms worn by decades of elbows, about basking in the warmth of a crackling coal fire and inspecting old engravings hung about the walls of a sitting room so homey that it might be your grandmother's parlor, if your grandmother lives in a nine-hundred-year-old house. You shift your toes closer to the glowing grate, then a smiling girl comes through the door carrying an enormous tray, which she bids you enjoy before departing, leaving you to contemplate scones, paper-thin sandwiches, raisin-crammed cake, and what must surely be one of the world's biggest pots full of steaming, fragrant tea.

It is an experience to be had nowhere else, this easeful partaking of good things and hot tea, this hour apart. One of the most endearing things about the English character is this ability to take food and drink and turn them not into some grand gustatory adventure but into a time of warmth and hospitality, of sociable and delectable sensations. With the tea that is poured from the pot, whether the tea be Chinese or Indian, the pot commonest clay or finest porcelain, comes a spell of as much understanding and sympathy, comfort and conviviality as we mortals are likely to now.

· 5 ·

Planning
Our
Afternoon Tea

A Japanese tea savant claimed long ago that there are two types of tea masters: the one who loves the ritual and the beautiful utensils, and the true devotee of tea who loves the metaphysical aspects.

Today I suppose he would say that the host or hostess more concerned with the maker's mark on the bottom of the teapot than with the spirit in which the tea is poured from the pot is missing the point. Yet even while admitting that the generosity and consideration with which the tea is served are more important than the specific details of its serving, we must also acknowledge that by its very nature afternoon tea has certain physical requirements. There must, of course, be tea to pour and something from which to pour it; there must be food and utensils with which to serve and eat it; there must be a setting of some sort; and there must—unless a solitary tea is contemplated—be guests, or at least, a guest.

The format of the afternoon reception long known in some circles here and abroad as the tea party offers us no help. We aren't aiming at masses of guests. We don't want the dining room table loaded down with silver candelabra, overpowering flower arrangements, a monstrous silver tea service, and plate after plate of cakes, sandwiches, bonbons,

91

salads, and ices. We don't want an event of such proportions that it takes several friends to help us serve it, and most of us don't have the neatly aproned and capped maids who discreetly replenished the tea tables of years gone by, then spirited away the dirty dishes.

We don't want a mathematical fete, planned by taking the number of guests to be invited and multiplying them by so many finger sandwiches, so many mints, so many ounces of salad, cups of tea, ounces of milk, slices of lemon, and cubes of sugar per person. We don't want the bother of accumulating and the responsibility of storing and caring for so much paraphernalia—the silver flatware, the silver tea service, the porcelain, the napkins, all of it coordinated to the last detail, all of it elegant to the point of stultification. We don't want the pretty food that somehow never quite lives up to its eye appeal—the fragile cakes that taste of cardboard when they taste of anything at all, the diminuitive sandwiches frosted with tinted mayonnaise, the perfect bonbons that coagulate in the mouth.

Yet in leaving the dullness of what we've been taught to think of as teas, we also leave the security of a known path and set ourselves on an itinerary where our only guideposts are those provided by our own taste and confidence. We don't have the strength of either the English or the Japanese tea traditions behind us; what we do have is the American genius for adaptability and for producing and enjoying, whatever the older cultures might think to the contrary, well-prepared food in an appealing setting. We aren't afraid of trying new things, and we are past masters at taking old ones and making them better.

The first step in successfully making this ceremony our own is the throwing out of old misconceptions about afternoon tea. If it isn't a massive reception, neither is it two fragile great-great aunts daintily eating angel food cake over cups of the palest green tea while they discuss the peccadillos of their younger relations. Its setting isn't confined to chintz-filled living rooms or to oak-beamed parlors with a tea table by a window overlooking a picturesque cathedral close. We don't have to have a lot of expensive equipment, a knack for teatime epigrams, or the skill of a professional pastry cook. Our most important devices are imagination and the willingness to experiment; and while there are no hard-and-fast rules that must be followed as we go along, there are certain things that it would probably help us to keep in mind as we adapt the pleasant custom of afternoon tea to suit our own way of doing things.

To begin with, we shouldn't forget that afternoon tea is a treat, not a necessity. It should be fun for us to plan and execute, something for us to enjoy with our guests. It's a small meal that doesn't require nearly the quantity or variety of food and accoutrements called for by a dinner party or even a luncheon; bread and butter, a good pot of tea, and the necessary number of cups and saucers make a perfectly acceptable tea if we haven't time or inclination for anything more. It's a portable meal: a sofa by the fire, a breakfast nook, an apartment balcony, a townhouse garden, a farmhouse porch, a penthouse terrace, a kitchen corner, any place that suits the season and our mood is a good place for serving tea. We can have one guest, ten guests, or no guests. Sometimes the nicest tea of all is the one we give ourselves. Even the time is more flexible than one might think. Because we are planning a small, less-structured social occasion, we can begin as early as two or three in the afternoon or as late as six, and while our guests will usually remain an hour, a really good conversation might carry us into a second hour or even a third.

Planning the tea. The teapot is eighteenth-century English porcelain, Worcester of the Dr. Wall period, painted with exotic birds.

This flexibility means that we can do things pretty much as we please—serve what we like, where we like, and to whom we like. Let's start by contemplating the ideal guest list. It is an old Chinese proverb that to drink tea with more than four guests is common. The precise number may be debatable, but the guest list should be kept small, partly because of the difficulties in serving tea properly to a large number, partly because the noise of more than a handful of people is antagonistic to the spirit of tea. A small number of guests allows the host or hostess to cultivate the intimacy and the spontaneity necessary for a successful gathering.

The personalities of the guests are also important. Not everyone is suited for the proper appreciation of an amusement as subtle as afternoon tea, as not everyone is suited for any other single activity we may ourselves enjoy. The ideal guest for afternoon tea is one who likes good conversation and good food and who is able to appreciate the atmosphere and aesthetics that make the occasion special. In assembling this ideal guest list and setting a day and hour, we have to remember that for us and for our guests this kind of occasion is usually easier to manage on Saturdays and Sundays, as most of us have weekday schedules and responsibilities that do not lend themselves to leisurely afternoon breaks.

Keeping in mind that the ideal number of guests is probably no more than five or six, we should decide if that is the number we are comfortable with. A lot of us function best when we can devote all our attention to one or two other people, and some of us need the stimulation that a few extra guests would provide. When we've settled on our personal ideal number, we can begin to think about the accoutrements we'll need to serve them.

The most basic item is the teapot. While we certainly won't need anything on the order of the tea cauldron at the great Lhasa cathedral that held twelve hundred gallons, we should have a pot big enough to serve at least one round to our ideal number of guests. On the other hand, it shouldn't be so big that we can't lift it comfortably and safely when it is full of tea. The pot should be stable, so that full or empty there is no chance of its tipping over, and it should be made of some material that will hold heat. It should have a lid that will stay on while we are pouring, a spout high enough so it won't dribble tea when the pot is full, and a handle that doesn't conduct the heat of the boiling water to our hand. To help keep the teapot hot, it is good to have a tea cozy of quilted fabric to slip over it.

Silver teapot, 1719, Thomas Folkingham, London. An octagonal shape.

Some tea connoisseurs like to have, in addition to the teapot, a separate pot for hot water. This lets them make the basic pot of tea very strong, knowing that they can use the water from the pot to adjust the strength of the tea to individual tastes.

A useful partner to the teapot and the hot water pot is the teakettle that can be carried to the tea table and set on its own trivet and burner so that fresh water can be boiled for a second pot of tea without the host or hostess leaving the guests. If we are going to make tea before our guests, we will probably also want to have a tea caddy from which to take the tea leaves and a spoon for the transfer of leaves to pot.

If we plan on serving coffee or hot chocolate along with the tea, we will need a coffee pot. For offering iced tea in the warmer months, it is helpful to have a pitcher, glasses, and iced teaspoons.

We will need containers for milk and for sugar and a dish for the sliced lemon. It is nice to have a waste bowl, which is a wide-mouthed container slightly larger than a cup into which the dregs of earlier cups of tea are discarded before subsequent cups are poured. To serve the sliced lemon, there should be a small fork of some kind (a lemon, pickle, olive, or seafood fork is about the right size), and for the sugar there should be either a sugar shell or tongs, depending on whether we prefer loose or cube sugar. For presenting the food, we need a cake plate or some other round platter and at least two or three additional plates or platters of varying sizes, a cake knife or pastry server, a marmalade jar and spoon, and a butter dish and knife. There are many other items that can be useful—such as bread warmers, tiered serving pieces, and footed cake stands—but they are not essential. It is, however, good to have some sort of not-too-large container in which to put a flower or two and a small bowl for fruit.

Porcelain chocolate pot, c. 1765, Meissen, Germany. A charming piece with painted decoration of flowers and orange scales.

To eat the food we will need a napkin, a small plate (salad or dessert size is about right), a teacup and saucer, a teaspoon and—if hot bread requiring butter is to be served—a small knife apiece. If we suspect that a guest may be uncomfortable eating with his or her hands, we might also want to provide a dessert or salad fork, although tea food is generally finger food. If sherry or Madeira is to be offered along with the tea, we will need a moderate-sized decanter as well as a small all-purpose wine glass apiece (the four-ounce size is fine).

However elaborate or simple the tea that we plan, this is all the equipment that we need or can use, and much of it can be eliminated if our teas are very simple. The point is that we can serve a very nice afternoon tea without shelves of china and silver. It may be that some of us had grandmothers with foresight, that is, who laid in service for twelve in silver, china, and linen, who delighted in accumulating interesting serving pieces, and who passed all of it on to us in immaculate condition, in which event all that we have to do is to stroll into the pantry and choose what suits the fancy of the day.

If, for whatever reason, our china cupboards aren't that well stocked, then we must do our own accumulating, which is probably better anyway since it lets us get what appeals to us rather than what appealed to grandmama.

We'll start with the teapot. In the three and a half centuries since western potters were first exposed to this utilitarian item, they have devoted considerable ingenuity to finding different shapes for it, and pots are made in all sizes, in silver, pewter, enamel, pottery, porcelain, and glass. Whether our tastes run to the antique or to the new, we can have a pot shaped like an animal, a fruit, a country cottage, or almost anything else. We can have pots that are dead-white, black, or any color in between, plain or painted with riotously colored scenes, smooth or embossed. Of course, most of us won't be buying the pot alone but a sugar and creamer besides, and these might as well match unless we find a very old pot that we love that has lost its mates along the way. Whether individual pot or tea set, we can buy something perfectly adequate for a few dollars in a department or specialty store or pay thousands in an antique shop.

As to whether the tea set should be metal or pottery or porcelain, we have to decide if the greater durability of silver or pewter is compensated for by the fact that metal does not hold warmth as well as earthenware. Metal sets do give us more versatility in that they can be used with different patterns of plates, serving pieces, and cups.

Silver tea utensils generally come in the following sets: teapot, sugar and creamer; teapot, coffee pot, sugar and creamer; teapot, coffee pot, sugar, creamer and waste bowl; teapot, coffee pot, sugar, creamer, waste bowl and kettle. Usually the matching tray, which is very useful, must be purchased separately. Shapes range from the severely angular to the graceful bell-shapes preferred in the days of Queen Anne. The pieces may have no decoration, incised decoration, or be repoussé, that is, the decoration may be formed in relief so that the silver seems to explode with flowers or fruit. Sterling tea sets are extremely expensive, silver-plated surprisingly reasonable.

Ceramic coffee pot, c. 1770, Liverpool, England. Painted with brilliantly colored oriental scenes. The English and European craze for chinoiserie lasted several decades, and this pot shows the fanciful Western view of the East.

If we prefer the feel of pottery or porcelain—and many do—we will probably have to buy our tea set by the piece from an open-stock list unless we buy an old set at auction or in an antique shop. Many makers of porcelain and pottery still offer the classic designs associated with tea. In porcelain, Oxford's *Ming Blossom,* Aynsley's *Bird of Paradise,* Wedgwood's *Kutani Crane,* Coalport's *Ming Rose,* Royal Crown Derby's *Old Imari*, Spode's *Siam*, and Noritake's *Nanking* are only a few currently available patterns that reflect the oriental influence. In fine pottery, the oriental feel is very strong in Spode's *Indian Tree*, Wedgwood's *Lotus*, Adam's *Chinese Bird*, Mason's *Manchu*, and Booth's *Real Old Willow*.

If we are attracted to the oriental shapes in pots and prefer tea bowls to teacups, we can find reasonably priced teapot-and-bowl sets at shops specializing in products of the Far East. These will not, as a rule, include a sugar and creamer since few Orientals use sugar or milk in their tea.

Craft shows are an excellent source for interesting and unusual pots, cups, and bowls if we like the Japanese way of intermingling various shapes, colors, and textures in our teaware.

There is no law that says everything must match, and it is fun to set a tea table with things that complement one another but don't necessarily duplicate every nuance of color or design. The only thing to be avoided here is fussiness—with several different patterns and colors it is possible for our table to look busy, and simplicity is what we aim at. Still, if we have a good sense of color and proportion, it is fun to haunt not only craft shows, but antique shops, auctions, garage sales, seconds' shops, and flea markets for bits and pieces to put together for an effect.

The plates and platters for serving the tea food can match the tea set or not; but if they do not they should be chosen very carefully so that they do not clash with it. Similarly, the individual plates can match the tea set or the serving plates, or they can be of a different pattern. If we're trying to accumulate an antique set, laboriously acquiring a piece or two at a time, it is unlikely that we will be able to find a set of plates to match the basic service. For that matter, we may not be able to find all three pieces of the tea service itself. Matching isn't important if the individual pieces look good together; and if we set a tea table that seems pleasing and harmonious to us, it will probably seem so to our guests as well.

Teacups can be the same pattern as the pot and serving pieces and plates, but—again—it isn't essential as long as everything looks good together. If we like the hot spiced tea of the Russians or the mint tea of the Middle East, we might want to consider getting glasses instead of cups. Meant for hot tea, these are somewhat taller than teacups and are set in metal holders.

The flatware that we use at tea—the teaspoons, sugar shell, butter knife, small individual knives, iced beverage spoon, lemon fork, marmalade spoon, cake knife—may be of silver, silverplate, pewter, or stainless steel. Simple patterns work better, as they look good with a greater variety of tea wares. Again, matching is largely a matter of preference as long as the flatware pieces resemble one another in scale and feel and are made of the same material.

If the tea caddy isn't going to leave the kitchen, all that matters is that it have a tight-fitting lid to preserve the freshness of the tea and to keep it from being contaminated by other substances. If we're going to use it at the tea table with the pot and kettle, we'll probably want an attractive one. Antique caddies are handsome and sometimes have locks on them, reminding us of how expensive tea once was. Today's caddies are made in many materials—porcelain, wood, pewter, brass, copper, silver—but among the most efficient and certainly the most economical are the tins decorated with colorful designs, some of which are chinoiserie in feeling, reflecting the Chinese origins of tea.

For linens, we will need a napkin for each guest. Also, if there is no obvious tea table and one must be improvised from a card table, drawing table, or one of those useful, portable, cardboard tables, we will need a cloth long enough to touch the floor and disguise the table's origins. This need not match the napkins as long as it is a complementary color and design. For that matter, it needn't officially be a table cloth; a pretty sheet cut and hemmed to size is sometimes even more attractive and almost always more economical.

The color, pattern, and texture of linens can be very useful in setting a mood. If our tea set is a plain white, an enormous variety of linens is available to us, suggesting a time of year, a degree of elegance, or a decorative motif. Even patterned tea sets lend themselves to very different linens. A friend of mine has a rose-sprigged set, all soft pinks and greens on white porcelain, that she uses with different sets of napkins at different times of the year—in the spring the palest pink, in the summer a sea-foam green, in the fall a darker green, and for Christmas white with lace trimming. Another friend has a set of old willow ware, in very strong blue on off-white. With it he sometimes uses napkins of a blue that almost exactly matches that of the pottery, but most of the time he prefers either dark red or bright yellow linens that offer a dramatic contrast to the tea set and dishes.

A lot of us have old cloths and napkins embroidered by patient hands decades ago, and these can be charming used with the right sort of tea service. A very sleek and modern set of white pottery looks surprisingly good with the dainty stitchery and somewhat faded colors of the old linens, and they are a natural with silver tea sets and delicately flowered dishes. Anyone who likes to do needlework might enjoy custom-designing his or her own patterns to get exactly the desired effect.

For a tea table, many of us will simply use a coffee table. Otherwise, a butler's tray table with a removable tray works very well for tea, and a tea cart is a pretty, practical serving medium although some fussy people think it is too casual.

Probably many of us can find most of what we need to set a very nice tea table by ransacking the stock of dishes and table accessories already on hand; but if we must accumulate, we should keep in mind at the outset that whatever we get must not only be bought, but stored and cared for. Silver does have to be polished; old dishes must be washed by hand; and the custom laundries that will do fancy linens are difficult to find. If we don't have much time for maintaining our possessions—and few of us do nowadays—we would probably be happier with tea wares that can be popped into the dishwasher and with linens that are in reality easy-care polyester blends.

Silver cake basket, 1785, Hester Bateman, London.

Unless we have storage to spare, we should avoid odds and ends that, however interesting in themselves, are so bizarre that they're unlikely to be very useful with anything else—unless we intend to use them as accent pieces. The simpler anything is, the more versatile it is.

In choosing all of our accoutrements, we should keep in mind that not only the appearance, but the feel of the utensils and the linens is important. To the masters of the Japanese tea ceremony the weight and balance, the texture and shape of the tea bowl was as important as its color and decoration. Tea drunk from an almost transparent porcelain teacup decorated with forget-me-nots seems actually to taste not better, not worse, but different from tea drunk from a heavy, handleless, earthenware bowl of the sort preferred by Orientals.

Something else we should not forget in choosing our tea wares and linens is the background against which they must be used. A novelty tea set in which the devil is the teapot and boiling cauldrons the creamer and sugar bowl may be fascinating on a picnic but merely odd in a living room furnished in Chinese Chippendale, nor is a set of old Imari ware going to be happy sitting on a rustic kitchen table. If we are tied to a setting with a very definite personality of its own, we will probably find a simpler pattern and neutral colors easier to work with, assuming that we don't want to create a tea service specifically designed to complement the setting.

While we needn't go to the extremes of Chou Wenfu, the Chinese scholar who was so attached to his teapot that he had it buried with him, we should make an effort to find a teapot and other wares that we enjoy using, for our enjoyment will communicate itself to our guests. And in assembling and choosing all of this—the dishes, the flatware, the linens—we should not forget that the point of the accoutrements is that they are useful items in a form of entertaining meant to please our guests, not to impress or intimidate them. That is why simplicity is to be preferred to the obviously expensive and rare. We flatter our guests by offering them an attractive table; by presenting an ostentatious one, we attempt to draw attention to ourselves.

Setting is as important as the tea service, and the most carefully thought-out and well-prepared tea will suffer from being presented in an ugly, noisy, or overpowering environment. It is not necessary to have an elegantly decorated drawing room complete with wood fire going in the Adam grate or a terrace overlooking stately lawns or—for that matter—the rooftops of New York City. The proper scene for afternoon tea is more a matter of details and frame of mind than an area of a certain size decorated in a particular style.

In Japan the tea hut or tearoom is a carefully designed environment meant for ceremonial tea drinking. The aesthetics of the room affect the ceremony and are, in turn, affected by it in the eyes of the guests. While we can hardly turn any part of our houses or apartments into a tearoom per se, there are many things that we can do to suggest a becoming ambience that will put both us and our guests in the proper frame of mind for enjoying tea. Even if our space and resources are limited, we can create one comfortable and pleasant place for afternoon tea. This will naturally be different for each of us, and its importance makes it worth our while to give it some thought.

For instance, old houses with their many nooks and crannies provide a treasure trove of possibilities. Alcoves off living rooms and dining rooms, breakfast rooms, oversized halls, and porches lend themselves to tea very easily. Space is more difficult to come by in newer houses, but they usually have one particularly attractive spot—an area by a large window overlooking a pretty yard for instance—that, with the addition of a small table and two or three comfortable chairs, can double as an ideal tea area. Even one-room apartments, called bed-sitting rooms in England, have potential. The space itself isn't what matters most, rather the spirit in which it is arranged, for the illusion of coziness and tranquility is almost as effective as the real thing.

Again, the aim is not opulence, but rather comfort and comeliness. Most of us have in our living rooms a sofa and a chair or two, as well as some sort of table nearby. If we arrange a companionable grouping, as indeed we probably have already to make the room more appealing for everyday use, we have the basic setting for afternoon tea. If we aren't thrilled by the fabrics of the seating pieces, we can throw quilts or colorful sheets over them and toss a few attractive pillows around. If we don't like the table but it's sturdy and a good size, we can cover it with a floor-length cloth. If our budgets don't yet run to much in the way of furniture, we can group pillows on a quilt or rug on the floor and set tea on a cloth in the center.

If it's winter and we're lucky enough to have a good fireplace, we can light a fire. If it's summer, and our windows overlook treetops, we can throw them open to the greenery and birdsong. If unpleasant outside noise is a problem, we can put on a favorite instrumental record or tune in a local FM station. On the wall we can hang a painting or photograph that, as in the Japanese tearooms, reflects the season and our mood, or we can put up a museum poster advertising an exhibition of the work of a favorite artist. This is the time to put out that new book we've just finished and can't wait to discuss with an appreciative friend. If we've a collection of any kind, it's fun to put it close to the tea area, as nothing is more interesting to talk about or reveals our true personality so much as what we choose to accumulate for the love of it, and an important part of a good tea is the development of rapport between us and our guests.

Food and drink are a very effective means of putting people at ease. While the menu will vary from tea to tea, there are some underlying considerations that we should keep in mind. As host or hostess our attitude is the single most important element in a good tea. If we are hot and tired from being too long in the kitchen, then we will not be sensitive enough to the mood of our guests to respond to them properly.

In planning our tea menus, we should take into account how much time we can reasonably allow ourselves for preparation or assembly of the food. One of the first lessons learned by Japanese child students of tea who are destined to become masters is respect for inanimate objects. Like the Japanese, we will have a successful tea only if every part of it is performed with consideration not only for our guests but also for the tea utensils and for the food and drink that we serve. We must also respect our own capacities and not be too ambitious in our menus. It is better to have one beautifully prepared dish and a well-brewed pot of tea than to offer our guests half a dozen platters of half-heartedly prepared food and bitter, lukewarm tea.

Historically, tea as a between-meal treat has been served with a variety of foods. At Dutch parties in the seventeenth century it was flavored with sugar and saffron, and offered with rich cakes. In the Dutch colony of New Amsterdam, soon to become New York, it was served with hot buns and waffles sprinkled with sugar and cinnamon. In the seventeenth and eighteenth centuries, buns were also a popular offering at English tea gardens, along with cakes and pastries. In the nineteenth century Japanese tea houses gave the tea drinker looking for light sustenance fruit, particularly watermelon and pears, and Japanese hostesses served cake with tea.

In England two kinds of afternoon tea evolved: a regular tea and a high tea. A high tea was essentially a substitute for the late evening meal, and meats, soups, and puddings were served along with bread and cake. By 1900 a typical regular English tea menu might consist of very thin bread and butter, some sort of cake (Dundee, Seed, or Madeira), tiny sandwiches (cucumber was a favorite), and a special bread (like scones or Sally Lunn). Travelers in Scotland in the 1920s would find that their tea at a small-town inn could include both white and brown bread, currant bread, gingerbread, jelly, and hot cakes and butter.

Tea in Russia might be served with a *dastarkhan,* or offering tray of treats: round cakes of sour-milk dough (*patyr*); candies, possibly the balls of roasted and ground walnuts known as *yanchmish;*pastries filled with nuts, pumpkin, or chopped vegetables and egg (*samsa*); and a bowl of fresh fruit (pomegranates, apricots, plums, pears, and grapes are favorites).

Today a full set tea in a good English tea shop would probably give the customer bread and butter, scones, two or three kinds of thin sandwiches, and a small selection of cakes.

Other foods may be served with afternoon tea, and even in England all sorts of salads and light luncheon-type dishes are available in some tea shops. There is, however, something appealing in not having to bother with forks, a throwback perhaps to our childhoods when eating everything possible with our hands was completely natural. Because eating with one's hands does tend to have a relaxing effect, contributing further to the cozy mood we are aiming at, most of the treats for which recipes are given in this book do not require forks, and only a few of the breads call for knives with which to spread butter or preserves.

In looking at the recipes and sample menus given later in the book or in improvising others, we should remember that there are several reasons for offering a variety of foods with tea. When small amounts of several dishes are provided, the guest need feel no embarrassment at not liking or being unable to eat any particular one. Besides, people are delighted with a choice of foods beyond any practical considerations. Just watch the pleasurable indecision on most faces at a buffet or in a cafeteria line. Even those who in the end choose only one or two dishes have enjoyed contemplating the rest of the food. Finally, and not least important, tea food is attractive, and a nicely arranged assortment of it adds an aesthetic element to the meal, as well as giving an air of plenty conducive to the feeling of ample hospitality that will make our guests feel that much more welcome. As for any leftovers, many tea foods will keep for days or even weeks in airtight containers.

If we're serving only one or two guests, and we know exactly what they will like, we should feel free to give them that one thing, beautifully prepared and presented. The one-dish tea is the perfect time to do something that must be served as soon as it is ready, as there is nothing to distract the cook from giving the last-minute details his or her best effort.

In deciding on our menu, we should keep in mind not only the considerations of time and money, but also those of atmosphere. Most tea foods smell delicious cooking—there are few things pleasanter in cool weather than to go into a house that smells of fresh-baked gingerbread, for example—but remember that not everyone enjoys all cooking aromas.

It goes without saying that dishes must be chosen very carefully so that their tastes are compatible without duplicating one another. We wouldn't want to serve Chocolate Citron Cake with Chocolate Dabs and Chocolate Muffins. On the other hand, while Curry Butter Sandwiches, Marble Spice Cake, and Ethel's Brown Sugar Chews taste nothing alike, each has such a distinctive flavor that serving them together will only startle the palates of our guests.

The way the assembled tea food will look is something else to consider. Since it forms a part of the decoration, it should lend itself to attractive presentation, that is, be varied in shape, size, and color. For example, Black Walnut Beauty Cake, Coconut Balls, Sugar Cookies, Scones, and Petticoat Tails are all white in color; and while there is nothing in their flavors to make their being served together objectionable, they would make for a monotonous-looking table. In the recipe section, sample menus are offered that avoid repetition or clashes in flavor, and these may be used as a starting point for other combinations.

Some of our guests may have religious dietary restrictions or be following low-calorie, low-fat, salt-free, or sugar-free diets, and we should try to have at least one thing that they can eat. The easiest way of doing this is to have fruit on hand—a small bowl of crisp, red-skinned apples or purple-skinned grapes adds enormously to the eye appeal of any table. Celery and carrot strips stood upright in a glass tumbler are another possibility. Also, many of the recipes can be adapted to take dietary requirements into account.

Unfortunately, some of our guests may restrict themselves out of culinary conservatism. Like the cliché, conservative Englishman, some are suspicious of the new and untried. If we have someone like this on our list, it is good to include at least one of the old standbys, something like Maggie's Gingerbread, Sugar Cookies, Corn Muffins, or Old-Fashioned Baking Powder Biscuits.

Finally, in putting together our tea menu, we must take into account how much time we will have for marketing. If the tea is impromptu and we have only an hour or so to get ready, we'll want to stick to one or two

Silver creamer, 1774, T. H., London. In the form of a cow with the tail for a handle and the cow's mouth for a spout. A popular shape for creamers and milk jugs.

things that may be quickly prepared and for which we already have the ingredients. Or we may want to dip into our emergency larder.

Even more important than the food is the tea, the kind and form being an individual preference, and, to some extent, a matter of experience and palate sensitivity. There are those who will not drink "real" tea, that is, tea made from the leaf of *camellia sinensis*. To them we can serve herb teas, coffee, cocoa, fruit beverages, or other liquids. A fuller discussion of all these drinks follows in the sample menus and recipes section.

The secret of a successful afternoon tea is to have planned it properly so that everything possible is done ahead of time. The rested and cheerful host or hostess is worth more to the guests than elaborate dishes or special decorating. What we aim at in our planning is a state of preparedness that allows an atmosphere not of escape from the world but of mental tranquility, one that encourages us to focus on the parts of our being that transcend the mundane considerations of jobs and duties, that lets us share our personal, innermost selves with one another.

· 6 ·

Serving
Afternoon Tea

Afternoon tea is a lot like a theatrical production—no matter how much time, material and thought have been put into it, it won't be successful unless the curtain is raised, the stage properly lit, and a mood created at the outset that encourages the members of the audience, that is, our guests, to enjoy themselves.

Because of this, first impressions are very important. If we are happy and relaxed when we open the door, if we greet our guests with enthusiasm, and lead them into an immaculate and imaginatively decorated setting, we are well on our way to a good tea. Their anticipation should be heightened from the beginning by what they see before them.

In the spring—with linens in the delicate shades of new grass or budding flowers, a bowl of daffodils or narcissi, a window open to the song of newly active birds, light and especially mouth-watering food—the brewing of one of the aromatic herbal teas like pennyroyal or lemon verbena will intensify the freshened spirits everyone feels at this time of year. With summer and the coming of hot weather, ferns in the window, a fan going lazily in the background, iced tea, and the lightest of food will give an illusion of coolness, a welcome oasis from the heat.

As fall approaches, the color and vibrancy of the season may be suggested by a bowl of red apples, an arrangement of miniature chrysanthemums, heartier food, and strong, brisk tea in the pot—Darjeeling or one of the spicy herbals like basil or fennel would be good. And if in winter a fire crackles invitingly on the hearth, pretty afghans are tossed across a chair to guard against stray chills, a bouquet of fresh flowers sits on the mantel, and the tea table is loaded with warm breads and spicy sandwiches, the guests will begin to relax and feel warm the minute they walk in the door. The steam that rises from the cup when the tea is poured offers a further visual barrier between the company and the outside cold, proof that in this charmed circle the winter weather is only an excuse for drawing closer together.

Pastry and tea served on modern tea set with floral decoration.

A nice touch at any time of year is an open bowl of potpourri near the tea area. Lavender, lemon peel, lemon balm, orange blossom, and rose bud are especially appropriate for spring. In the summertime, scents that suggest cool woodlands are pleasant, among them angelica root, cedar wood, patchouli herb, and woodruff. Aromas that seem particularly evocative of autumn include bay leaves, coriander, mace, marjoram leaves, rosemary, sage, and spearmint. Allspice, cinnamon, frankincense, ginger, nutmeg, and orange peel are very effective in winter.

Once the guests have absorbed the overall atmosphere, their attention will naturally turn to the tea table. If we have planned properly, the food will offer some variety in color, shape, and texture, and it will be attractively but simply arranged. Its arrangement should have dimension, that is, not everything should be one layer or be displayed on the same shape and size of plate. A heap of scones or biscuits on a medium-sized serving plate looks more appealing than a layer spread out over the surface of a larger plate. Decorated cakes or cookies that cannot be stacked look best in one layer on a round, flat serving plate. When cakes or breads are cut into squares ahead of time, the individual pieces look better stacked on a smaller plate rather than left fitted together on a larger. Large, particularly fancy items that are left intact show up well on footed cake stands. Celery and carrot sticks are prettier stood loosely in a glass or tumbler than laid flat in a dish. Fruit should be washed and dried thoroughly, then arranged unpeeled and uncut in an appropriate, not-too-large container. If this will not fit on the tea table, it may be put on another table in the area.

The tea service itself, whether pot for hot tea or pitcher for iced, sits on its tray at the end of the table. If it does not have a matching tray, it is a nice touch to lay a small cloth or napkin that matches the other linens across a plain tray and to set the pot or pitcher, the sugar and cream, sugar shell or tongs, the lemon plate, lemon fork, and the waste bowl upon it. If there is to be a separate pot of hot water or a pot of coffee or chocolate, it also sits on the tray. The kettle and burner, if used, may sit on a nearby table or stand if there is no room on or next to the tray.

The arrangement of these items on the tray is a matter of size and use. The teapot, along with the hot-water pot and coffee or chocolate pot, sits at the back of the tray, the sugar bowl in front and to one side, the creamer in front and to the other side, the waste bowl in front of the pot, slightly behind and between the sugar and creamer. The plate of lemon sits at the front of the tray, with the lemon fork lying atop it. The sugar shell or tongs may be placed in the sugar container, the lid of which is removed. The spouts of the teapot, coffee pot, and creamer should face the same way. During the course of the afternoon, these items should remain on the tray and not be intermingled with the food or be set on other tables. This is not only a matter of appearance—it makes the serving of subsequent cups easier.

Traditionally the serving of tea follows a pattern of sorts. Pouring is handled by the hostess, by a female guest appointed by the host in a

Afternoon tea with biscuits, cake, cookies, tea buns, and tea in a contemporary ceramic pot.

womanless household, or by the host of an all-male gathering. This custom of the female dispensing tea and food while the male greeted guests doubtless originated in the fact that once upon a time it was always the woman who had prepared or supervised the preparation of the food. The old masculine role, meanwhile, was family protector and guardian of the gate. And in eras when the female was supposed to be shy and retiring as a mark of ladyhood, it must have seemed more appropriate for the hostess to hide behind the teapot. Nowadays, many men cook well and take pleasure in what they've prepared.

Today, if a man is giving the tea, he should pour. If a woman is giving the tea, then pouring is her responsibility. If it is a couple providing the hospitality, then whoever feels more comfortable pouring should handle this hardly onerous chore. But unless there is some physical reason why the host or hostess cannot handle the teapot, servants should not come into it. This is supposed to be an occasion for interaction between us and our guests, a time when we show our respect for them and our pleasure at having them with us by serving them personally.

The serving of the tea is a common-sense procedure; the point is to get the beverage from the pot into the guest's cup with a minimum of fuss. The host or hostess sits or stands beside or behind the tea service, pouring a cup for each guest in turn. If there is a separate pot of hot water, the guest is asked how strong he or she would like the tea, then the tea is poured into the cup, the amount depending on the strength of the brew, and hot water is added so that the cup is no more than two-thirds to three-quarters full, then sugar, milk, or lemon is offered. There is no single accepted combination: more than 25 percent of Americans drink tea with milk and sugar, another 25 percent with sugar alone. Fifteen percent use sugar and lemon, 8 percent milk alone, 2 percent lemon alone; and 14 percent drink it without anything added. The remainder either don't care or add a variety of things. The person pouring must remember never to combine lemon and milk, as it will curdle, an interesting but definitely unappetizing process.

For subsequent cups, if there are only one or two guests, each may help himself or herself, or the host or hostess may repeat the initial process. First, of course, the guest's cup must be emptied of the dregs, which are poured into the waste bowl. If there are several guests, it will probably be simpler if the host or hostess pours subsequent cups, especially if space is limited. Everyone will realize how awkward it would be to have guests getting up and down and crowding around the tea service.

Coffee is served in the same manner as tea, but chocolate needs only to be poured from the pot since it is sweetened and milk is added during its preparation. If fruit juice, sherry, or Madeira is available and the decanter is on the tea table, whoever is pouring may also serve these if a guest prefers them to tea.

As for the food, it is a graceful gesture for the host or hostess to say to a guest something like, "Do try one of the cakes—it's an old recipe of my grandmother's," or "The sandwiches are filled with that cheese you like so well." On no account, however, should food be forced on a guest either at the beginning or during the tea. Our duty ends when we have paid the company the compliment of offering them food made and arranged with care. We should never ask why a guest is not eating, and we should never apologize for any presumed problem with the food.

The food remains on the tea table throughout the afternoon. As it is food that simply sits and looks good on the plate even hours later, there is no need for banishing it from sight. Also, teacups are left with the guests unless a guest specifically asks that the cup be removed. This is because many will refuse a second cup of tea immediately following the first, then after a time will decide to have one after all.

The main thing that we should keep in mind is that offering the food and drink in a graceful fashion is only a prelude to the development of good rapport between us and our guests. That is why we should not become obsessed with details, but should try to make the overall occasion a pleasant one for the gathering. If a guest makes a mistake, say accidentally keeping the sugar shell after helping him- or herself to sugar, no notice should be taken. If the guest calls attention to the mistake, it should be passed over as trivial, the sort of thing that anyone might do. And if we make an error ourselves, we should cover it as discreetly as possible and move right along.

We should never be so concerned with the ritual that we lose our sense of spontaneity and gaiety. We can't be like the Orientals who take lessons in "this politest of arts," who regulate every motion from the ceremonial bringing in and arranging of the utensils to their removal after a regimented tea has been served. In our culture, too much precision not only intimidates possibly unknowledgeable guests, it also seems pretentious. Worst of all, it's dull, the last thing that any host or hostess can afford to be.

As for what goes on once the tea is poured, the scones are being munched, and the scent of potpourri drifts lazily over the proceedings, that is up to us and our guests, but certain activities seem to lend themselves to tea while others do not. Unless something very special and apropos is being offered—like a concert or a program on a topic of interest to everyone present—teatime is not the time for television or radio. Soft music can add to the mood of the moment, but by and large it should stay in the background and not become the focus of the gathering. Some aficionados retire from the tea table to the card table or to a game of chess. The *rinkan* fanciers of old Japan would doubtless see a natural affinity between tea and modern hot tubs. Some people like to talk about the food and drink offered to them, not in the competitive spirit of the *tōcha* game but as a matter of mutual interest. The tea table provides an ideal atmosphere for talking about books, about music, about the way of the world. Traditionally, it is gossip that is supposed to be most at home here, "love and scandal," according to Henry Fielding, "being the best sweetners of tea."

The tea table is also the place for confidences and for reciprocal understanding, tea and sympathy being as connected in the vernacular as tea and toast, but it is more than a place for "comfortable advice." Handled properly, it creates a very evocative backdrop for romance.

Silver tea and coffee service, 1799, Hennell, English.

Unlike the Edwardian lords and ladies, we don't have sticks and gloves to lay upon the drawing room floor; and when we shut our doors, it is unlikely that there are servants to listen on the other side of them. Yet even in these more broad-minded times, there is something definitely delicious about love in the afternoon. Finding ourselves in a private, attractive setting, confronted by food that sets a mood of casual intimacy, our guest list pared to that one special person, we are almost bound to grow closer.

Afternoon tea in an oriental mood, using Chinese-style pot and tea bowls. The food includes cake, bread and butter, carrot curls and celery sticks, and tiny biscuits.

If romance is on our mind, we could do worse than invest in a set of tea ware in the *Blue Willow* pattern and tell our guest the sad but hopelessly romantic legend that is associated with it. The story is that of Koong-se, the beautiful daughter of a wealthy manufacturer, and of her love for Chang, her father's secretary. The two-storied house in the middle of the pattern is where Koong-se lived with her proud father, but in spite of their wealth and position she fell hopelessly in love with Chang, a mere employee. This infuriated her father, and he dismissed his secretary and ordered him to go away. Seeking to improve the family's position still further, the father then betrothed Koong-se to a wealthy, dissipated nobleman.

In despair Koong-se ran away to meet her lover Chang. The men on the bridge pursued them as they fled in the boat. Eventually they landed on the island in the upper left of the pattern, built a home, and began to farm. Inspired by his love for Koong-se, Chang was so successful that people began to talk about him, and the dissipated nobleman to whom Koong-se had been betrothed learned where the lovers were. The nobleman confronted Chang and killed him, probably expecting the beautiful Koong-se to plead for forgiveness and mercy. Instead, she set fire to the home that she and Chang had built and threw herself into the flames, where she perished. The gods, all-knowing, all-beneficient, as is the way of gods, put a curse on the nobleman and transformed the spirits of Koong-se and Chang into the two immortal doves who fly forever together in the topmost center of the pattern.

And if that doesn't soften up our special guest, we can always resort to that tried and true method of reading the tea leaves. Unlike Miss Mitford's sweet old maid who saw "strangers in her tea-cup," we can make certain that we see what pleases us in the cup of our guest. To read the tea leaves, we should use black leaves in brewing our tea, leaves not too small in size, as the larger are easier to read. When our guest has finished the tea, we then take the cup and, if not enough leaves remain at the bottom, remove a spoonful at random from the pot to add to them, after which we pour a small amount of water over the leaves and ask our guest to make a secret wish. What we hope, naturally, is that it involves us. Then we hold the cup in our hands and rotate it slowly, gradually beginning to tip it away from us and downward so that the water begins to trickle into the saucer beneath, after which we carefully set the cup upside down onto the saucer to let any remaining water drain from the leaves. Turning the cup right side up we next study the distribution of the tea leaves around the inside of the cup, looking for leaves that suggest or are shaped like certain things—people, animals, cars, boats, planes, houses, anything at all. Then, knowing what we do, or have guessed, or would like to be so, we interpret the leaves in the context of our guest's life and try to learn if we have touched upon the secret wish. Since considerable poetic license is allowed, we may even see ourselves in the tea leaves!

Whether we share a table of treats with a group of friends, one very special dish with a very special friend, or find contentment in a solitary pot and a piece of cinnamon toast, when we lift the steaming cup to our lips we link our lives with faraway places and faraway times. Our spirits touch those of Shên Nung, "the Divine Cultivator," who legend says thousands of years ago in China first accidentally brewed tea, and of Bodhidharma, the Buddhist saint who wept for his failure to stay awake and whose bitter tears touched the ground from which sprang the tea plant that banished sleep. We stand at the elbow of Lu Yu as he wrote in the *Ch'a Ching* his belief that the tea ceremony embodied the harmony of the universe; we travel alongside the monk Eisai as he brought tea seeds from the Zen Buddhist monasteries of China to Japan and introduced the first shoguns to the pleasures of drinking tea. We marvel at the large tea parties of the *kwampaku* Hideyoshi who both used and loved *cha-no-yu,* and we imagine the feelings of his tea master Rikyū as he made ceremonial tea for the last time and then died by his own hand. We sympathize with the tea masters of the Tokugawas who tried to retain the meaning of tea in the midst of luxury and self-indulgence.

We read the shop bill of Garraway's Coffee House that first advertised tea for sale to the English. We sip tea and eat cake with Dryden and his

An afternoon tea setting with a contemporary ironstone teaset on the tea table.

mistress in an arbor at the Mulberry Gardens; we marvel at Dr. Johnson, "whose kettle has scarcely time to cool; who with tea amuses the evening, with tea solaces the midnight, and with tea welcomes the morning." We listen to the cheerful tinkle of tea things in Regency vicarages, endure stuffy Victorian tea parties, sit under ancient oaks on green velvet lawns, not knowing as we sip our tea that an age is ending.

In the long march of history, ages are always ending, for the ebb and flow of politics, economics, religious theories, and aesthetic trends is as ceaseless as the tide and sometimes almost as regular. Yet some things never change, and these have to do not with matters of theory or even what is seen as contemporary reality, but with the heart that if it is to live must touch another, and another. To survive as civilized beings we need respect for ourselves, concern for others, and the ability to make the best possible use of the resources our own day allows us. We must cultivate our friends and delight in giving them pleasure, in presenting them with an opportunity to experience a time away from the purely physical requirements of life, a time to be devoted to emotional and aesthetic concerns.

In an era when social custom and the requirements of economic survival seem to have made each of us a solitary island, we can still build a bridge to our particular, private world. We can bake a cake, brew a good pot of tea, and offer ourselves with generosity. We have shared the best that we have, and no one can say fairer than that.

PART II

Beverages for Afternoon Tea

· 7 ·

What to Put
in the
Teapot

Tea was a food before it was a beverage. It was made into balls and cooked or mixed with other foods in primitive casseroles. In different parts of the world its leaves have been pickled or tossed with sugar, oil, and vinegar for salads. A traditional recipe from Tibet calls for tea leaves to be crushed and steamed, then mixed with rice, orange peel, spices, milk, and onions. In colonial days, some New Englanders brewed tea leaves for hours, then ate them with a touch of salt and butter. In Japan, even now, there are those who like to pour hot tea over rice and eat it with salted seafood and pickles.

Fortunately for us, tea is used primarily today as a beverage, one of the most popular in the U.S. Most American tea drinkers are content to buy blends off the supermarket shelf, and most of these blends are of black teas. About 98 percent of American tea fanciers drink black tea; and acceptable though the black blends may be, those who drink nothing else miss a fascinating range of flavors. Anyone ready to explore the world of tea beyond the impressive frontiers established by Messrs. Lipton, Bigelow, et al, will find many good and even great teas ready to be tried. Specialty food stores and quite a few mail-order sources offer a wide selection of both blended and unblended teas. Because the blends are individual to the establishment, there is little point in going into the combinations available, but almost any supplier of fine teas will offer at least some of the following unblended varieties: Oolongs; green teas such as Gunpowder, Pan-fired, Imperial Gunpowder, and Young Hyson; and blacks like Assam, Ceylon, Darjeeling, Keemun, and Lapsang Souchong.

Best-known of the Oolongs is that from Formosa, marketed appropriately as Formosa Oolong. This tea has the richness of the lighter blacks and the delicacy of the greens. It is an amber brew best drunk without the addition of milk, and because of its color and sparkle, it has come to be known as the champagne of teas. Some Oolong also comes from Mainland China, but it is of a coarser type and more suitable for spicy meals than for afternoon tea.

Green teas, almost all of which at one time came from China, are now also processed in quantity in Japan, Formosa, and India. So little tea is exported from Japan that you are unlikely to be able to pick and choose, but the grades range from Extra Choicest, the best, down to Dust, the least-desirable, and the tea is named according to leaf-style and manufacturing method: Pan-fired, Guri, Basket-fired, and Natural Leaf. Formosan and Chinese greens, in descending order of quality, may be sold as Gunpowder, Young Hyson, Imperial Gunpowder, Hyson, Twankay, Hyson Skin, and Dust. Green teas from India are marketed from the best grade of Fine Young Hyson to the least-desirable of Dust, with Young Hyson, Hyson No. 1, Twankay, Sowmee, and Fannings in between, in descending order of quality.

In China and Japan, green tea remains by far the most widely drunk type, and green teas have at various times been very popular in the West as well. In the early nineteenth century, Miss Mitford's "quiet little girl" could describe her role in the English household of *Our Village* as "an excellent hander of muffins and cake; a connoisseur in green tea." Today, however, even in England, black tea has become an overwhelming favorite; and although one is usually offered a choice between "India or China," most people sitting down to afternoon tea seem to prefer the "India" or black tea.

Delicious as the best blacks are, green teas have a pronounced appeal of their own. Of all teas, they are the lowest in caffeine content and offer a lightness and delicacy not found in other true teas. In fact, the best greens are sometimes called the white wine of teas.

The finest black teas come from India, Ceylon, China, and Formosa. Assam, grown in the province of the same name in northeastern India, one of the few areas where the tea plant is native, is probably the strongest of the well-known blacks. A rich, thick, heavy brew with a penetrating flavor and good color, Assam is frequently blended with less pungent varieties. Straight, it is so strong that even confirmed coffee drinkers like it.

From Sri Lanka comes the tea known as Ceylon, frequently marketed as an Orange Pekoe, a term describing leaf size. High-grown is the best grade. This makes a strong but mellow brew with a delicate flavor. As a tea expert poetically put it long ago, Ceylon has an aroma like "flowers in new-mown hay."

The best-known of the world's great black teas is Darjeeling, grown in the foothills of the Himalayas in India. Particularly fragrant, Darjeeling has a rich but delicate flavor and makes an attractive reddish brew. This is the favorite tea of many connoisseurs.

Keemun comes from northern China. Aromatic with a sweet, almost perfume-like undertone, it is gentle but strong on the palate. A thick, full-bodied brew, it mixes well with milk. It is sometimes called the Burgundy of China teas.

From both Mainland China and Formosa comes Lapsang Souchong, one of the most-distinctive teas. It has a smoky flavor that is almost overpowering to the uninitiated or unsuspecting. Thick and rich, it is an attractive, clear, orange brew that people either love or hate.

Mr. Jennings, that curious Victorian clergyman in Le Fanu's supernatural tale "Green Tea," voiced the theory that "Every one who sets about writing in earnest does his work . . . *on* something—tea, or coffee, or tobacco . . . I began to take a little green tea. I found the effect pleasanter, it cleared and intensified the power of thought."

Like Mr. Jennings, who delved too deeply into ancient metaphysics and quite literally ended, poor man, with a monkey on his back, most of us like our tea to match our mood. Our household is no exception. A cozy hour by the living-room fire with the shutters drawn against the passing traffic on the wet streets of a rainy city afternoon in the fall calls for one type of brew. Quite a different tea is put in a Thermos and carried to Lover's Leap on a snowy January day at Applespring in the North Carolina mountains.

More than the weather affects the choice of teas. The tea that we serve to a guest who shares with the eminent Dr. Johnson the habit of being a "hardened and shameless tea drinker" is a fuller-bodied brew than that poured for the visitor who rarely touches tea.

As with wines, different teas lend themselves to different menus as well as moods. If you're serving a delicately flavored tea treat, one of the green teas or possibly an Oolong would be nice. A spicy recipe calls for a strong black tea.

The point is to experiment with several teas and find two or three quite different in "tone" that please you, then match them to the season, the menu, and the mood. This is not an expensive undertaking. Many tea suppliers offer sampler packages, allowing you to try several different kinds of tea in small quantities. Fine teas can be bought by the pound for a price that averages out to only a few cents a cup, and smaller quantities may cost somewhat more but are still surprisingly economical. Tea holds very well if kept in an airtight container in a cool, dark storage area, making it easy to keep several kinds on hand at all times.

Having chosen the tea or teas that you like best, remember that even the greatest leaf can be ruined by indifferent brewing. Through the centuries since the leaves of *camellia sinensis* first fell by chance into boiling water there have been quite a few approaches to brewing tea, but they have resolved themselves into a simple, no-nonsense method that never fails if carefully followed.

To Make a Good Pot of Tea

Tea, 1 teaspoon per serving	Kettle
Water, 2 cups per serving	Tea cozy
	Teapot
	Teaspoon

1. Start with immaculate utensils, since tea picks up alien flavors all too easily, and the least hint of oiliness spoils the brew.
2. Draw cold water from the tap into the kettle and set on stove on high heat. (While choosing exactly the right water for the preparation of tea has been considered a part of the art of brewing in China to the extent that it has been satirized in literature by a character not daring to make tea until she could produce "rainwater saved from the year before" or even melt "snow that I collected from the plum trees five years ago," modern tap water seems to fit adequately the old Chinese

proverb requirement of running-water from the mountains being the best for tea, especially as much of it comes from reservoirs on higher ground. If you make a practice of not drinking your city's water, use bottled spring water.)

3. While waiting for the kettle to boil, fill the teapot with warm water and let it stand for several minutes. This warms the material of which the teapot is made so that the heat of the brew itself will not be dissipated. When it is thoroughly warmed, empty the teapot and spoon in one exact teaspoonful of tea leaves for each two cups to be served.

4. As soon as the water in the kettle reaches a rolling boil (steam will rise as a steady vapor from the kettle spout and the water will actually be rolling as in waves), take the teapot to the kettle (never the kettle to the pot), and pour boiling water over the tea leaves. The length of time that must be allowed for the infusion will vary from tea to tea, according to the variety and the strength preferred. As William Lyon Phelps pointed out, the English like their "tea so strong that . . . it has a hairy flavor." Few Americans have that much fortitude, yet no one enjoys a brew so weak and characterless that it could pass for colored hot water. This is why it is necessary to experiment and know your tea before preparing it for guests. Sometimes an infusion of as little as three or four minutes is adequate, sometimes several minutes longer may be required. While the tea is brewing, keep the teapot covered with a cloth or cozy to keep it warm.

5. If you'd like to experiment with creating your own scented or spiced teas, the herbs or flavorings should be added to the tea leaves before the boiling water is poured over them. Mint is a nice addition, as is dried lemon or orange peel. Whole allspice or cloves will add zip to any brew if you like a spicy undertone.

In brewing tea, some people prefer to use tea bags or tea ball infusers instead of loose leaves. This has the advantage of enabling one to remove the ball or bag the instant the tea has reached the proper strength and color, thus keeping the tea from growing bitter and too dark. A tea ball infuser may be made of mesh or perforated metal and is simply a container that may be filled with the correct amount of loose tea and lowered into the teapot by a handle or chain. Some purists think that the metal of such infusers—usually chrome or stainless steel—imparts an undesirable quality to the brew, and prefer to use a bamboo strainer.

The convenience of tea bags is so obvious that I mention them

Tea paraphernalia—contemporary silverplated teapot, tea bags, teaspoon, mesh tea ball, tea strainer, tea infuser ball, tea infuser spoon, and tin tea caddy.

primarily to point out that if you do prefer tea bags but want a tea that isn't available in that form, you can make your own of plain, white, loose-weave cotton with a foldover top to contain the leaves. Also, some tea merchants sell small, reusable cotton containers for this purpose. You simply fill each bag with the amount of straight or blended tea that you prefer, adding any spices or herbs, then store the bags in an airtight container until needed.

If you do make your own bags, you'll be following an old American tradition. Tea bags were invented by the operator of a modest wholesale tea and coffee shop in New York's spice district who decided in 1908 that the small metal cans then generally used for tea samples had become too expensive. Looking for a substitute container, he had small bags sewn of silk, which he then filled with tea. His customers not only didn't object to the change—they began to brew the samples in the bags; and when they came back to order tea, many of them asked that it be put in the same sort of bags.

If you don't like bags—and they can be a soggy mess—but do like to make individual cups of tea, tea-infuser spoons offer the convenience of tea bags at a considerable saving.

Volumes could be written about the proper strength and color of tea, but there is only one infallible guide—your own taste. If you try a tea in different strengths and find one that you like best, then that is the correct brew for you. And remember, to enjoy tea at its best, drink it as soon as possible after brewing.

If you'd like a hot tea that is different, here are two recipes to enliven the dullest winter afternoon.

ALMOND TEA

A nice, spicy tea for cold days. May be prepared ahead, strained and reheated, but is best when freshly made.

4 teaspoons green tea	Kettle
3 teaspoons black tea	Measuring cups and spoons
4 whole cardamoms	Nut chopper
⅓ cup blanched and chopped	
almonds	
1 small cinnamon stick	
2 whole cloves	
5 cups water	

1. Combine all ingredients, bring to a boil and simmer gently for 20 minutes.
2. Serve hot. You may prefer to sweeten tea by adding ⅓ to ½ cup granulated sugar to mixture before pouring into teapot.

Makes five generous cups.

HOT CRANBERRY TEA

Especially good on cold days: A nice, spice smell, and it will keep several days in an airtight container in refrigerator.

4 cups cranberry juice cocktail   Measuring cups and spoons
1 cinnamon stick   Saucepan, large, heavy
½ teaspoon whole cloves
6 teaspoons black tea
1 quart (4 cups) water
½ cup honey
¼ cup granulated sugar

1. Combine cranberry juice and spices in saucepan, bring almost to a boil, reduce heat, and leave over low heat for half an hour.
2. Meanwhile brew tea in water.
3. Add tea to cranberry juice mixture. If to be served at once, add honey and sugar. If to be served later, store cranberry/tea mixture in refrigerator and add sugar and honey just before reheating.

Makes six generous servings.

In the summertime there are those who find hot tea too, well, hot. For them, iced tea is a good substitute. Like tea bags, an American novelty almost unknown in the rest of the world, iced tea was discovered by an Englishman who had a large exhibit promoting Indian and Ceylon tea at the St. Louis Exhibition of 1904. It was a very hot summer, as summers have a way of being in St. Louis, and thirsty fairgoers streamed by the tea exhibit on their way to get ices. The enterprising Englishman decided if they wanted something cold, he'd give it to them, so he made a batch of exceptionally strong tea, dumped ice in it, and the new drink was born.

TO MAKE A PITCHER OF GOOD ICED TEA

Tea, 1½ teaspoons per serving   Kettle
Water, 1 cup per serving   Pitcher, covered
(Flavored ice cubes)   Teapot
                                  Teaspoon

1. Draw cold water from the tap into the kettle and put onto the stove top on high heat.
2. Put into the teapot 1½ teaspoons of tea leaves for each glass to be served.
3. As soon as the water in the kettle reaches a rolling boil, pour boiling water over the tea leaves. Let the infusion continue long enough to produce a strong brew but not long enough to get bitter, then strain out leaves immediately.
4. Store in a covered pitcher until thoroughly cool, then serve over ice cubes.
5. For a nice touch, use flavored ice cubes made by taking 2 tablespoons lemon juice or 4 tablespoons orange juice, apricot juice, or other fruit juice, and dilute with enough cool water to fill the ice-cube tray before putting it in the freezer. When the cubes are hard, pour the cooled tea over them and serve. Finely crushed mint sprinkled atop the cubes is a flavorful last-minute addition.

HERB TEAS

For people who cannot or will not drink so-called true tea, look to the herb teas. There are literally thousands of possibilities, since tea can be made from any non-poisonous substance that can be brewed in water. The following are only a few of the more common.

Because there are so many herb teas and because each has a personality all its own, a certain amount of experimentation may be required before you find the varieties you prefer. Along the way you will discover that there are some that you take to at once, others that don't appeal to you at all. The following pointers may save you a little time in your search for the ones that you'll like best.

For a minty flavor, try bee balm, birch, catnip, hyssop, pennyroyal, peppermint, and spearmint. If you like spicy beverages, consider agrimony, basil, cloves, celery, fennel, ginger, hops, marjoram, thyme, and Yerba Santa. Sweet teas include anise, cinnamon, coltsfoot, fenugreek, hawthorn, licorice, linden, mallow, and pennyroyal.

Among the fruity teas are agrimony, lemon grass, lemon verbena, and rose hip. Teas with especially fine aromas are agrimony, angelica, anise, basil, bay, bee balm, borage, catnip, celery, cinnamon, coltsfoot, fennel, fenugreek, goldenrod, juniper, lavender, lemon verbena, linden, motherwort, pennyroyal, red raspberry, rosemary, sage, valerian, Yerba Buena, and Yerba Santa.

Along with the other health benefits claimed for them, most herb teas are free of caffeine, a stimulant found in true tea that some people cannot tolerate. And although caffeine contributes significantly to the effect gained from drinking true tea, some of these caffeineless teas taste much like their true-tea relatives: angelica, wild snowball (also known as New Jersey Tea), and Labrador tea are all like oriental teas, and woodruff is something like Darjeeling.

While many health-food and other specialty food stores carry herb teas, as do the coffee and tea suppliers who have traditionally handled at least some herbs and spices, there are other ways of getting the raw material. If you're a devoteé of Euell Gibbons or a grown-up Scout who recalls with fondness foraging in the woods on camping trips, then get yourself a plant identification guide and some waterproof boots, and start looking. Just be very careful. Not everything that grows in the wild is safe for human consumption.

If woods-rambling doesn't appeal to you, take a look around your yard or the yards of your nearest and dearest—you may be surprised at what you find. A lot of Southern backsteps, for example, at one time had mint planted by them for use in the ubiquitous and very welcome iced tea of summer. Hardy perennial herbs useful for tea that may be flourishing unsung many years after their original planting include comfrey, pennyroyal, hyssop, woodruff, angelica, horehound, spearmint, sage, peppermint, lemon balm, and catnip. Several years ago when we bought a small farm in the mountains of North Carolina, we found ourselves the possessors of a hedge of monster-sized rose bushes that annually produce enough rose hips to make tea for a regiment without the birds noticing that their picking rights have been invaded.

You can, of course, plant any herbs that you especially like. In Atlanta we have for years grown our own basil, lemon balm, and spearmint for tea. All it takes is a few square feet of growing space, in either a yard or window box. Plants or, if you want to do it from scratch, seed may be ordered from seed catalogues or bought at local garden centers. The herbs are easy to take care of, pretty to look at, nice to smell, and useful in the kitchen, making their cultivation a rewarding as well as an inexpensive hobby.

However you obtain your herbs, when you reach the point of preparation, you should exercise the same care in making herb tea as in making tea from the leaves of *camellia sinensis.*

TO MAKE A POT OF GOOD HERB TEA

Herb leaves, shredded	Kettle
(amount will vary according	Tea cozy
to herb)	Teapot
Water, 2 cups per serving	Teaspoon

1. Draw cold water from the tap into the kettle and put onto the stove top on high heat.
2. While waiting for the kettle to boil, fill the teapot with warm water and let it stand for several minutes. This warms the teapot so the heat of the brew itself will not be dissipated. When it is thoroughly warmed, empty the teapot and spoon in the herb leaves. The amount will vary from one herb to another. To start with, you might try 2-3 teaspoons of leaves for each cup of water. If this proves too much or too little for the individual herb, adjust the quantity until you have it to your liking.
3. As soon as the water in the kettle reaches a rolling boil, take the teapot to the kettle and pour boiling water over the leaves. Herb teas may require brewing anywhere from 5 to 20 minutes, so it is especially important to keep the teapot insulated with a cozy or thick, clean cloth while the infusion takes place.
4. Remember that herb teas may not be as pronounced in color as true tea while their flavors may be stronger. Some herbs, in fact, have extremely pronounced tastes that may not appeal to everyone. The minty and lemony teas seem to have wide appeal, as do the spice teas, but there are those who quail before sage and marjoram and some of the other teas whose flavors are not normally associated with beverages.

There are many fine teas, both herbal and true, but no one likes all of them, at least no one whom I've ever encountered. When you're serving a guest whose taste you're not sure of, don't offer a tea that's so strong or so unusual that the others present may not want even to try it. If you yourself are addicted to Lapsang Souchong or one of the other strongly scented, pungently flavored teas and can't face teatime without it, then provide an alternative for your guest.

If you're entertaining people who are tea lovers, then it's fun to stage a tasting party. Using either infuser spoons or tea bags, you can let them sample several different kinds of tea. All you'll need are a large kettle of boiling water, cups, a waste container for the dregs and—of course—the teas. Many teas are now available in tea-bag form at grocery stores, and tea merchants can often supply fine teas in bag form. For a tea-tasting party, it's better to keep the food simple and not highly flavored.

No matter which tea or teas you choose to serve, with what menu, and to how many people, there are five vital points to remember: the tea should be stored in a cool, dry place in an airtight container; the utensils used in its preparation should be spotlessly clean; the brewing should proceed without interruption; the teapot should be kept warm while the tea is brewing; and the tea should be drunk as soon after brewing as possible, preferably within a few minutes.

Tea should never be rewarmed, and spent tea leaves should not be used in an attempt to brew a second pot. (One or two green teas, actually, are known for their ability to produce two or even three brewings from one measurement of leaves, but by and large reusing the leaves of most teas gives a result that is either tasteless or bitter.)

There are those who, no matter how fine the tea or careful the brewing, simply do not like tea, usually because they have never had a good brew. Sometimes you can get them to try a tea, but often they will refuse more than a sip or two, which they do not even taste in their eagerness to swallow so that they can tell you again, "Sorry, but I've never cared for tea." If you suspect that you may have a resolute non-tea-drinker on your guest list, it makes sense to provide an alternative beverage, the most obvious of which is coffee.

COFFEE

When the patriotic fervor of the American Revolution caused tea—so strongly identified with the British—to lose favor, it was coffee that replaced it as America's favorite beverage, and it was coffee that went west with the wagon trains, the settlers, and the soldiers, just as it is coffee that today remains the country's favorite hot drink.

Coffee had been known for many centuries before it came to America.

Like tea, it was first eaten as a food. At a later period, the berries remaining after the coffee shrub had bloomed were fermented and combined with cold water to produce a primitive wine. It was less than one thousand years ago that the Arabs began boiling the coffee bean in water to make a hot drink.

Also like tea, coffee was originally associated with medicine and religion, and coffee-drinking only gradually came to be accepted as something done for pleasure and as a stimulus to secular intellectual activity. The habit spread from the Near East, carried to Europe by Venetian traders in the sixteenth century and known in both England and its huge colony America by the mid-seventeenth century.

Today the United States is the world's major importer of coffee, bringing in more than ten pounds per capita annually, yet coffee grows in only one place on American soil—in the Kona district of Hawaii, on the slopes of Mauna Loa, an active volcano. The coffee produced there is highly prized, but there is not much of it and the remainder of our vast consumption comes from the rest of the world.

Originally cultivated only by the Arabs, coffee today is grown in many areas, most notably in South America, Central America, Africa, the West Indies, and Asia. Of the several varieties of the coffee shrub, most coffee, including all that of the finest quality, comes from the *coffea arabica,* a plant indigenous to Ethiopia but now grown in most coffee-producing areas of the world.

On its way from shrub to cup, coffee is handled differently from tea. When ripe, the fruit of the coffee shrub is hand-picked and split, revealing the seed, or coffee bean, which is then dried, graded, sorted, packed, and sent to the nearest port for shipment. Unlike tea, which is processed before shipping and is usable when shipped, the green coffee bean must be processed when it reaches its destination. The character of the finished coffee is affected not only by the conditions under which it was grown, but also by the way that it is roasted, that is, exposed to heat for varying periods of time depending on the type of roast desired. When roasted, the coffee bean decreases in weight, increases in volume, darkens from pale green to a deep brown, and begins to smell and taste like coffee.

There are several types of roasts, ranging from the light to the very dark. Most popular in the United States is the so-called American or brown roast, also known as city roast. This is a light roast and not particularly hearty. The darkest roast is Italian or Espresso, long familiar to the coffee-house habitué and frequenter of Italian restaurants. Between these two extremes is French roast, which is not as dark as the Italian but is considerably darker than American roast. The degree of roast, incidentally, is not a question of strength, which has to do with the amount of any given roast that is used in brewing the coffee, but of flavor.

As with tea, most coffee imported into the United States is blended, the point being to combine the best qualities of several different coffees; for example, the smoothness of one with the richness of another. An expert blender can also allow for differences in growing conditions from year to year to maintain a consistently high quality. Large-scale coffee blenders—like mass-market tea blenders—tend to avoid scarce or costly coffees to make it easier and more economical to reproduce a given taste from one season to the next. Consistency at a reasonable price is their aim, not necessarily the best taste.

Like tea, coffee is very susceptible to humidity and to odors from other substances, and must be carefully stored once roasted and ground. Its shelf life is shorter than that of tea, for the roasted whole bean remains fresh for only five or six weeks, while ground coffee begins to deteriorate after two weeks. Refrigerating or freezing in an airtight container will help to preserve freshness longer.

A roasted coffee bean that is fresh will feel brittle when squeezed, and ground coffee betrays its staleness by losing some of the characteristic aroma of the roast and by "packing" due to even a faint trace of moisture. Brewing a stale coffee will produce a beverage that is bitter and lacking in the fragrance and flavor normally expected.

Coffee may be bought in three forms: the green bean, the roasted whole bean, and ground. At one time most people roasted their own coffee. While the basic process is simple enough—the application of heat to bring out the bean's essential characteristics—the development over the years of commercial equipment that in professional hands can control the process to produce the exact roast desired makes home-roasting unnecessary. If you do want to try your hand, whether just for the fun of it or because the green beans hold longer than the roasted, find a specialty store that handles fine coffees and get them to supply you with both the green beans and a few tips on home-roasting.

Not many people roast their own coffee anymore, but many coffee connoisseurs prefer to buy the roasted whole bean and grind their own as needed. There are several serviceable grinders on the market, some quite inexpensive, and grinding your own coffee has the advantage of extra freshness and also of giving you the precise grind you want at the moment. The roasted whole bean, as mentioned before, will hold considerably longer than ground coffee.

If you have a good local source for the coffee you prefer, the simplest way of buying it is in the form of a grind. There are essentially four types of grind: powder, fine, regular, and coarse; and it is very important to choose the correct grind for the equipment to be used in making the coffee, which in turn is determined by the method of brewing that you prefer.

There are several methods of preparing coffee: boiling, steeping, drip or percolation, pumping percolation, and filtration. Boiling, the oldest technique and the simplest, is a process where a powder grind is boiled in a small pot. The roast used is dark, and the coffee is boiled twice and rested, then boiled a third time before being poured as a froth into small, individual cups. The resulting coffee is usually known as Turkish or Greek coffee.

Another version involves boiling a coarse grind in a large pot, then straining the brew to filter out the grounds before serving.

In steeping, a regular grind is put into boiling water and the water kept warm, but not boiling, for five or six minutes while the steeping process takes place. At the end of this time the grounds are strained out of the brew.

In the drip or percolation process, hot water is poured over a fine grind and drips through the small holes in the basket or holder containing the coffee. At no time does the water stand in contact with the grounds.

In the pumping percolation process a regular grind is suspended in a basket in a pot of cold water which, as it is heated, passes repeatedly through the grounds. When the brewing time has elapsed, the basket of grounds is removed.

The filtration process, recommended by many modern-day coffee experts, employs one of two methods. A two-compartment utensil is used in which steam pressure draws the hot water into contact with the coffee, then forces its withdrawal as a clear, flavorful brew—this is known as the vacuum principle. Even simpler, boiling water is poured through a paper or cloth filter filled with a fine grind; and when the water has filtered through the medium holding the coffee, the filter is removed and discarded and the coffee, after stirring, is ready to serve.

Espresso, which requires a fine grind also, utilizes a filtration process requiring special machines that extract maximum results through the use of steam pressure.

Your present coffee-making equipment will employ one of these principles, and to get the best possible cup of coffee from it requires following the directions provided with your pot, percolator, or machine. Be especially sure that you are using the correct grind, which should be specified in the instructions.

If you're not satisfied with your present coffee-making equipment and are thinking of trying another method, keep in mind that the ideal brewing device is one that is easily controlled, quickly cleaned, consistent in performance, and the size closest to that which you will need most often.

It used to be said that Americans, while not very fastidious in their other gustatory tastes, demanded and made the best coffee in the world. This reputation has suffered because of increasing dependence on indifferently blended mass-market coffees and because the relatively simple process for making good coffee seems to be honored more by being slighted than observed. It seems today that what many Americans call "good" coffee is simply that which corresponds most nearly to the degree of bitterness and shade of dark brown presented by the "Stygian stuff" that they themselves brew so perfunctorily at home.

In fact, both the tea and coffee brewed throughout much of the land have tended to become simply dark and acrid hot beverages. Our suffering taste buds might be forgiven for identifying with the indignant turn-of-the-century *Punch* character who proclaimed, "Look here, Steward, if this is coffee, I want tea; but if this is tea, then I wish for coffee."

It needn't be that way. Coffee merchants, specialty food stores, and even some grocery stores offer a variety of excellent coffees that may be roasted and ground to order. As for equipment, there are probably more kinds for sale now than ever before. Making a really excellent cup of coffee requires nothing more than experimenting to discover which brewing method and which coffee you like best, storing the dry coffee properly, brewing each batch with care, and drinking the coffee as soon after brewing as possible. Contrary to popular supposition, coffee—like tea—does not rewarm well.

While good coffee is a pleasure at any time, it is a necessity if it is to be served at afternoon tea, for the only excuse for its presence is that it appeals more to a guest than even a fine tea, something that a poor or commonplace brew is unlikely to do.

When you choose a coffee for an occasion like this, make it a special coffee, one that your guests do not encounter in every cafeteria or restaurant. If there's a specialty store that sells coffee in your area, visit it to see the wide array available. Many such shops offer samples or even tastings of their more popular blends and straights. If there isn't a convenient store selling fine coffee, get catalogues from two or three of the merchants willing to sell by mail (list in the Appendix)—many of them offer sampler packages, containing small amounts of several different kinds of coffees. Both local and mail-order specialty stores will usually have a house blend, a dependable choice as a rule because it is on this blend that the store is resting its coffee-blending reputation. In addition to its own blend, a store specializing in fine coffee will offer a variety of blends and straights.

The coffees that are especially suitable for the afternoon tea table are the flavorful, aromatic brews like Ethiopian Harrar, Jamaican Blue Mountain, Guatemalan High Grown, Venezuelan Maracaibo, Ethiopian Djimmah, Cameroon Arabica, Kenya AA, Venezuelan Tachira, and—when you're lucky enough to find it unblended—Hawaiian Kona. Apart from these delicious straights, my personal favorite is a good Vienna Roast, whose rich, mellow flavor will add interest to the blandest afternoon.

COFFEE

The cinnamon adds a special flavor especially good with Vienna Roast.

FOR EACH CUP DESIRED:

1½ to 2 teaspoons ground coffee	Coffeemaker
	Measuring cups and spoons
1 cup water	
¼ teaspoon ground cinnamon	

Make coffee in your usual way, except add cinnamon to mixture before brewing. Serve hot and fresh with separate containers of sugar and whipped cream.

ALTERNATE METHOD:

2 tablespoons coffee beans, freshly roasted	Kettle
	Measuring cups and spoons
¼ teaspoon ground cinnamon	Mortar and pestle
1 cup water	

1. Pound coffee beans to a fine powder.
2. Bring water to a boil in the kettle, add coffee powder, and boil for 1 minute.
3. Add cinnamon, and bring to second boil.
4. Let sit off heat for a minute or two, allowing the sediment to settle to the bottom.
5. Serve with separate containers of sugar and whipped cream.

Multiply above by number of cups desired.

ICED COFFEE

Nice on a hot day for coffee lovers.

4 cups strong, fresh coffee	Coffeemaker
1 cup half-and-half	Measuring cups and spoons
3 tablespoons sifted granulated sugar	Pitcher, large
	Sifter and small bowl
Coffee ice cubes	Tray, ice

1. Make strong coffee and combine in pitcher with half-and-half and sugar, stir well, then refrigerate for several hours.
2. Make coffee ice cubes by filling ice tray with cool or lukewarm fresh coffee, then freezing.
3. To serve, place two coffee ice cubes in each glass and fill three-quarters full of coffee mixture.

Makes six to eight servings.

CHOCOLATE

Sometimes neither tea nor coffee seems exactly right, leading one to think of hot chocolate, a childhood favorite that's just as appealing to adults on dark, dreary days when the outside cold calls for something warm, rich, and nourishing inside.

Long prized by the Aztec Indians, cocoa was introduced to Europe by Hernando Cortez, the sixteenth-century Spanish conquistador who conquered Mexico and ordered expeditions through Central America. The new drink he found quickly established itself in European society, and in England the same coffee houses that introduced tea and coffee to Londoners also offered cocoa, and on menus that were in some ways similar to those of a latter-day afternoon tea. Ladies of quality began to drink chocolate for breakfast, and there were establishments that designated themselves as chocolate houses, most notably the Cocoa-Tree, which acted in the early eighteenth century as an informal club for leading Tories.

Introduced as a beverage, chocolate ultimately came to be used as a food ingredient, which further increased demand for the substance that the Aztecs had valued as a stimulant. Today there are enough chocolate addicts to support an industry which turns out not only sweets but such diverse offshoots as luxury tours to Switzerland, during which the participants visit leading chocolate manufactories and sample their wares. There is even a newsletter devoted to the love of chocolate in all its forms, put out not by the industry but by one chocolate-lover for other chocolate-lovers.

Demand, in fact, is more consistent than supply, for the cocoa bean proves bashful some years. That is why some of the more nervous moments of the commodities market have to do with cocoa futures. The investor who bets that it will be a poor year for production and buys cocoa futures can lose a lot of money if the cocoa tree confounds expectations and yields a bumper crop, flooding the market with cocoa beans and depressing the price. It is not only nature that the cocoa crop has to contend with. Although it is indigenous only to Mexico, Central America, and parts of South America, the cocoa tree is now cultivated in tropical Africa as well, and several of these are areas where political instability sometimes affects agricultural production.

The processing of cocoa is different from that of tea or coffee. A member of the Sterculia family, the *Theobroma cacao* produces a pod-like fruit which, when picked and opened, contains twenty to fifty seeds, each about the size of an almond. These seeds are removed from the fruit's pulp and allowed to ferment for about a week. The fermentation process removes their bitterness, darkens them to a reddish color, and releases a fragrant aroma. Afterwards the seeds are dried and then shipped to manufacturers, mostly American and European, where they are processed.

At the manufacturing plant the seeds are roasted and crushed. The husks are sorted out and ground to be used as fuel, or even in cheap grades of cocoa. The remaining material, which is minute seed-like matter, is ground again to produce an oily liquid which solidifies into chocolate. If cocoa is desired, a further process extracts part of the oil and grinds the remaining chocolate into a fine powder. The oil removed is known as cocoa butter and is used in the manufacture of medicines and cosmetics.

Chocolate for cooking is most often marketed as a solid, usually packaged in one-ounce squares but sometimes in larger blocks, in unsweetened, semi-sweetened, sweetened, and even flavored form. Unless otherwise specified, recipes for either beverages or foods that call for chocolate refer to the unsweetened variety. Cocoa has always been sold as an unsweetened powder, until recently, and the unsweetened form is still preferred for cooking purposes.

Unlike tea and coffee, chocolate seems not to have attracted much historical criticism on health or moral grounds, although it has prompted at least one bit of doggerel:

> Tea, although an Oriental,
> Is a gentleman at least;
> Cocoa is a cad and coward,
> Cocoa is a vulgar beast.

So wrote G. K. Chesterton, but there will be nothing beastly about the beverage you serve your guests if you follow these instructions carefully.

CHOCOLATE

Rich, sweet, and very good; marvelous for cold weather, especially if your guest doesn't like tea or coffee. *May* be made a few hours ahead and reheated, but it won't be quite as good. Cream should be whipped at last minute.

⅓ cup grated unsweetened baking chocolate dissolved in ¼ cup boiling water
1¾ cups water
1¾ cups milk
⅔ cup granulated sugar
½ cup heavy cream
¼ teaspoon vanilla extract
1 tablespoon confectioners sugar
⅛ teaspoon cinnamon

Bowl, small
Electric mixer and small bowl
Measuring cups and spoons
Saucepan, medium, heavy, and stirring spoon
Sifter, fine-mesh

1. Over medium heat bring water and chocolate to a boil and let simmer 10 minutes.
2. Add milk, bring to a second boil, and simmer for 20 minutes, stirring occasionally.
3. Add granulated sugar, stirring well, and let simmer while you whip the cream.
4. To whip the cream, combine cream, vanilla, and confectioners sugar; beat at high speed until thick. (Cream will whip better if bowl and beaters have been chilled.) Put whipped cream in a chilled serving bowl and sprinkle with sifted cinnamon.
5. Put chocolate in warmed pot and serve with a generous tablespoon of cream on top of each cup.

Makes six cups.

ICED COCOA

Cool, chocolate-flavored creaminess for a hot day.

1 teaspoon cocoa	Kettle
3 teaspoons granulated sugar	Measuring cups and spoons
½ cup boiling water	Pitcher, covered
⅓ cup half-and-half	Spoon, stirring
(1 tablespoon whipped cream)	

1. Pour boiling water over cocoa and sugar and combine thoroughly.
2. Add half-and-half and stir until combined.
3. Refrigerate until cold, then serve in small glasses over crushed ice or—if a richer effect is desired—omit the ice and top the drink with a tablespoon of whipped cream.

Makes approximately one cup.

FRUIT BEVERAGES

Although tea, coffee, and chocolate are the usual beverages served at afternoon tea, there are times when something different is called for. The following fruit-based drinks make a nice change, especially in the hot summer months.

GINGER AND LEMON WATER

An exhilarating taste for a hot day. Will keep several days in refrigerator in covered pitcher.

2 teaspoons chopped fresh ginger root	Chopper
6 tablespoons brown sugar	Measuring cups and spoons
5 tablespoons lemon juice	Pitcher, large
3 cups water	Tray, ice
Lemon ice cubes	
Fresh mint, chopped	

1. Combine all ingredients except the mint and ice cubes and refrigerate several hours.
2. Serve over lemon ice cubes (made by combining 2 tablespoons lemon juice with enough water to fill tray, then freezing), garnished with mint.

Makes six small glasses.

GRAPEFRUIT SHRUB

A tangy version of a Victorian favorite for hot weather. May be bottled months ahead, using the hot-water-bath canning method.

1 cup grapefruit juice	Measuring cups
1¼ cups granulated sugar	Pitcher
¼ cup white wine vinegar	Saucepan, heavy
	Spoon, stirring

1. Combine juice and sugar in a saucepan and simmer until sugar dissolves.
2. Stir in vinegar.
3. Refrigerate until cold, and pour over crushed ice in beverage glasses, allowing ¾ cup per serving.

Makes approximately two cups.

LEMONADE

Always refreshing.

2 tablespoons granulated sugar	Juicer
1 cup hot water	Kettle
¼ cup lemon juice	Measuring cups and spoons
Lemon ice cubes	Pitcher and long-handled spoon

1. Dissolve sugar in hot water. Add lemon juice and mix thoroughly.
2. Serve over lemon ice cubes (made by freezing 2 tablespoons of lemon juice and enough water to fill an ice tray.)

Makes one serving. Multiply quantities by number of servings desired.

ORANGE AND LIME COOLER

A refreshing citrus combination for sultry summer days.

1 cup orange juice	Measuring cups and spoons
¾ tablespoon lime juice	Shaker
Pinch of salt	
¼ cup crushed ice	

1. Combine all ingredients and shake thoroughly.
2. Serve at once in iced beverage glasses, allowing about ¾ cup per serving.

Makes one and one-half cups.

STRAWBERRY WATER

Delicious on a hot day, and a good way to use berries that are still good but too ripe for whole use.

2 cups ripe hulled strawberries	Blender
1 cup granulated sugar	Juicer
5 cups cold water	Measuring cups and spoons
4 tablespoons lemon juice	Pitcher
	Spoon, long-handled

1. Put berries, sugar, and 2 cups of water into blender and liquefy.
2. Stir in remaining water and lemon juice, and refrigerate until serving.

Makes about eight glasses.

SPIRITS

It is perfectly acceptable to offer a decanter of sherry or Madeira along with tea. The two basic types of sherry are finos and olorosos. The finos are pale and dry, more suitable as an aperitif. The olorosos are heavy, dark, and sweet but less fragrant than finos. "Brown" and "cream" sherries are olorosos, and one of these is probably what would appeal to most guests at teatime. As for Madeira, there are four types, of which bual or boal is probably most suitable for afternoon tea, as it is rich, full, heavy, and well-balanced.

In the winter, and particularly at holiday time, many guests seem to enjoy an old English favorite, Mulled Wine.

MULLED WINE

May be poured from a teapot or ladled from a punch bowl. Use regular teacups. Makes the place smell wonderful, and is especially delicious in cold weather.

1½ cups water	Measuring cups
3 cups claret	Saucepan, heavy, large
¾ cup granulated sugar	
1 lemon, unpeeled and thinly sliced	
4 whole cloves	
3 crushed allspice berries	
2 small sticks cinnamon	

1. Over medium heat in heavy saucepan, combine all ingredients and heat just to boiling point.
2. Serve as soon as possible.

Makes about seven punch cups.

CHOOSING THE TEA BEVERAGE

In choosing beverages for afternoon tea, keep in mind that balance is important. Don't overpower a delicate green tea by serving it with Mulled Wine as the alternative beverage, or be so repetitious as to offer Lemon Verbena tea with Lemonade. Let the season speak through your choice—in the spring, green tea, Formosa Oolong, or one of the more-delicate herb teas; in the winter, Assam or Almond Tea. And give your guests a choice if you aren't sure of what they'd like best—tea and coffee, tea and a cooler, or tea and sherry—but don't trivialize a fine tea by offering too many other sorts of drinks. The aim isn't to produce a liquid smörgåsbord, but to offer one or two really exceptional beverages.

Above all, whichever beverage or beverages you choose, prepare the recipe with as much care and precision as you would a fine pastry or tender bread.

PART III

Tea Foods

· 8 ·

Recipes and Sample Menus

There is something about the kind of food that is served with afternoon tea that brings memories of childhood holidays: picnics on the Fourth of July; family dinners at Thanksgiving and Christmas; and birthday parties when our own special cake was ceremoniously presented. Perhaps it is these associations that make tea food seem such fun, that and the fact that it suggests two of America's favorite purveyors of edibles— the bakery and the delicatessen.

The recipes that follow are, for the most part, treat foods: delicious breads, handsome cakes, mouth-watering confections, pretty cookies, and flavorful sandwiches. These recipes, or the ideas that inspired them, came from a variety of sources: friends and relatives; nineteenth-century cookbooks, both English and American; and food eaten while wandering here and abroad. The recipes are, in fact, a personal history of sorts, and their names alone evoke for me a series of happy images. Maggie's Gingerbread was my somewhat haughty but very wonderful grandmother's favorite recipe for her favorite sweet bread, and Ethel's Brown Sugar Chews came from my other grandmother, a down-to-earth woman who liked her sweets as straightforward as her well-organized life. Ruth's Crunchy Chocolate Mounds are from a recipe adapted by my aunt, whose way with cakes and candies, pies and puddings is family legend. Carrie's Molasses Bars, Pat's Spice Cookies, Jessie Lee's Quick Crumpets, Great-Aunt Minnie's Candied Grapefruit Peel, and Mrs. Witherspoon's Raisin and Nut Sandwich were shared by friends with whom I have spent many happy hours over the teacups, some of the recipes having come down in their families, some of their own devising.

Quite a lot of the recipes bring back memories of special places. Apricot Treats, Chocolate Raisin Delights, and Coconut Balls make me remember a brisk afternoon in late summer in a dimly lit confectionery shop in Ogunquit, Maine, lined with glass cases full of row after row of sugarplums, hard candies, French creams, bonbons, fondants, toffees, nougats, and fudges of a bewildering variety. Cheese Straws mean sultry summer days in Savannah, Georgia, and a bakery in the Victorian district shaded by gigantic live oaks. Cranberry Muffins are a fall morning in a cozy inn on the outskirts of Provincetown, Massachusetts, with Cape Cod at our back and the blue-green water of the bay sparkling in the distance. Burnt-Sugar Cake is a restaurant hidden in the hills of western Virginia on a day when snow fell so thickly that it looked like ready-made snowballs.

But—appropriately—it is mostly England, Wales, and Scotland that figure in these memories. It was in the sun-dappled yard of a farmhouse in Suffolk that we first had crumpets, hot from the oven and dripping with butter that coated our fingertips almost unnoticed as we gazed at the beauty around us. On all sides lush, green swells flecked with Queen Anne's Lace gave the land the look of a gentle, foam-touched sea, and the garden in which we sat—sheltered by the branches of an ancient apple tree—offered irises, coxcombs, daisies, and peonies as the only bright colors in this soft-green land-locked wave of grass.

As for scones, they are the one thing to be found on almost all tea menus throughout Britain, and the first time we had them was in a tiny cafeteria in Glastonbury, site of a famous ruined abbey. It was, to say the least, a utilitarian sort of place with stark-white walls and worn linoleum on the floor; but the scones were plump and fresh and served with clotted cream and strawberry preserves, and through the plate-glass window the main street meandered on the dark, wet November afternoon as it has through the centuries since this minute Somerset town attracted pilgrims from far and wide.

Since then we have had scones all over Britain in surroundings that ranged from converted castle keep to food concession stand by the sea, but the smell of them baking brings back the memory of the first time we made them ourselves, in tiny Church Cottage, which nestles in a quiet Welsh hamlet a few miles inland from Cardigan. The cottage, of stone with narrow Gothic-arched windows, is an early Victorian doll-house of a place that is owned by the Landmark Trust and rented out as a home away from home for travelers who want the experience of actually living in the area rather than merely passing through. Like other Landmark properties we've stayed in, Church Cottage boasts a well-equipped, modern kitchen that tempts the visitor to cook; and when we found ourselves with a jug of honey bought from a beekeeper whose hives we could see from the kitchen windows, and a pound of melt-in-the-mouth Welsh butter from a shop in Newcastle Emlyn, what more natural to try our hand at than scones? And nothing could have been better than the taste of them, oven-hot and heaped with honey and butter, as we sat on the small stone terrace outside the kitchen door and listened to bees buzzing lazily in the soft May sunshine.

Huron Cakes call to mind a funny little tea shop in Ludlow that in retrospect seems to have been ten feet wide and fifty feet deep with a row of tables down each side at which shoppers and family groups attacked plates piled high with breads, cakes, pastries, and sandwiches. The gloom of the windowless place was broken only by red-shaded lamps that cast a warm glow over the menus brought by a smiling waitress, and it was a shock to step back into the brightness of early summer on a street of Georgian brick and Tudor half-timbering. Eating the sweet, cookie-like cakes with their dollop of tart jelly, we walked to the ruined castle, once one of the most important in the Border Country between England and Wales. We ate the last of the cakes standing in a stone chamber with a barred window that looked out over a landscape that might have been A. E. Housman's "idle hill of summer, sleepy with the flow of streams." Then we walked back to our inn, the sixteenth-century Feathers, by way of St. Lawrence's Church, where Housman's ashes lie in the churchyard, the paradoxical nature of the poet-scholar now still instead of roaming

> The happy highways where I went
> And cannot come again.

Apple Dumpling Tarts from a bakery in a half-timbered building at Tewkesbury. Shortbread in the blind harper's cottage at Alton Towers overlooking the enchanted gardens created by Charles, fifteenth Earl of

Shrewsbury, early in the nineteenth century. Palmiers, from a Stafford bakery, eaten on the roof of Tudor Tixall Gatehouse overlooking fields of grazing cattle with peculiar, flat-bottomed craft moving lazily down the Staffordshire and Worcestershire Canal beyond. Meringues in the belvedere of the Gothic Temple at Stowe with dozens of temples, grottoes, obelisks, and monuments scattered about the vast Capability Brown park that was once the playground of the Dukes of Buckingham. Lemon Tea Biscuits on a train between Edinburgh and Inverness; Bread and Butter Sandwiches on the banks of Loch Tarbert; Scottish Shortbread from a bakery in Glasgow.

Before you begin mixing a recipe, all ingredients should be on hand.

There are few pastimes more pleasant than the association of interesting places with beautiful food; and while neither opportunity nor fancy may have carried you to these particular spots, you can recreate for yourself and your guests both the menu and ambience of an English tea. Following are many recipes for many delicious treats, as well as sample menus, but as much fun as it is to plan and prepare special foods for sharing with people we care about, we must never lose sight of the fact that it should be ourselves and the spirit of our home that we give our guests as much as it is "a perpetual feast of nectared sweets."

It was a pleasure developing and collecting these recipes. Whether friendly gifts, the product of travels, the result of happy accident, or traditional recipes with stories that stretch back into the mists of American and English history, they have delighted us and our guests. May you have as much fun with them as we have had, and may your teapot never grow cold.

Testing Conditions

These recipes were developed and tested in a home kitchen at an altitude of slightly more than one thousand feet. The recipes were tested using the best-quality ingredients: butter where specified, otherwise corn-oil margarine or polyunsaturated oils as specified; soft, white plain flour where all-purpose flour is called for and other flours and grains as specified; fresh nuts and coconut; whipping cream where heavy cream is called for and half-and-half, milk, milk powder, and sour cream as specified; top-quality block cheese freshly grated; fresh vegetables, fruits and juices unless dried or canned are specified; the freshest-possible eggs; fresh spices and extracts; newly picked herbs; fresh baking chocolate and cocoa as specified; fresh baking powder; and—for the sandwiches— fresh bread that was sliced just before use, unless otherwise indicated.

The emphasis on quality and freshness is intentional, for the best of cooks and recipes may be sabotaged by inferior ingredients. It scarcely seems worth taking the time to prepare special foods if we aren't going to do everything possible to ensure the best results.

INGREDIENT SUBSTITUTION

It is my experience that the ingredients indicated give the most appealing result, but there are times when it may be necessary or desirable to make substitutions. Since these recipes are for special-occasion foods not meant to be served every day, the richness of the ingredients in some of them should not pose a problem for most guests. If it does, it is often possible to make certain substitutions without ruining the recipe, although its texture and flavor will be altered to some extent.

Except for Scottish Shortbread, Coconut Sugar Drops, Sherry Drops, Black Walnut Beauty Cake, and Palmiers, corn-oil margarine may be substituted for butter without catastrophic changes in taste and texture. Substituting oil for either butter or margarine, however, will adversely affect both taste and texture.

Substituting honey, fructose, or other sweeteners for granulated sugar will change the flavor to the extent that your palate is sensitive to the different undertones of these sweeteners; more important, the texture will be altered considerably. Also, it will be necessary to adjust both the amount of sweetener and liquid to be used. To add honey in place of granulated sugar, reduce by one-eighth the amount called for and reduce the liquid by two to three tablespoons for each cup of honey so incorporated, and—unless the recipe includes sour milk or cream—add a pinch of baking soda.

If you want to substitute one of the low-calorie, artificial sweeteners, read the sweetener's label to see how it compares with sugar in its intensity and adjust the amount accordingly; also, reduce by one to two tablespoons each cup of liquid called for. Brown sugar and white sugar are not interchangeable because the finished product made from one is completely different in taste and texture from that made with the other. Substituting dark-brown sugar for light-brown gives the recipe a much stronger taste; substituting light for dark gives a more delicate flavor. Granulated and confectioners sugar are not interchangeable.

Whole-wheat pastry flour may be substituted, cup for cup, for the all-purpose flour specified in the bread recipes; although the taste and color will change and the texture be somewhat altered, many people like the difference. In the recipes that specify whole-wheat flour, a combination whole-grain flour may be substituted. Where cake flour is called for, all-purpose flour may be substituted at a ratio of seven-eighths of a cup of all-purpose for each cup of cake flour, but the cake or cookie will not be as light. Self-rising flour may be substituted for all-purpose by omitting the baking powder and salt specified, but it does not give a consistently satisfactory result in many recipes, and the plain all-purpose flour is much more versatile.

Nonfat or low-fat milk may be substituted for half-and-half and half-and-half for cream, but the result will lack the rich smoothness contributed by the creamier liquid. If a recipe calls for buttermilk, you may instead use—cup for cup—lukewarm sweet milk to which lemon juice or white vinegar was added ten to fifteen minutes before, giving the mixture time to clabber (use a ratio of one tablespoon lemon juice or vinegar to each cup of milk).

Usually one kind of nut may be substituted for another, but as a rule peanuts and other nuts should not be interchanged. Also, do not use salted nuts in place of unsalted. In recipes calling for coconut, freshly chopped or grated is preferable, but you may substitute commercially prepared baking coconut, measure for measure. Do not substitute quick oats for rolled oats when specified, as the desired crunchy quality will be adversely affected.

If you must substitute sweetened baking chocolate for unsweetened— the variety specified in all these recipes—decrease the amount of sugar called for by four tablespoons per cup. To substitute cocoa for unsweetened chocolate, use three tablespoons of cocoa and one tablespoon of corn-oil margarine or butter for each square of chocolate indicated.

To substitute salted butter for sweet, decrease the amount of salt specified by one-half. To add sweet in place of salted, increase the amount of salt specified by one-fourth.

If you must use a salt substitute, ask your doctor about its intensity as compared to ordinary salt and adjust the recipes accordingly. If you run out of baking powder or suspect that yours may not be fresh, you can make your own. For each cup of flour specified, mix together one-half teaspoon of salt, two teaspoons of cream of tartar, and one teaspoon of baking soda, and use immediately. This mixture will not hold, so do not try to prepare it ahead of time.

Do not interchange whole and ground spices or herbs, as a measure of ground is stronger than an identical measure of whole and also disperses throughout the batter or mix in a more regular fashion. Substituting one kind of flavoring for another—for example, ground cloves for cinnamon—will change the taste of a recipe to the extent of the spice's or extract's prominence in it, and such substitutions are tricky because few spices are of equal flavoring value. To use the same example, a teaspoon of ground cloves is three to four times the strength of a like amount of ground cinnamon. Spice or extract substitution calls for careful experimentation, but it does sometimes produce very interesting results.

STOCKING THE TEA PANTRY

In any sort of cooking, it makes sense to keep an assortment of tools and basic ingredients on hand. While few of us have the storage space to hoard every piece of available equipment and every conceivable recipe constituent, we can analyze the kinds of dishes we like best and set aside a cabinet or a few shelves to hold the necessary cooking materials and tools.

If you are particularly fond of spicy things, then you should have a selection of spices on hand, at the least ginger, cinnamon, cloves, and allspice. If your favorite bread is Baking Powder Biscuits, you'll want to keep available all-purpose white flour, baking powder, salt, corn-oil margarine, and milk. If the sweets you like best are chocolate flavored, stock a small amount of baking chocolate, cocoa, semi-sweet bits, and vanilla flavoring. Buy and keep at hand the ingredients that you are almost certain to use on a regular basis; and if you have the space and the budget, gradually add to your private store to allow impromptu experimentation.

Don't overlook the refrigerator as a valuable storage space. A trick to make last-minute teas less of a hassle is to keep tiny containers full of various toppings—for example, grated coconut, chocolate curls, chopped nuts—in the refrigerator. Mayonnaise keeps well in a good refrigerator container and can be tossed together with canned salmon, tuna, and crab from your pantry shelves for a quick, tasty sandwich.

Find a good source for sandwich breads, and try to keep at least one kind on hand, whether white, whole-wheat, rye, or pumpernickel. It is also helpful to assemble a small collection of jams, jellies, marmalades or preserves, as these can be used to decorate fast-but-plain cakes and cookies, and are also good in sandwich fillings or served with hot, plain breads and butter.

Another good idea is to bake one or two of the "keeper" recipes (listed in the recipe categories that follow) to keep on hand at all times, and for emergencies don't overlook the convenience of high-quality, commercially prepared cakes and cookies that will stay fresh as long as their containers are sealed and they are not subjected to heat. My own favorites in this line are Stollen, a fruity, buttery cake of German origin, which must be kept in the refrigerator; Panettone, a dry fruit-and-nut cake from Italy; and Lebkuchen, a spicy German cookie.

COOKING EQUIPMENT

As with ingredients and the storage problem, so it is with equipment, possibly even more so since there seems to be an army of manufacturers working fulltime to add to the already large array of appliances, utensils, and gadgets meant for the kitchen. Many of these are undeniably useful, but buying and storing even a fraction of this output would be beyond almost any cook. The tool lists given with these recipes are aimed at the average cook, one whose kitchen is equipped with certain appliances and tools but not necessarily all.

It may be that you have a tool superior for the purpose to that specified; if so, by all means use it. If, on the other hand, you don't have the listed utensil and don't want to buy and store it, improvise. Some of the items listed may strike you as superfluous. Perhaps you prefer to use a whisk for beating egg whites rather than an electric mixer, or possibly you consider the egg separator a waste of time. You may prefer to grate onto a sheet of wax paper or a paper towel rather than into a small bowl. The tools' list is intended primarily as a shorthand clue to the kind and variety of preparation activities the recipe calls for. Generally, the shorter the list of equipment, the more quickly the recipe may be prepared.

PREPARATION AND BAKING

The recipes have been organized to present clearly at the outset the exact ingredients required, as well as helpful equipment, followed by instructions that incorporate a logical sequence of preparation steps.

When a recipe calls for a baking sheet, dish, or pan to be greased, this should be done with the same kind of shortening specified in the recipe.

For example, if the recipe calls for sweet butter, then take an extra tablespoon or so of softened sweet butter and thoroughly coat the cooking utensil. If the utensil is to be floured, sift a small additional amount of the same flour specified in the ingredients' list over the sides and bottom of the greased pan.

When a certain kind and size of cooking utensil is shown, you may, of course, use a different size or kind, but cooking times, oven temperatures, and textures will often be affected. In my testing, most of the utensils specified were stainless steel or baker's black steel with the exception of the muffin tins and the deep cake pans, which were of medium-weight aluminum. If you use glass pans or lightweight aluminum, reduce the oven temperatures by 25° and expect a heavier, darker crust. If you want to use a baking pan of a different shape, try to keep it the same volume as the suggested pan. For instance, a 10″ round cake pan that is 1½″ deep contains 79 square inches, while a rectangular pan measuring 11″ x 7″ x 1½″ holds 77 square inches, and a 9″ x 1½″ round pan holds 64 square inches, identical to the volume of an 8″ x 8″ x 1½″ pan. If you try to use a pan that does not hold as much volume, the batter may overflow during cooking, while a too-large pan may make the baked cake or bread rise or brown imperfectly. A deeper pan, even if of the same volume, will require a slightly lower oven temperature and a longer cooking time, and a shallower pan will require a shorter cooking time.

Ideally, the batter should fill between one-half and two-thirds of the pan before baking. If you want to make muffins or cupcakes instead of loaf- or cake-sized recipes, fill each muffin tin two-thirds full and decrease the baking time by approximately fifteen percent, keeping a close watch on the oven the first time you bake the different shape and size.

Cooking times were tested, unless otherwise indicated, using the oven of a conventional electric range. If you want to use another cooking appliance, then adjust the cooking times according to the capabilities stated in the instructions that came with your particular equipment.

Cakes and breads are done when a cake tester inserted in the center comes out clean, when the center springs back at once when depressed lightly with a fingertip or the back of a spoon, or when cake or bread begins to pull slightly away from the edges of the pan. The crust of tarts and pastries is done when lightly browned and firm to the touch. For crumpets and skillet-baked tea cakes, thorough browning on both sides is the key. Cookies should be done when baked the length of time called for, as long as they were shaped and sized as specified. Cookies burn very easily, so they require almost second-to-second watching toward the end of their baking. Cookies should be removed from heat once they start to brown unless otherwise indicated, then removed at once to cake racks to cool. If left on the hot baking sheet they will continue to cook and may even scorch on the bottom.

Cooking times and conditions may be affected by high altitude. If you live at an altitude higher than 3,000 feet, you will get better results by adjusting certain of the instructions, as follows:

1. Underbeat eggs, or use them cold instead of at room temperature;
2. Decrease baking powder by approximately 12%;
3. Decrease baking soda by approximately 12%;
4. Decrease sugar by approximately 12%;
5. Increase liquid by about 18%;
6. Raise the baking temperature slightly;
7. Grease and flour pans very carefully or line them with wax paper, as they are more prone to stick.

SCALE OF RECIPES

You will notice that these recipes make relatively small amounts. This is partly because some of the best teas are given for one special guest so that an enormous mound of any one thing is not called for. Also, if you like to serve more than one dish, no matter how many guests you may have, the smaller quantity means that more of what you prepare will be eaten at its best.

If you want more of a particular recipe, you can double the ingredients called for, remembering that, if you plan on cooking the double batch all at once, you will need double the cooking utensils, and that different oven positions require different cooking times. The center of a rack placed approximately two-thirds from the bottom of the oven is the ideal position for most baking. If you must place a pan or baking sheet closer to the heating element, watch it carefully to guard against burning on the bottom. Cookies are especially vulnerable to a close proximity to bottom heat.

There are some recipes that lend themselves to being mixed in larger batches because they can be held before cooking, giving you the choice of serving them freshly baked on several occasions when there may not have been time to prepare the recipe from scratch. Doughs that hold well uncooked include those of:

Cardamom Rusks   Apricot Snaps
Scottish Shortbread   Carrie's Molasses Bars
Brandy Bites   Orange-Almond Rounds
Sugar Cookies   Apple Dumpling Turnovers
Pat's Spice Cookies   (crust only)
Pepper Pretties   Petticoat Tails
Scones

The dough must, of course, be refrigerated in an airtight container until ready to be cooked. You can freeze the dough to keep it longer, but cookies freeze better if prebaked, divided into layers, and wrapped in freezer paper. To freshen before serving, crisp for a minute or two in a 300° F. oven.

Baking Ahead

Cake and bread batter should be baked as soon as mixed unless otherwise indicated, but several of the cakes may be mixed and baked, then frozen. Just prepare according to the recipe, bake, and cool completely, then seal with freezer wrap. Unfrosted, they will retain their flavor for three to four months except for spice cakes which alter flavor very rapidly. A few hours before serving, the cake should be removed from the freezer, unwrapped, and thawed. After thawing, it may be iced or sprinkled with sugar. Cakes that freeze especially well include:

Black Walnut Beauty   Sally White
Coconut Supreme   Candy Bar
Madeira   Delicate
Raisin Squares   Delicious No-Cholesterol

Sometimes you won't use something you've baked, or some will be left over. Proper storage will save most of these dishes for another day, and sometimes even another week. Unless otherwise indicated put the item, once cooked and cooled, in an absolutely airtight container in a dry, cool place. Almost all of these recipes are at their peak within a few days of preparation, but even if you find yourself with something that is by no means unedible but is no longer quite good enough to serve in its original state, you can often salvage it.

To restore tired cookies, preheat the oven to 300° F. and put in one layer of cookies on an ungreased baking sheet for no more than a minute or two on the very top rack. Slightly stale cake makes good "bread" for sweet sandwiches like Pineapple Cream or Pecan and Cream Cheese. Just cut away any frosting and shape the cake in a rectangular block from which you can cut slices ¼-inch to ½-inch thick and as large as you like. Then coat with a sweet sandwich filling. Or you can toast the cake slices and serve warm, either plain or with butter, jelly, or honey. Either cakes or cookies when stale can be crumbled to use in puddings.

Stale bread can be toasted as above or used in casseroles that are based on somewhat dried-out bread. Pastries can be crumbled, but not too finely, very quickly toasted, and served warm over ice cream or sweet gelatin puddings.

Candy that has become too hard can also be used as ice cream topping. Nuts may sometimes be revived by a few minutes in a 300° F. oven, stirred frequently.

THE TEA MENU

In planning a tea menu the usual object is to have enough, but not so much that afterwards you are faced with a disposal problem. To this end there are several considerations to be kept in mind at the outset, among them: the number of people you plan to serve; the amount of money you want to spend; your cooking skills; and the time you can devote to preparation on the day itself.

A barebones approach is to prepare pretty much what you think your guests will eat and no more. Any of the following recipes will give you a more-than-generous serving for two to four people. If there are to be more guests, add an additional item for each two to three people. Think of yourself as a stingy chef in a Chinese restaurant putting together the set group dinner, and you will come up with about the minimum that you can put before guests and be sure that everyone has a reasonable portion.

As to the amount of money you want to spend, while none of the following recipes is likely to break a bank account, some of them are undeniably more economical to prepare than others. Some of the best in terms of both taste and pocketbook are the spice-based recipes, but even though they use only small amounts of spices, if you do not have the spices that they require already on hand, their initial cost mounts rapidly. This is also true of recipes that are otherwise economical but require small amounts of brandy or sherry.

Within categories, you will find that these recipes will give you the most for your money:

Breads:
Alabama Rice Muffins, Bran Biscuits, Chocolate Muffins, Cinnamon Toast, Corn Muffins, Irish Soda Bread, Old-Fashioned Baking Powder Biscuits, Premium Crackers, Sandwich Biscuits, Scones.

Cakes:
Burnt-Sugar, Madeira.

Confections:
Great-Aunt Minnie's Candied Grapefruit Peel, Peppermint Drops.

Cookies:
Chocolate Dabs.

Sandwiches:
Bread and Butter, Basil and Onion, Cucumber and Butter, Curry Butter, Eggy Olive, Olive and Cream Cheese, Tomato Butter, Tomato Cheddar, Watercress and Butter.

Pastries:
Meringues, Petticoat Tails.

The level of your cooking skills and patience is known only to you. There is no dish in these recipes that would be beyond even an impatient novice cook if the instructions are carefully followed, and some of the things are exceptionally fast and easy to make, as follows:

Breads:
Cinnamon Toast, Irish Soda Bread, Maggie's Gingerbread, Pecan Drop Biscuits.

Cakes:
Ethel's Brown Sugar Chews.

Confections:
Aromatic Pecans, Coconut Balls, Curried Cashews, Sesame Balls, Sugared Almonds.

Cookies:
Chocolate Dabs, Ruth's Crunchy Chocolate Mounds.

Sandwiches:
Bread and Butter, Cucumber and Butter, Curry Butter, Mrs. Witherspoon's Raisin and Nut, Olive and Cream Cheese, Pineapple Cream, Thunder and Lightning, Tomato Butter, Watercress and Butter.

Pastries:
Meringues.

At the other end of the scale, either more difficult or especially time consuming, are:

Cakes:
Boston Cream, Dundee, Marble Spice.

Confections:
Great-Aunt Minnie's Candied Grapefruit Peel.

Cookies:
Ischeler Tortelettes.

Sandwiches:
Carrot Cream, Potted Shrimp, Salmon Mayonnaise Pinwheel.

Pastries:
Linzer, Palmiers.

Often it isn't the degree of difficulty or even the time required that restricts menu choices, but rather when the preparation must take place. To help you plan a tea for a day when you have limited time for preparation, here are categories that range from things that may be made and kept on hand indefinitely (as indicated in the individual recipes) to those that must be prepared and eaten immediately.

The Keepers:
Cardamom Rusks, Premium Crackers, Scottish Shortbread, Apricot Treats, Aromatic Pecans, Coconut Balls, Curried Cashews, Great-Aunt Minnie's Candied Grapefruit Peel, Sugared Almonds, Pat's Spice Cookies, Pepper Pretties, Yorkshire Parkin, Peppermint Drops.

If stored in an airtight container in a cool, dry place, these recipes will keep a surprisingly long time. Many of them are also easy to make; and if you enjoy this kind of entertaining, it is handy to keep two or three of them on hand all the time to serve at impromptu teas.

May Be Made as Much as a Week Before Use:

Breads:
Bran Biscuits, Buckwheat Nut Bread, Butterscotch Curls, Chocolate Muffins, Irish Soda Bread, Maggie's Gingerbread, Old-Fashioned Baking Powder Biscuits, Pecan Drop Biscuits, Scones.

Cakes:
Almond and Citron, Bangor Brownies, Black Walnut Beauty, Burnt-Sugar, Candy Bar, Chocolate Citron, Chocolate Delight, Coconut Fruit, Coconut Supreme, Coffee Spice, Currant Tea Cakes, Delicate, Delicious No-Cholesterol, Dundee, Ethel's Brown Sugar Chews, Farmhouse, Hazelnut Squares, Madeira, Marble Spice, Orange Surprise, Raisin Squares, Rock Cakes, Sally White, Tennessee Black.

Confections:
Chocolate Cream Drops, Chocolate Raisin Delights, Coffee Creams, Orange Creams, Peanut Butter Bits, Poppy Seed Toffee.

Cookies:
Apricot Snaps, Brandy Bites, Carrie's Molasses Bars, Chocolate Dabs, Coconut Sugar Drops, Florentines, Grandma's Oatmeal, Orange-Almond Rounds, Pecan Pats, Ruth's Crunchy Chocolate Mounds, Sherry Drops, Sugar Cookies, Swedish Sprits, Viennese Crescents.

Pastries:
Petticoat Tails.

May Be Made on Day Before Use:

Breads:
Alabama Rice Muffins, Almond Bran Muffins, Banana Nut Bread, Cheese Straws, Easy Raisin Bread, Herb Loaf, Lemon Tea Biscuits, Orange Nut Bread, Quick Cinnamon Buns, Sandwich Biscuits, Whole Wheat Gingerbread.

Cakes:
Blackberry Spice, Boston Cream (separate parts may be made ahead, but assembly should take place on day), Caraway Seed, Eccles Cakes, Goldenglow, Honey Drop, Madeleines, Maple Nut Cakes, Orange and Cashew, Red Currant Jelly Roll (sponge only).

Confections:
No-Cook Divinity Drops, Sesame Balls.

Cookies:
Huron Cake Drops, Ischeler Tortelettes, Savory Crisps.

Sandwiches:
Basil and Onion, Bread and Butter, Curry Butter, Eggy Olive, Jam and Butter, Mrs. Witherspoon's

Raisin and Nut, Mushroom, Olive and Cream Cheese, Parmesan Egg, Pecan and Cream Cheese, Watercress and Butter.

Sandwich Fillings:
Carrot Cream, Crab and Olive, Lemon Crab, Pineapple Cream, Potted Shrimp, Salmon with Capers, Salmon Mayonnaise Pinwheel, Tomato Butter, Tomato Cheddar.

Pastries:
Linzer, Palmiers. Several others may be made day ahead, then assembled on day of serving, including: Apple Dumpling Turnovers (crust only), Grapefruit Tartlets, Lemon Curd Tartlets, Mocha Tartlets.

Must Be Made on Day of Use:

Breads:
Apple Walnut Muffins, Cinnamon Toast, Corn Muffins, Cranberry Muffins, Herb Loaf, Honey Lemon Sesame Bread, Jessie Lee's Quick Crumpets, Parsley Stars, Sally Lunn, Sweet Tea Buns.

Cakes:
Apricot Tea Cakes, Boston Cream Cakes (assembly only), Red Currant Jelly Roll (assembly only).

Cookies:
Orange Lace.

Pastries:
Apple Dumpling Turnovers, Tartlets—Grapefruit, Lemon Curd, Mocha (assembly only).

Sandwiches:
Cucumber and Butter, Pimento Pecan, Salmon Mayonnaise Pinwheel (sponge only), Thunder and Lightning, Tuna Almond.

If you would like to create a tea based on English dishes long served at this time of day, here are traditional English tea offerings included in the recipes:

Breads:
Jessie Lee's Quick Crumpets, Maggie's Gingerbread, Sally Lunn, Scones, Scottish Shortbread, Yorkshire Parkin.

Cakes:
Caraway Seed, Dundee, Eccles, Farmhouse, Madeira, Rock.

Cookies:
Chocolate Dabs, Florentines, Huron Drops.

Sandwiches:
Bread and Butter, Cucumber and Butter, Jam and Butter, Potted Shrimp, Thunder and Lightning, Tomato Cheddar, Watercress and Butter.

Pastries:
Apple Dumpling Turnovers, Petticoat Tails.

If you're one of those brave cooks who honestly enjoys cooking in front of your guests and have the sort of kitchen that lends itself to this, Jessie Lee's Quick Crumpets and Apricot Tea Cakes are good choices. They're easily mixed, quickly cooked, and are absolutely delicious if eaten fresh from the stove dripping with butter.

There are other dishes that are best eaten warm, including most of the muffins.

Some of the dishes either must be made ahead or profit greatly from a day's seasoning, including:

Banana Nut Bread, Whole Wheat Gingerbread, Yorkshire Parkin, Blackberry Spice Cake, Chocolate Citron Cake, Ethel's Brown Sugar Chews, Marble Spice Cake, Great-Aunt Minnie's Candied Grapefruit Peel, and Carrie's Molasses Bars.

Don't forget the importance of ambience. Some foods seem to fit certain seasons of the year. Hot breads and spicy treats make a winter tea especially inviting, and fruity recipes seem to taste extra good in the spring and fall. Summer's hot weather makes light, delicate breads, cakes, and cookies more inviting than their heavier, more highly seasoned counterparts. You can add to the sense of timeliness—and give dieting friends a break—by including a fruit in your menu: apples in the fall, hothouse grapes in the winter, citrus in the spring, peaches or nectarines in the summer. A glass of washed and trimmed celery stalks or carrot sticks is a good addition to the tea table at any time of the year.

If you want to feature an especially delicious or attractive fruit, choose a baked treat that will complement it. Particularly good with fruit are:

> Almond Bran Muffins, Bran Biscuits, Cardamom Rusks, Cheese Straws, Irish Soda Bread, Old-Fashioned Baking Powder Biscuits, Pecan Drop Biscuits, Premium Crackers, Scottish Shortbread, Farmhouse Cake, Madeira Cake, Madeleines, Carrie's Molasses Bars, Sugar Cookies, Bread and Butter Sandwiches, Petticoat Tails.

While planning your menu, keep in mind the importance of choosing dishes with compatible but not identical flavors, and of different colors and shapes. As to quantity, your guests shouldn't be overwhelmed, but neither should they feel that by taking a piece of something they're depriving the other guests. An ample, attractively arranged assortment of tea food is a principal mood setter for any tea.

Sample Menus

Week-Ahead Menus:

Menu #1: Scones (to be served cold with preserves)
              Aromatic Pecans
              Raisin Squares with Brandy Icing
              Celery

Menu #2: Cardamom Rusks
              Candy Bar Cake
              Apricot Treats
              Oranges

Menu #3: Baking Powder Biscuits (to be served cold)
Florentines
Farmhouse Cake
Apples

DAY-AHEAD MENUS:

Menu #1: Blackberry Spice Cake
Sugar Cookies
Eggy Olive Sandwich
Celery

Menu #2: Banana Nut Bread
Coconut Balls
Parmesan Egg Sandwich
Celery

Menu #3: Easy Raisin Bread
Madeleines
Watercress and Butter Sandwich
Apples

ON-DAY MENUS:

Menu #1: Cranberry Muffins
Sugared Almonds
Crab and Olive Sandwiches
Celery

Menu #2: Honey Lemon Sesame Bread
Cucumber and Butter Sandwiches
Pimento Pecan Sandwiches
Apples

Menu #3: Sally Lunn
Red Currant Jelly Roll
Carrot Cream Sandwiches
Mrs. Witherspoon's Raisin and Nut Sandwich
Celery

WEEK-AHEAD TRADITIONAL TEA MENU:

Scones (to be served cold with preserves and cream)
Dundee Cake
Petticoat Tails
Celery

DAY-AHEAD TRADITIONAL ENGLISH TEA MENU:

Scottish Shortbread
Eccles Cakes
Watercress and Butter Sandwich
Celery

ON-DAY TRADITIONAL ENGLISH TEA MENU:

Jessie Lee's Quick Crumpets
Caraway Seed Cake
Chocolate Dabs
Tomato Cheddar Sandwich
Bread and Butter Sandwich
Celery

Use the above menus as guides for putting together your own favorite combinations. Develop a repertoire of tea foods, and you'll find this to be one of the easiest, most delightful ways of entertaining. Before making any recipe for guests, it is always best to make at least one trial run. Read the listing of ingredients and tools and assemble what's needed before you begin. Then prepare the recipe, making any changes called for by special diet requirements or by the use of equipment different from that specified. Keep track of anything you changed, then if the dish turns out exactly to your liking, you can note the changes you made in the recipe. Also, record any observations you may have on the procedure or the result; then when you're making the same thing for your guests, you will have the benefit of both my experience and your own.

· 9 ·

Breads

ALABAMA RICE MUFFINS

An old-time recipe that is best when served hot.

1¼ cups all-purpose flour	Cake tester
½ teaspoon salt	Egg separator
1½ teaspoons double-acting	Electric mixer, medium bowl,
baking powder	and two small bowls
½ cup sour cream	Measuring cups and spoons
⅛ teaspoon baking soda	Muffin pan, 2″ cup, greased
⅛ cup water	Sifter and small bowl
¼ cup granulated sugar	Spatula for folding
1 large egg, separated	Spoon, stirring
½ cup cold, boiled white rice	

1. Preheat oven to 400° F.
2. Sift together flour, salt, and baking powder, and set aside.
3. In small bowl, add water and baking soda to sour cream and beat at medium speed for 1 minute, then set aside.
4. In medium bowl cream together the sugar and egg yolk until lemon colored.

5. To the sugar/egg yolk mixture add the flour mixture and cream mixture in alternate thirds, beating continuously until smooth, then stir in rice and set aside.
6. Beat the egg white until stiff but not dry and fold gently into the batter.
7. Spoon the muffin cups two-thirds full and bake approximately 25 minutes, or until lightly browned and a cake tester inserted in center of a muffin comes out clean.
8. Serve at once with corn-oil margarine or butter.

Makes about twelve 2" muffins. Will keep several days in an airtight container, but is much better fresh and hot.

ALMOND BRAN MUFFINS

A light, delicate taste and a good contrast to sweeter offerings.

1 egg, separated	Egg separator
1 tablespoon lightly salted butter, softened	Electric mixer and two small bowls
½ cup finely ground blanched almonds	Measuring cups and spoons
	Muffin tin, 1" cup size, greased
½ teaspoon double-acting baking powder	Nut grinder
	Spatula for folding
1 tablespoon bran	

1. Preheat oven to 325° F.
2. Beat egg yolk until lemon colored. Add butter and beat at high speed until mixture is creamy.
3. Add almonds and baking powder, beating at low speed until thoroughly blended. Set aside.
4. Beat egg white until stiff but not dry, and fold into the creamed mixture along with the bran.
5. Spoon into muffin tins. (Do not smooth tops, as effect won't be as pretty.) Bake until set and light brown, 12–15 minutes.

Makes twelve 1" muffins. May be served warm or cold. Will hold two days in an airtight container.

APPLE WALNUT MUFFINS

Not only tastes good but has an especially delicious aroma while baking, making it ideal for a last-minute tea treat.

MUFFINS:

1½ cups all-purpose flour	Butter melter
⅓ cup granulated sugar	Cake tester
2 teaspoons double-acting baking powder	Ladle, small
	Measuring cups and spoons
½ teaspoon salt	Muffin tin, 2″ cups, greased
½ cup dry nonfat milk	Nut chopper
½ teaspoon cinnamon	Pastry fork and medium bowl
¼ cup butter, melted	Spoon and small bowl
1 large egg	
½ cup water	
1½ cups finely chopped, peeled apple	

TOPPING:

⅓ cup firmly packed brown
   sugar
⅔ cup finely chopped English
   walnuts
½ teaspoon cinnamon

1. Preheat oven to 375° F.
2. Combine flour, sugar, baking powder, salt, powdered milk, and ½ teaspoon cinnamon.
3. Add butter, egg, water, and apple, blending with quick strokes. A light touch is important here. Too much stirring will make muffins heavy.
4. Fill tins two-thirds full.
5. Combine all topping ingredients and spoon over tops of uncooked muffins.
6. Bake until cake tester inserted in center of center muffin comes out clean, about 20 minutes.

Makes twelve 2″ muffins. Will hold two or three days in an airtight container, but is best served hot from the oven.

Banana Nut Bread

A delicious, moist banana bread flavored with black walnuts.

2 cups sifted all-purpose flour	Baking Pan, 9¼″ x 5¼″ x 2¾″,
1 teaspoon baking soda	greased, bottom lined with
½ teaspoon baking powder	wax paper
½ teaspoon salt	Cake rack
½ cup corn oil	Cake tester
½ cup granulated sugar	Electric mixer and medium bowl
½ cup light-brown sugar, firmly	Fork and small bowl
packed	Measuring cups and spoons
2 eggs, beaten	Nut chopper
4 bananas, mashed	Sifter and medium bowl
3 tablespoons milk	Whisk and small bowl
½ teaspoon vanilla extract	
¾ cup chopped black walnuts	

1. Preheat oven to 350° F.
2. Sift flour, soda, baking powder, and salt together; set aside.
3. Beat oil and sugar together until creamy. Add eggs and bananas, beating continuously.
4. In alternate thirds add flour mixture, milk, and vanilla to sugar mixture, beating at slow speed, then stir in nuts.
5. Pour into baking pan and bake until light brown and cake tester inserted in center comes out clean.
6. Remove from heat and let rest in pan for 10 minutes, then remove from pan to cake rack and allow to cool completely.

Makes one loaf that may be cut into eighteen ½″ slices. For best results, make the day before use. Will hold well in an airtight container for several days.

BRAN BISCUITS

A rougher textured biscuit good with fruit and cheese.

¼ cup bran	Baking sheet, greased
¾ cup unbleached flour	Biscuit cutter, 1″ round
2½ teaspoons double-acting	Butter melter
baking powder	Fork and medium bowl
⅓ teaspoon salt	Measuring cups and spoons
1½ tablespoons granulated sugar	Rolling pin
½ cup water, as required	Wax paper, two sheets, flour-
1 tablespoon corn-oil	dusted
margarine, melted	

1. Preheat oven to 450° F.
2. Combine dry ingredients and add enough water to make a soft dough.
3. Add melted margarine and mix thoroughly.
4. Form into a ball and, between wax paper, roll approximately ¼″ thick.
5. Cut into 1″ rounds, place 1½″ apart on baking sheet, and bake until puffed and lightly browned, 12–15 minutes.

Makes about eighteen 1″ biscuits. Serve at once with corn-oil margarine or butter. Will keep one week in an airtight container. May be served cold as well as hot.

BUCKWHEAT NUT BREAD

The tang of the citrus and crunchiness of the nuts really bring out the character of the buckwheat.

1 cup buckwheat flour

1 cup all-purpose flour

⅛ teaspoon salt

2 teaspoons double-acting baking powder

¼ teaspoon baking soda

⅓ cup chopped pecans

2 tablespoons chopped, candied orange peel

¾ cup low-fat milk

⅓ cup dark molasses

Baking pan, 9¼″ x 5¼″ x 2¾″, greased, bottom lined with wax paper

Cake tester

Fork, large

Measuring cups and spoons

Sifter and large bowl

1. Preheat oven to 350° F.
2. Sift together all dry ingredients except nuts and peel.
3. Add pecans, orange peel, milk, and molasses and mix thoroughly.
4. Pour into baking pan and let stand for 20 minutes.
5. Bake until cake tester inserted in center comes out clean, about 45 minutes.

Makes one loaf, or about eighteen ½″ slices. Serve hot with corn-oil margarine or butter. Will hold one week in an airtight container. Good cold as well as hot.

BUTTERSCOTCH CURLS

A mild butterscotch flavor.

1 cup all-purpose flour

2 teaspoons double-acting
  baking powder

⅓ teaspoon salt

2 tablespoons corn-oil
  margarine, chilled and cut
  into bits

⅓ cup low-fat milk

2 tablespoons corn-oil
  margarine, melted

¼ cup light-brown sugar

Baking sheet, greased

Butter melter

Knife, small, sharp

Measuring cups and spoons

Pastry brush

Rolling pin

Sifter and medium bowl

Wax paper, two sheets, flour-
  dusted

1. Preheat oven to 375° F.
2. Sift together dry ingredients, then work in the chilled margarine with your fingertips until mealy.
3. Add enough milk to make a soft dough and knead lightly.
4. Roll ¼″ thick between sheets of wax paper and coat on one side with the melted margarine.
5. Sprinkle evenly with brown sugar and roll as for jelly roll.
6. Cut in 1″ pieces and stand on end on baking sheet.
7. Bake until rolls are lightly browned and the center curls up, about 30 minutes.

Makes about ten "curls." May be served hot or cold. Will keep one week in an airtight container.

CARDAMOM RUSKS

An aromatic alternative to commercial rusks and much more economical. On the tea table they're irresistible—people eat them like peanuts.

½ cup corn-oil margarine	Baking sheet, greased
2½ cups all-purpose flour	Butter melter
2 teaspoons double-acting	Cake racks
baking powder	Electric mixer and medium bowl
½ teaspoon salt	Knife, small, sharp
1 egg	Measuring cups and spoons
½ cup granulated sugar	Plastic wrap
¾ teaspoon ground cardamom	Sifter and medium bowl
½ teaspoon vanilla extract	Spatula, small, metal
¼ cup milk	

1. Melt and cool margarine; set aside.
2. Sift flour, baking powder, and salt together; set aside.
3. Beat egg until thick and pale-lemon colored; gradually add sugar, beating continuously, then margarine, cardamom, and vanilla until thoroughly combined.
4. To egg mixture add flour mixture and milk alternately in thirds, beating continuously at slow speed, until thoroughly combined. Dough will be stiff.
5. Cover bowl with plastic wrap and refrigerate at least one hour.
6. Preheat oven to 375° F.
7. Remove dough from refrigerator, shape into balls approximately 1" in diameter, and place 1" apart on baking sheet. Using back of spatula, gently flatten tops, being careful not to exert too much pressure and make balls spread.
8. Bake until light gold, 14–16 minutes.
9. Remove from heat and turn oven to 300° F.
10. Split balls horizontally with sharp knife. Arrange halves with cut sides up on baking sheet, return to oven when it reaches 300° F., and bake them until they are dry and crisp but still light gold, about 15 minutes.
11. Remove rusks from baking sheet to racks and allow to cool completely before putting into airtight container.

Makes seventy to eighty rusks. Because they keep so long—several weeks in an airtight container—they're ideal for periodic baking.

CHEESE STRAWS

A nice and buttery cheese taste.

⅓ cup lightly salted butter, cut into bits
⅔ cup all-purpose flour
⅛ teaspoon cayenne powder
¼ teaspoon salt
½ cup extra-sharp Cheddar cheese, grated

Baking sheet, ungreased
Cake racks and metal spatula
Fork and medium bowl
Grater, medium-toothed
Knife, small, sharp
Measuring cups and spoons
Rolling pin
Wax paper, two sheets, flour-dusted

1. Preheat oven to 350° F.
2. Put butter, flour, cayenne, and salt in bowl and work lightly with your fingertips until combined.
3. Add cheese and mix thoroughly.
4. Roll between floured wax paper to ⅛" thickness and cut into ½" x 2" strips.
5. Place 2" apart on baking sheet and bake until set and light brown, 12–15 minutes.
6. Remove at once to cake racks to cool.

Makes thirty-six straws. Will keep four days in airtight container.

CHOCOLATE MUFFINS

A pretty, springy muffin.

1 cup all-purpose flour	Butter melter
2 teaspoons double-acting	Egg separator
baking powder	Electric mixer and small bowl
¼ teaspoon salt	Ladle, small
⅓ cup plus 1 tablespoon milk	Measuring cups and spoons
2 eggs, separated	Muffin tins, 1″ size, greased
½ cup granulated sugar	Pastry fork and medium bowl
⅓ cup cocoa	Sifter and small bowl
1 tablespoon butter, melted	Spatula
	Whisk and small bowl

1. Preheat oven to 400° F.
2. Sift flour, baking powder, salt, sugar, and cocoa into small bowl, then resift into medium bowl. Add milk and beaten egg yolks, mixing thoroughly. Stir in melted butter. Set aside.
3. In small bowl of mixer, beat egg whites until stiff but not dry, then fold gently into batter, mixing no more than necessary as overmixing will keep the muffins from being properly light.
4. Pour batter into muffin cups, filling each two-thirds full.
5. Bake until muffins are fluffy and firm to the touch, 15–20 minutes.
6. Remove from heat at once.

Makes twenty-four 1″ muffins. Serve hot, with or without butter and/or strawberry preserves. May also be baked in a loaf pan to use for chocolate sandwich bread, provided that time is adjusted to size of pan or pans used, and the bread is cooked until cake tester inserted in center comes out clean. Will keep one week in airtight container.

CINNAMON TOAST

Fast and tasty.

1 5″ loaf of unsliced white sandwich bread	Bread knife
	Measuring spoons
2 tablespoons corn-oil margarine	Spreader
3 teaspoons granulated sugar, mixed with ⅓ teaspoon ground cinnamon	Toaster oven

1. Slice loaf into ½″ slices and remove crusts.
2. Toast until lightly brown on both sides.
3. Remove from heat and while still warm spread one side with margarine.
4. Sprinkle each margarine-coated side with the cinnamon/sugar mixture until lightly but evenly coated.
5. Just prior to serving, place in warm oven just long enough to melt sugar.

Makes ten ½″ slices. Serve hot.

CORN MUFFINS

A version of one of America's favorite breads that is very suitable for afternoon tea.

¾ cup yellow, coarse-ground cornmeal	Cake tester
¼ cup soy flour	Ladle, small
½ teaspoon salt	Measuring cups and spoons
2 teaspoons baking powder	Muffin tin, 2″ cup, greased
1 teaspoon sugar	Pastry fork
4 teaspoons corn oil	Sifter and medium bowl
1 large egg	
1 cup milk	

1. Preheat oven to 400° F.
2. Sift dry ingredients together.
3. Add corn oil, egg, and milk, and mix only until just combined. Do not overmix, as this will make muffins heavy.
4. Fill muffin cups three-quarters full. Bake until browned and a cake tester inserted in center of a muffin comes out clean, about 15 minutes.

Makes twelve 2″ muffins. Serve at once with butter or corn-oil margarine.

CRANBERRY MUFFINS

Tart and tasty. This is a good year-round bread, for cranberries may be bought relatively cheaply during their season and frozen for later use without appreciable loss of quality.

2 cups all-purpose flour	Chopper for cranberries
1 tablespoon double-acting baking powder	Electric mixer, medium bowl, and small bowl
½ teaspoon salt	Fork
¼ cup corn-oil margarine	Grater, fine-toothed
¼ cup granulated sugar	Measuring cups and spoons
1 egg, beaten	Muffin tins, 2″ cup, greased
1 cup milk	Nut chopper
1 cup finely chopped cranberries	Sifter and two medium bowls
1 teaspoon finely grated lemon rind	Spatula
½ cup chopped English walnuts	Whisk and small bowl

1. Preheat oven to 400° F.
2. Sift flour, baking powder, and salt together; then resift. Set aside.
3. Cream margarine, sugar, and egg until fluffy. Using fork, add sifted dry ingredients in thirds, alternately with milk, stirring gently and just enough to incorporate flour mixture. Mixture will be lumpy.
4. Gently fold in cranberries, lemon rind, and walnuts.
5. Fill muffin tin cups two-thirds full. (Put an inch of water into any empty cups.) Bake until light brown and springy to the touch, about 25 minutes.

Makes approximately sixteen 2″ muffins. They should be served at once since they do not hold well.

EASY RAISIN BREAD

A hearty fruit bread that is especially good warm, but is also delicious cold because it strengthens in flavor the day after baking.

1 cup whole wheat flour	Baking pan, 9¼" x 5¼" x 2¾",
1 cup unbleached white bread flour	greased
	Cake tester
½ cup granulated sugar	Fork and large bowl
¼ cup dark-brown sugar, packed	Measuring cups and spoons
	Sifter
1 tablespoon double-acting baking powder	Whisk and small bowl
½ teaspoon salt	
1⅛ cups milk	
1 egg, beaten	
1 cup raisins	

1. Preheat oven to 375° F.
2. Sift flours, sugars, baking powder, and salt into bowl.
3. Add milk, stirring until thoroughly combined, then add egg and beat mixture for 2 minutes.
4. Stir in raisins.
5. Pour batter (it will be thick) into pan. Bake until browned and cake tester inserted in center comes out clean, about 25 minutes.
6. Remove from pan at once.

Makes eighteen ½" slices. Serve warm with butter. Will hold several days in an airtight container.

HERB LOAF

A hearty loaf especially welcome on cool days. Good for guests who aren't fond of sweets.

3 cups sifted whole wheat flour	Baking pan, 9¼″ x 5¼″ x 2¾″,
2 tablespoons double-acting	greased
baking powder	Butter melter
¼ cup dark-brown sugar, packed	Cake tester
½ teaspoon marjoram	Measuring cups and spoons
1 teaspoon celery seed	Oven toaster
1 tablespoon sesame seed, toasted	Pastry fork and medium bowl
1 teaspoon seasoned salt	Sifter and medium bowl
¼ cup corn-oil margarine, melted	Whisk and small bowl
1¼ cups milk	
2 eggs, beaten	

1. Preheat oven to 350° F.
2. Resift flour, then sift again with baking powder, sugar, marjoram, and seasoned salt. Add celery seed.
3. Add sesame seed, reserving ½ teaspoon for garnish, then set flour mixture aside.
4. Combine eggs, milk, and margarine.
5. Pour liquid combination over flour mixture, stirring only until flour is just moistened. Do not overstir.
6. Pour gently into baking pan, sprinkle with reserved sesame seed, and bake until browned and cake tester inserted in center comes out clean, about one hour.
7. Cool in pan 8–10 minutes, then remove.

Makes eighteen ½″ slices. Serve hot with butter or margarine. Will hold several days in an airtight container, but is best served hot.

HONEY LEMON SESAME BREAD

A sweet, citrus bread that's very good.

BREAD:

1¼ cups all-purpose flour

2 tablespoons nonfat dry milk

2 teaspoons double-acting
   baking powder

½ teaspoon salt

¼ cup corn-oil margarine

½ cup honey

2 medium eggs

2 tablespoons lemon juice

1 tablespoon grated lemon rind

½ cup sesame seeds

Baking pan, 8″ x 8″ x 2″, greased

Cake tester

Electric mixer and medium bowl

Fork and small bowl

Grater, fine-toothed, and small
   bowl

Measuring cups and spoons

Sifter and two small bowls

TOPPING:

2 tablespoons lemon juice and
   3 tablespoons honey,
   thoroughly mixed

1. Preheat oven to 350° F.
2. Sift flour, milk powder, baking powder, and salt, then resift. Set aside.
3. Cream margarine and honey thoroughly. Add eggs, lemon juice, and lemon rind, beating continuously. Add sesame seed, beating continuously.
4. Gradually add flour mixture, beating at low speed.
5. Pour dough into baking pan. Bake until lightly browned and cake tester inserted in center comes out clean, about 20 minutes.
6. Remove from oven and, without removing cake from pan, immediately prick top of bread in a dozen places with a toothpick or the cake tester. Pour topping over cake and let rest in pan for 10 minutes.
7. Remove cake from pan, cut into 2″ squares.

Makes sixteen 2″ squares. Serve warm. Will hold two or three days in an airtight container, but is best if served fresh from the oven.

Irish Soda Bread

Hard and crusty outside, soft inside, and absolutely delicious.

2 cups all-purpose flour	Baking sheet, greased
½ teaspoon baking soda	Fork and medium bowl
½ teaspoon salt	Measuring cups and spoons
⅔ cup milk with 1 teaspoon	Sifter
vinegar added	

1. Preheat oven to 425° F.
2. Sift together flour, soda, and salt.
3. Slowly stir in milk mixture until dough can be formed into a sticky ball. If mixture is crumbly, add another tablespoon or two of sour milk.
4. Divide dough into six equal portions, form into balls, and set on baking sheet 3" apart.
5. Bake until exterior is light brown and crusty, about 25 minutes.

Makes six 3" rolls. Best served hot with butter, but good cold as well. Will keep one week in an airtight container.

JESSIE LEE'S QUICK CRUMPETS

While not exactly the same as the traditional yeast version that once was the favorite of the English tea table, these are very good and take only a few minutes to make.

1 cup sifted all-purpose flour	Baking sheet, large
1½ teaspoons double-acting baking powder	Butter melter
	Fork and medium bowl
¼ teaspoon salt	Knife, sharp
1 tablespoon corn-oil margarine, melted	Ladle, small
	Measuring cups and spoons
¾ cup milk	Muffin rings, 3" size
Margarine for cooking (3–4 tablespoons)	Sifter and small bowl
	Skillet with cover, large, preferably electric
	Spatula, large

1. Mix together flour, baking powder, salt, and melted margarine.
2. Add milk. If dough is not thin enough to pour from ladle, add another spoonful or two of milk.
3. If using electric skillet, turn setting to 350° F.; when it has begun to warm, put in 2 tablespoons margarine. If using skillet atop stove, turn heat to medium-high and add margarine.
4. When margarine has melted, position as many muffin rings as the skillet will hold and fill each no more than half-full of the thin dough. Cover the skillet and let crumpets cook until browned on bottom side, about 5 minutes. (Dough will puff up slightly over top of muffin rings.)
5. Remove muffin rings, turn over immediately, and allow crumpets to brown on other side. If necessary, add more margarine to keep bottom of skillet just moist.
6. Remove from skillet at once and, when cool enough to handle, cut in half and toast until lightly browned.

Makes ten 3" crumpets. Serve hot with margarine and your favorite jelly or marmalade. They must be served immediately after toasting or they get soggy. Crumpets may be prepared and split ahead of time, but it is necessary to toast them at the time of serving.

LEMON TEA BISCUITS

In these lemony biscuits the tartness of the fruit goes nicely with the bread texture.

1½ cups all-purpose flour	Baking sheet
½ teaspoon salt	Cookie cutter, 2″ round
2 teaspoons double-acting baking powder	Fork and medium bowl
	Grater and small bowl
¼ teaspoon baking soda	Measuring cups and spoons
2 tablespoons corn-oil margarine, chilled and cut into bits	Pastry brush
	Rolling pin
1 teaspoon grated lemon rind	Wax paper, two sheets, flour-dusted
½ cup milk to which has been added 2 tablespoons lemon juice	
1 tablespoon corn-oil margarine, melted	

1. Preheat oven to 450° F.
2. Combine flour, salt, baking powder, and soda.
3. Using your fingertips, work in chilled margarine until texture of mixture is mealy, then stir in grated rind.
4. Stir in lemon-soured milk, combining thoroughly, and knead lightly into a ball.
5. Roll to ¼″ thickness between sheets of wax paper, cut into rounds, and place 1½″ apart on baking sheet. Brush tops with melted margarine.
6. Bake until well-risen and light brown, 10–12 minutes.

Makes about fifteen 2″ biscuits. They will hold three days in an airtight container. May be served cold, but are best hot.

MAGGIE'S GINGERBREAD

A spicy bread loved by our great-grandparents.

¾ cup granulated sugar,
  1 teaspoon salt and enough
  sweet syrup (maple mixed
  with honey) to make 1 cup
  in all
2 teaspoons ground ginger
1 teaspoon ground cinnamon
1 teaspoon ground allspice
2 large eggs
½ cup milk, 1 teaspoon soda,
  and 1 teaspoon vinegar,
  mixed together
2½ cups all-purpose flour
½ cup corn-oil margarine, melted

Butter melter
Cake pan, 9″ tube, greased and
  floured
Cake rack
Cake tester
Electric mixer and medium bowl
Measuring cups and spoons

1. Preheat oven to 350° F.
2. In mixer bowl combine all ingredients and blend at medium speed until mixture is smooth.
3. Pour into cake pan. Bake until browned and a tester inserted in highest portion comes out clean, about 30 minutes.
4. Remove pan to rack and let cool for five minutes before removing cake.

Makes one 9″ tube cake. Good hot or cold. If served warm, butter or firm corn-oil margarine is a good accompaniment. It will keep for a week in an airtight container.

OLD-FASHIONED BAKING POWDER BISCUITS

A very old and easy recipe for what is probably America's favorite bread.

1 cup sifted, all-purpose flour	Baking sheet, ungreased
2 teaspoons double-acting baking powder	Biscuit cutter, 1″ round
¼ teaspoon salt	Measuring cups and spoons
2 tablespoons corn-oil margarine	Pastry fork and medium bowl
⅓ cup milk	Rolling pin
	Sifter and small bowl
	Wax paper, two sheets, flour-dusted

1. Preheat oven to 450° F.
2. Sift together flour, baking powder, and salt.
3. Blend margarine and flour mixture with your fingertips until particles are mealy.
4. Add milk, stirring only until a very soft dough is formed.
5. Knead no more than a minute.
6. Place dough between floured sides of wax paper and roll to ½″ thickness. Cut in 1″ rounds.
7. Arrange ½″ apart on baking sheet.
8. Bake until well-risen and lightly browned, about 15 minutes. This will make a high, fluffy biscuit.

Makes about twenty 1″ biscuits. Best served hot with corn-oil margarine, but also good served cold with chutney. In an airtight container it will hold for two weeks.

ORANGE NUT BREAD

A delicious sweet bread with a strong orange flavor.

1 medium orange	Baking pan, 8″ x 8″ x 2″,
Boiling water	greased
Seedless raisins	Butter melter
1 teaspoon baking soda	Cake tester
1 cup light-brown sugar	Food chopper
2 tablespoons corn-oil	Fork and large bowl
margarine, melted	Juicer
1 teaspoon vanilla extract	Kettle
1 egg, beaten	Measuring cups and spoons
1 teaspoon double-acting	Nut chopper
baking powder	Whisk and small bowl
2 cups unbleached flour	
½ cup chopped pecans	

1. Preheat oven to 350° F.
2. Squeeze juice from orange into one-cup measure, and add boiling water to fill cup.
3. Chop orange shell, and to its pulp add enough raisins to equal 1 cup.
4. Put orange pulp/raisin mixture into bowl and add orange juice/water mixture, soda, sugar, margarine, vanilla, egg, flour, and baking powder, stirring well after each addition. When thoroughly blended, stir in nuts.
5. Pour into pan. Bake until browned and cake tester inserted in center comes out clean, about 25 minutes.

Makes sixteen 2″ squares. May be served warm or cold. Will keep four days in an airtight container.

PARSLEY STARS

A pretty bread, especially appropriate for Christmas.

¼ cup grated mild onion	Baking sheet, greased
¼ cup sesame oil	Cookie cutter, star-shaped
⅛ cup water	Grater, medium-toothed
1 large egg, lightly beaten	Herb mincer
1½ cups all-purpose flour	Measuring cups and spoons
2 tablespoons sesame seed,	Pastry fork and medium bowl
toasted	Plastic wrap
½ teaspoon granulated sugar	Rolling pin
¾ teaspoon double-acting	Toaster oven
baking powder	Wax paper, greased and
½ teaspoon salt	floured on one side
Dash white pepper	Whisk and small bowl
3 tablespoons parsley, minced	

1. Combine onion, oil, water, and egg; then add remaining ingredients, mixing until thoroughly combined. Dough will be sticky and elastic.
2. Wrap dough in plastic wrap and refrigerate 1 hour.
3. Set oven to 350° F.
4. Remove dough from refrigerator, place between greased and floured sheets of wax paper, and roll to ⅛" thickness.
5. Cut in star shapes and place on baking sheet.
6. Bake until lightly browned, 8 to 10 minutes.

Makes twenty-five 2" stars. Best if served warm.

Pecan Drop Biscuits

Fast and good, especially with honey.

1 cup all-purpose flour	Baking sheet, ungreased
1 teaspoon granulated sugar	Cookie dropper or spoon
½ teaspoon salt	Fork and medium bowl
1 tablespoon baking powder	Measuring cups and spoons
⅓ cup chopped pecans	Nut chopper
⅓ cup milk	Sifter and small bowl
3 tablespoons safflower oil	

1. Preheat oven to 400° F.
2. Sift together flour, sugar, salt, and baking powder.
3. Add pecans and mix well.
4. Stir in milk and oil until thoroughly combined.
5. Drop by teaspoonfuls onto baking sheet 1½" apart.
6. Bake until lightly browned, 12–15 minutes.

Makes about sixteen 1½" biscuits. Best if served hot, but also good cold. Will keep one week in an airtight container.

Premium Crackers

Very fresh tasting, crisp, and a nice foil for sweet tea offerings.

¾ tablespoon lightly salted butter, cut into small pieces

1 cup all-purpose flour

½ teaspoon salt

⅛–¼ cup milk

Baking sheet covered with baking parchment

Bowl, medium

Canape cutters or small, sharp knife

Measuring cups and spoons

Rolling pin

Wax paper, two sheets

1. Preheat oven to 350° F.
2. Combine butter, flour, and salt, kneading with fingertips until mealy.
3. By the teaspoonful, add just enough milk to make a dough so stiff that it can be formed into a hard, firm ball.
4. Put dough between 2 sheets of wax paper and roll to ⅛" thickness. With small, sharp knife or canape cutters, cut dough into desired cracker shapes. (If you prefer a flavored cracker, at this point coat the top of each cracker with melted butter and sprinkle with your choice of cinnamon sugar, garlic salt, seasoned salt, etc.)
5. Bake until slightly puffed and light brown, 10–11 minutes.

Makes about eighty ½" crackers or nine 3"-square crackers. Will keep indefinitely in an airtight container.

QUICK CINNAMON BUNS

A quick, tasty version of a favorite yeast bread. Smells wonderful cooking.

2 tablespoons granulated sugar

2¼ cups all-purpose flour

½ teaspoon salt

4 teaspoons double-acting baking powder

2 tablespoons corn-oil margarine, chilled and cut into bits

1 egg, beaten

½ cup water

2 tablespoons corn-oil margarine, melted

6 tablespoons granulated sugar

2 teaspoons ground cinnamon

4 tablespoons raisins

3 tablespoons corn-oil margarine, softened

3 tablespoons dark-brown sugar

Baking pan, heavy (preferably iron), with sides

Electric mixer and small bowl

Fork and large bowl

Knife, small, sharp

Measuring cups and spoons

Pastry brush

Rolling pin

Sifter and medium bowl

Wax paper, two sheets, flour-dusted

Whisk and two small bowls

1. Preheat oven to 425° F.
2. Sift together 2 tablespoons granulated sugar, flour, salt, and baking powder, then work in chilled margarine with your fingertips until mealy.
3. Combine egg and water and mix with dry ingredients to make a soft dough.
4. Roll between wax paper to ¼" thickness, then brush on one side with melted margarine.
5. Combine 6 tablespoons granulated sugar, cinnamon, and raisins, and sprinkle evenly over margarine-coated dough.
6. Roll as for jelly roll and slice into 2" pieces.
7. Cream together softened margarine and brown sugar and spread on the bottom and sides of baking pan.

8. Lay the cinnamon pinwheels in the pan, side by side, and let stand for 15 minutes.
9. Put into oven and bake 25 minutes, then remove from pan at once, turning upside down to serve.

Makes ten to twelve buns. Will hold two or three days in an airtight container, but is best if served at once.

SALLY LUNN

A fast version of the traditional English tea bread, this is a very light bread with an interesting texture.

1 cup sifted all-purpose flour	Baking pan, 8″ x 8″ x 2″,
1½ teaspoons double-acting	greased
baking powder	Cake tester
⅓ teaspoon salt	Electric mixer and medium
¼ cup corn-oil margarine,	bowl
softened	Measuring cups and spoons
¼ cup granulated sugar	Pastry fork
2 large eggs	Sifter and two small bowls
½ cup milk	

1. Preheat oven to 425° F.
2. Sift flour, baking powder, and salt together; set aside.
3. Cream margarine and sugar until fluffy, then beat in eggs, one at a time.
4. Add flour mixture and milk alternately to margarine mixture, beating continuously at low speed until ingredients are just blended. (Overbeating coarsens baking powder bread.)
5. Pour batter into baking pan. Bake until browned and cake tester inserted in center comes out clean, 20–25 minutes.
6. Remove at once from pan.

Makes sixteen 2″ squares. Will hold two days in an airtight container, but is best served hot from the oven, with margarine or butter.

SANDWICH BISCUITS

A favorite of those who like their tea treats plain and good.

1¼ cups all-purpose flour	Baking sheet, greased
2 teaspoons double-acting baking powder	Butter melter
	Fork, large
½ teaspoon salt	Knife, small, sharp
1½ tablespoons corn-oil margarine, chilled and cut into bits	Measuring cups and spoons
	Pastry brush
	Rolling pin
⅓ cup low-fat milk	Sifter and medium bowl
2 tablespoons corn-oil margarine, melted	Wax paper, four sheets, flour-dusted

EGG WASH:

1 beaten egg yolk and ¼ cup
cream, thoroughly combined

1. Preheat oven to 450° F.
2. Sift together the dry ingredients and work in the chilled margarine with your fingertips until mealy.
3. Add enough milk to make a soft dough and knead lightly.
4. Divide dough into two equal portions and roll between wax paper to ⅛" thickness.
5. Brush one sheet of dough with the melted margarine, top with the second sheet, and cut into 1½" squares.
6. Place 1½" apart on baking sheet and brush tops with Egg Wash.
7. Bake until lightly browned, approximately 12 minutes.

Makes about twelve "sandwiches." Will keep several days in an airtight container, but is best if served hot from the oven.

SCONES

The traditional English tea bread, this very old bread was baked on a stone or griddle before the introduction of ovens.

2½ cups all-purpose flour	Baking sheet, greased
1 teaspoon double-acting baking powder	Biscuit cutter, 2½″ round
	Measuring cups and spoons
1 tablespoon granulated sugar	Pastry brush
½ teaspoon salt	Pastry fork and large, chilled bowl
3 tablespoons corn-oil margarine, cut into bits and chilled	Rolling pin
	Wax paper, 2 sheets, flour-dusted
1 egg, beaten to froth	Whisk and small bowl
½ cup milk	
1 teaspoon granulated sugar	

1. Preheat oven to 400° F.
2. In chilled bowl, mix together flour, baking powder, 1 tablespoon sugar, salt, and margarine. Using your fingertips, rub until mixture looks like coarse meal.
3. Reserve 1 tablespoon of frothy egg; combine remainder of egg with the milk and add to flour mixture.
4. Using fork, mix until dough forms a ball.
5. Place dough between floured sides of wax paper and roll to ¼″ thickness.
6. Cut into rounds and arrange on baking sheet 1″ apart.
7. Coat tops of rounds with reserved egg, and sprinkle with 1 teaspoon sugar.
8. Bake in middle of oven until light brown, about 15 minutes.

Makes ten to twelve 2½″ scones. If served hot from the oven serve whole for guests to split. Serve with butter or corn-oil margarine and your favorite marmalade. May also be split into halves and toasted to rewarm immediately before serving. If served cold with whipped, unsweetened heavy cream (clotted cream) and preserves, do not split. Will keep in airtight container one week.

SCOTTISH SHORTBREAD

A traditional cookie-like bread that literally melts in the mouth.

1 cup sweet butter, softened	Baking sheet, greased
½ cup granulated sugar	Cake racks
2½ cups sifted all-purpose flour	Cookie cutter or small, sharp knife
	Electric mixer and medium bowl
	Fork
	Measuring cups and spoons
	Rolling pin
	Sifter and medium bowl
	Wax paper, two sheets, flour-dusted

1. Preheat oven to 350° F.
2. Cream butter and sugar together until fluffy, then continue to beat at lower speed and gradually blend in flour, beating until consistency is smooth.
3. Form dough into ball and place between floured sides of wax paper and roll to ½" thickness.
4. Cut into desired shapes, then prick all over in an even pattern with fork tines.
5. Place 1" apart on baking sheet and bake in middle of oven until firm and very lightly browned, about 25 minutes.
6. Transfer to cake racks and cool completely.

Makes approximately twenty 1½" squares. For best results, do not substitute another shortening for butter, since nothing else gives the shortbread the proper texture or taste. Will keep several weeks in an airtight container.

Sweet Tea Buns

Sweet and eggy. A Victorian recipe updated.

½ cup corn-oil margarine	Egg separator
1 cup granulated sugar	Electric mixer and two
½ teaspoon vanilla extract	medium bowls
¾ cup all-purpose flour	Fork
5 egg whites	Measuring cups and spoons
	Muffin tin, 2″ cups, greased
	Spoon

1. Preheat oven to 375° F.
2. Cream margarine and sugar together until fluffy. Add vanilla, then gradually add flour, beating continuously at low speed. Set aside.
3. With mixer at highest speed, beat egg whites until stiff but not dry; stir lightly into dough.
4. Fill muffin tins one-half full and bake until set and browned, 20–25 minutes.

Makes eighteen to twenty buns. Should be served at once, hot.

WHOLE WHEAT GINGERBREAD

An old recipe for gingerbread—with a difference.

¼ cup corn-oil margarine	Baking pan, 9¼" x 5¼" x 2¾",
¾ cup dark molasses	greased and floured, the
2 tablespoons granulated sugar	bottom lined with wax paper
1 cup all-purpose flour	Cake rack
1 cup whole wheat flour	Cake tester
2 tablespoons chopped	Fork and large bowl
candied lemon peel	Fork and small cup
¼ cup raisins	Measuring cups and spoons
¼ cup chopped English walnuts	Saucepan, heavy, small
½ teaspoon ground ginger	Whisk and small bowl
¼ teaspoon ground mace	
½ teaspoon ground	
cinnamon	
¼ teaspoon salt	
1 large egg, beaten	
½ teaspoon baking soda	
dissolved in 2 tablespoons	
milk	

1. Preheat oven to 350° F.
2. In small saucepan over low heat melt margarine, molasses, and sugar, then set aside to cool.
3. Combine flours, peel, raisins, nuts, spices, and salt.
4. Stir the egg into the cooled molasses mixture and add to the dry ingredients along with the milk and soda mixture.
5. Combine thoroughly, pour into baking pan, and bake until cake tester inserted in center comes out clean, 50–60 minutes.
6. Remove from heat and let rest in pan for 10 minutes, then remove to cake rack to cool before serving.

Makes one loaf, or approximately eighteen ½" slices. Is best if allowed to ripen for a day before cutting. Will hold four to five days in an airtight container.

Yorkshire Parkin

An old English recipe.

¼ cup corn-oil margarine, melted

6 tablespoons molasses

1½ tablespoons granulated sugar

1 egg, beaten

⅛ teaspoon salt

¼ teaspoon baking soda

½ teaspoon ground ginger

⅛ teaspoon ground allspice

¼ teaspoon ground cinnamon

½ cup all-purpose flour

1 cup regular oatmeal

Baking pan, 8" x 8" x 2", greased

Butter melter

Cake rack

Cake tester

Fork and large bowl

Measuring cups and spoons

Whisk and small bowl

1. Preheat oven to 350° F.
2. Combine melted margarine with molasses, then add sugar, egg, salt, soda, spices, flour, and oatmeal, mixing well.
3. Pour into baking pan and bake until cake tester inserted in center comes out clean, 25–35 minutes.
4. Remove from heat and let cool completely in pan.

Makes sixteen 2" squares. Let ripen for one week in an airtight container before serving. Will keep two to three weeks.

· 10 ·

Cakes

ALMOND AND CITRON CAKE

A light, delicious tea cake.

1 cup all-purpose flour
½ teaspoon salt
½ teaspoon baking powder
⅛ teaspoon ground mace
½ cup corn-oil margarine,
    softened
½ cup granulated sugar
3 eggs, separated
2 tablespoons brandy
½ cup blanched chopped
    almonds
½ cup chopped candied citron
    peel
2 tablespoons confectioners
    sugar

Baking pan, 8″ x 8″ x 2″,
    greased, the bottom lined
    with wax paper
Cake rack
Cake tester
Egg separator
Electric mixer, medium bowl,
    and small bowl
Knife, small, sharp, and
    chopping board
Measuring cups and spoons
Sifter and medium bowl
Spatula for folding

205

1. Preheat oven to 350° F.
2. Sift together flour, salt, baking powder, and mace; then re-sift and set aside.
3. In medium bowl of mixer, cream margarine and granulated sugar until fluffy, then add egg yolks and brandy and beat until lemon colored.
4. To egg yolk-margarine mixture slowly add the dry ingredients, beating constantly at low speed, then set aside.
5. Beat egg whites until stiff but not dry and fold gently into the batter along with the nuts and peel.
6. Pour into baking pan and bake until cake tester inserted in center comes out clean, about 25 minutes.
7. Let rest in pan away from heat for 10 minutes, then remove from pan and let cool thoroughly on cake rack before dusting with sifted confectioners sugar.

Makes sixteen 2" squares. Will keep one week in an airtight container.

APRICOT TEA CAKES

These were a Victorian favorite at the tea table—very good.

½ cup granulated sugar	Butter melter
1 teaspoon double-acting baking powder	Chopping board and small, sharp knife
1 cup all-purpose flour	Electric skillet and metal spatula
¾ cup milk	Fork and medium bowl
1 egg	Muffin rings, greased, 3"
1 tablespoon butter, melted	
¾ cup diced apricot (use canned fruit, thoroughly drained, if fresh is unavailable)	
Sweet butter for cooking, about 3 tablespoons	

1. Mix together, in order given, sugar, baking powder, flour, milk, and egg, mixing just long enough to blend thoroughly. (Batter will be slightly lumpy.)
2. Add butter and apricot, stirring just long enough to blend.

3. Set electric skillet to 350° F. and put part of butter in it, then cover. If you do not have an electric skillet, use a heavy, flat-bottomed skillet atop a stove eye set on medium.
4. When butter has melted, place as many muffin rings in skillet as it will hold without crowding, pour batter into each to one-half of ring's depth, then cover skillet.
5. When cakes are thoroughly browned on bottom, 2–4 minutes, remove rings, and turn cakes over to brown on other side, leaving skillet uncovered. Add remainder of butter if necessary.
6. When cakes have browned on other side, remove to heated plate.

Makes about eight 3" tea cakes. These do not keep well, so should be eaten at once, with butter.

BANGOR BROWNIES

A crunchy, chewy favorite.

1 cup all-purpose flour	Baking pan, 8" x 8" x 2",
1 teaspoon double-acting	greased, the bottom lined
baking powder	with greased wax paper
⅟₁₆ teaspoon salt	Butter melter
¼ cup corn-oil margarine,	Cake rack
melted	Chocolate melter
1 cup molasses	Chopping board and sharp
1 egg	knife
2 squares (2 ounces) baking	Fork and large bowl
chocolate, melted	Measuring cups and spoons
1 cup chopped pecans	Nut chopper
	Sifter and small bowl

1. Preheat oven to 325° F.
2. Sift together flour, baking powder, and salt; set aside.
3. In large bowl combine margarine, molasses, egg, and chocolate.
4. Add flour mixture and pecans, incorporating thoroughly.
5. Spread batter evenly in baking pan, and bake until done, approximately 15 minutes (top will be crusty, but the inside somewhat soft).
6. Remove from pan at once and cut into 2" squares to be cooled on cake rack.

Makes sixteen 2" squares. Will hold one week in an airtight container.

BLACK WALNUT BEAUTY CAKE

A beautiful tea cake with a dense texture and unusual flavor.

1⅔ cups all-purpose flour	Baking pan, 8″ round, greased
1½ teaspoons double-acting	and floured, the bottom lined
baking powder	with wax paper
⅛ teaspoon salt	Cake rack
⅓ cup sweet butter, softened	Cake tester
1 cup granulated sugar	Egg separator
1 teaspoon vanilla extract	Electric mixer, large bowl, and
⅔ cup half-and-half	medium bowl
⅓ cup chopped black walnuts	Fork
2 egg whites	Measuring cups and spoons
Black Walnut Frosting	Nut chopper
(recipe follows)	Sifter and medium bowl
	Spatula

1. Preheat oven to 350° F.
2. Sift flour, baking powder, and salt. Resift and set aside.
3. Cream butter, sugar, and vanilla until fluffy.
4. Add flour mixture and milk alternately in thirds to butter mixture, beating continuously at low speed, and incorporating each well before adding next third.
5. Stir in black walnuts and set aside.
6. Beat egg whites until stiff.
7. Stir 2 tablespoons of stiff whites into dough, then carefully fold in remainder of whites.
8. Pour into baking pan. Bake until lightly browned and cake tester inserted in center comes out clean, about 50 minutes.
9. Cool pan on cake rack for 10 minutes, then remove cake, peel paper from bottom and place on cake rack.
10. When completely cool, frost with Black Walnut Frosting.

Black Walnut Frosting

2 cups confectioners sugar	Electric mixer and small bowl
¾ cup sweet butter, softened	Measuring cups and spoons
¼ teaspoon vanilla extract	Nut chopper
⅛ cup milk	Spreader
¼ cup chopped black walnuts	

1. Cream together sugar, butter, vanilla, and milk until fluffy.
2. Spread thickly over top and sides of cake.
3. Sprinkle black walnuts across the top.

Makes one 8" round cake. Frosted, this cake will hold very well in an airtight container for about one week. The cake may also be frozen, unfrosted. Thaw, then frost just prior to serving.

BLACKBERRY SPICE CAKE

The blackberry-walnut combination is irresistible.

2 cups all-purpose flour	Baking pan, 9¼" x 5¼" x 2¾",
1 teaspoon ground allspice	greased and floured, the
1 teaspoon ground cloves	bottom lined with greased
1 teaspoon ground cinnamon	and floured wax paper
1 teaspoon ground nutmeg	Cake rack
4 eggs	Cake tester
¾ cup corn-oil margarine,	Electric mixer and medium
softened	bowl
1 cup granulated sugar	Measuring cups and spoons
1 cup seedless blackberry jam	Sifter and medium bowl
¾ cup buttermilk combined	Whisk and small bowl
with 1 teaspoon baking soda	
English Walnut Frosting	
(recipe follows)	

1. Preheat oven to 350° F.
2. Sift together flour and spices; set aside.
3. Whisk eggs until lightly beaten; set aside.

4. Cream butter and sugar together until fluffy, then add eggs and jam, beating continuously.
5. Add flour and buttermilk mixtures alternately, beating continuously.
6. Pour into baking pan and bake until tester inserted in center comes out clean, about 35 minutes.
7. Set pan on rack to cool, then remove cake to oblong platter and spread with English Walnut Frosting.

English Walnut Frosting

1 cup granulated sugar	Egg separator
1 cup light-brown sugar, packed	Measuring cups and spoons
¾ cup half-and-half	Saucepan, large and heavy;
¼ cup corn-oil margarine	stirring spoon, preferably
1 egg yolk	wooden
¾ cup English walnuts, broken	Spreader
¼ teaspoon vanilla extract	

1. In saucepan combine sugars, half-and-half, margarine, and egg yolk.
2. Cook over medium heat, stirring constantly, until sugar is dissolved.
3. Continue to stir as mixture comes to a boil, then cook over medium heat, stirring constantly, until it thickens, about 10 minutes.
4. Remove saucepan from heat and add walnuts and vanilla.
5. Cool until spreadable, then use as topping for Blackberry Spice Cake.

Makes eighteen ½" slices when cut for serving. Let cake rest for one day before cutting and serving, as this improves the flavor greatly. The cake will hold four days after baking in an airtight container.

Boston Cream Cakes

Delicate, with a heavenly taste and texture.

CAKE

½ cup sweet butter	Baking sheet, greased
1 cup hot water	Cake racks
1 cup sifted all-purpose flour	Measuring cups and spoons
3 eggs	Saucepan, large, heavy, and stirring spoon
	Sifter and small bowl
	Spoon, large

1. Put butter and water into saucepan over medium heat.
2. When mixture boils, stir in flour, and continue to stir until very smooth. Set aside to cool.
3. When dough is completely cool, set oven at 400° F. Then add the eggs to the dough, one at a time, stirring well after each addition.
4. Drop by large spoonfuls 2″ apart on baking sheet.
5. Bake until set and palest brown, about 15 minutes.
6. Remove at once to cake racks to cool.

FILLING

2 cups milk	Double boiler, large; and stirring spoon
2 eggs, beaten	
½ cup cornstarch	Measuring cups and spoons
1 cup granulated sugar	Whisk and small bowl
1 teaspoon sweet butter	
¾ teaspoon lemon extract	

1. Put two thirds of milk into top half of double boiler and bring slowly to a boil.
2. Meanwhile, stir eggs, cornstarch, and sugar into remaining milk.
3. As soon as milk is about to boil, add egg mixture and stir continuously until thickened, about 3 minutes.
4. Remove from heat and add butter.
5. When cool, add lemon extract, stirring well.

ASSEMBLY

Cakes	Knife, small, sharp
Filling	Spoon

1. Open cakes carefully on one side with knife and fill with custard.
2. Serve as soon as possible.

Makes about twelve 3" cakes. If you want to make this ahead, wait until as close as possible to serving time before putting the filling into the cakes.

BURNT-SUGAR CAKE

A spongy texture and pretty color combination—but rich!

⅓ cup plus 1 tablespoon granulated sugar

⅓ cup plus 1 tablespoon boiling water

⅓ cup corn-oil margarine, softened

½ teaspoon vanilla extract

1 egg, separated

1½ cups sifted cake flour

1½ teaspoons double-acting baking powder

¼ teaspoon salt

⅓ cup plus 1 tablespoon milk

Burnt-Sugar Frosting (recipe follows)

Cake pan, 8" round, greased, the bottom lined with wax paper

Cake rack

Cake tester

Egg separator

Electric mixer, medium bowl, and small bowl

Kettle

Measuring cups and spoons

Saucepan, small, heavy, and stirring spoon

Sifter and small bowl

1. Preheat oven to 375° F.
2. In saucepan heat sugar until brown and just beginning to smoke, stirring constantly. Gradually stir in boiling water, remove from heat, and set aside to cool thoroughly.
3. In medium bowl of mixer cream together margarine and sugar until fluffy. Gradually beat in ¼ cup of the burnt-sugar syrup. Add vanilla and egg yolk, beating continuously. Add flour, baking powder, and salt alternately with milk, beating on slow speed until smooth, then set aside.
4. Beat egg white until stiff, then fold gently into the batter, mixing no more than necessary.

5. Pour into cake pan. Bake until lightly browned and cake tester inserted in center comes out clean, about 20 minutes.
6. Remove at once from pan to cake rack and, when cool, frost with Burnt-Sugar Frosting.

Burnt-Sugar Frosting

3 tablespoons corn-oil margarine, softened	Electric mixer and small bowl
1 cup confectioners sugar	Measuring cups and spoons
¼ teaspoon salt	Spreader
¾ teaspoon vanilla	
Remainder of burnt-sugar syrup	
1 tablespoon cream	

1. Cream margarine until fluffy.
2. Add remaining ingredients, beating at highest speed until of spreading consistency.

Makes one 8″ round cake. Will hold up to one week in an airtight container in the refrigerator.

CANDY BAR CAKE

A soft cake that tastes surprisingly like a candy for grownups.

2 cups sifted all-purpose flour

1 teaspoon double-acting
baking powder

1 cup granulated sugar

½ cup sweet butter, softened

⅔ cup milk

½ teaspoon vanilla extract

4 egg whites

1 cup semi-sweet chocolate
chips

1 cup grated coconut

Baking pan, 9¼" x 5¼" x 2¾",
greased and floured

Cake rack

Cake tester

Egg separator

Electric mixer, medium bowl,
and small bowl

Grater, medium-toothed, for
coconut

Measuring cups and spoons

Sifter, medium bowl, and small
bowl

Spatula for folding

1. Preheat oven to 350° F.
2. Sift flour and baking powder together; set aside.
3. Cream sugar and butter until fluffy.
4. Add half the milk, beating continuously at low speed, then half the flour mixture, beating continuously; repeat with remaining flour and milk.
5. Add vanilla and beat at medium speed for 3 minutes; set aside.
6. Beat egg whites until stiff but not dry and fold into dough.
7. Fold chocolate chips and coconut into dough.
8. Pour into baking pan. Bake until lightly browned and cake tester inserted in center comes out clean, about 50 minutes.
9. When done, let rest in pan away from heat 10 minutes, then remove cake to rack to cool completely.
10. Slice at serving time, not before.

Makes eighteen ½" slices. Will keep up to one week in an airtight container.

CARAWAY SEED CAKE

A softer, tastier version of an old teatime standby.

1 ⅓ cups all-purpose flour

2 teaspoons double-acting
   baking powder

3 eggs

½ cup lightly salted butter,
   softened

½ cup granulated sugar

1 teaspoon vanilla extract

2 teaspoons caraway seeds

¼ cup milk

Baking pan, 8″ x 8″ x 2″,
   greased

Cake rack

Cake tester

Electric mixer, medium bowl,
   and small bowl

Measuring cups and spoons

Sifter and small bowl

1. Preheat oven to 350° F.
2. Sift flour and baking powder together; set aside.
3. Cream butter and sugar until fluffy; set aside.
4. Beat eggs until light and lemon colored.
5. Add vanilla, butter mixture, and caraway seeds to eggs, beating continuously at low speed.
6. Add flour mixture alternately with milk, beating continuously at low speed.
7. Pour into baking pan. Bake until golden and a cake tester inserted in center comes out clean, 35–45 minutes.
8. Remove from heat and let rest in pan for 10 minutes, then remove from pan to cake rack to cool completely.
9. Just prior to serving, cut into 2″ squares and arrange on cake plate.

Makes sixteen 2″ squares. Best if served within one day of baking.

CHOCOLATE CITRON CAKE

A cake that smells like Christmas, it can also serve as a bread for sweet sandwiches.

1 cup plus 2 tablespoons sifted cake flour	Baking pan, 9¼" x 5¼" x 2¾", greased and floured
¾ teaspoon double-acting baking powder	Cake rack
	Cake tester
¼ teaspoon ground cloves	Electric mixer and medium bowl
½ teaspoon ground cinnamon	Grater, fine-toothed, and small bowl
¼ teaspoon ground nutmeg	
¼ cup lightly salted butter, softened	Measuring cups and spoons
	Sifter and small bowl
¾ cup granulated sugar	
2 eggs	
2 ounces grated sweet baking chocolate	
⅓ cup finely grated citron (lemon and orange peel mixed)	
½ cup milk	
Confectioners sugar	

1. Preheat oven to 350° F.
2. Sift flour, baking powder, and spices together; set aside.
3. Cream butter and sugar until fluffy.
4. Add eggs one at a time, beating continuously.
5. Add chocolate and citron, beating continuously.
6. Add flour and milk alternately in fourths, beating continuously at low speed.
7. Pour into baking pan and bake until cake tester inserted in center comes out clean, 45–50 minutes.
8. Remove from oven and let cake rest in pan for ten minutes, then remove cake from pan and put on cake rack to cool.
9. When completely cool, dust with confectioners sugar.

Makes eighteen ½" slices. Will keep up to one week in an airtight container.

CHOCOLATE DELIGHT CAKE

This cake has a marvelous, rich texture.

1 cup buttermilk
½ cup lightly salted butter
1½ ounces unsweetened baking
   chocolate (1½ squares)
2 cups sifted all-purpose flour
1 teaspoon baking soda
1 teaspoon vanilla extract
2 cups light-brown sugar,
   packed
2 eggs
Coffee Pecan Topping
(recipe follows)

Baking pan, 13″ x 9″ x 2″,
   greased and floured
Cake rack
Cake tester
Electric mixer and medium
   bowl
Measuring cups and spoons
Saucepan, small
Sifter and medium bowl

1. Preheat oven to 350° F.
2. Melt butter and chocolate in buttermilk over low heat; do not allow to boil.
3. Meanwhile, sift flour and baking soda together; set aside.
4. Pour melted buttermilk mixture into mixer's bowl; add sugar and eggs, and beat on medium speed for 2 minutes.
5. Gradually add flour mixture, beating continuously at low speed.
6. Add vanilla.
7. Pour into baking pan and bake until cake tester inserted in center comes out clean, 20–30 minutes.
8. Remove from heat but leave cake in pan while Coffee Pecan Topping is made.

Coffee Pecan Topping

½ cup heavy cream
½ ounce unsweetened baking
   chocolate
½ teaspoon instant coffee
1 tablespoon granulated sugar
1 cup chopped pecans

Measuring cups and spoons
Saucepan, small, heavy, and
   stirring spoon

1. Melt cream, chocolate, coffee, and sugar together over low heat, and boil until thickened.
2. Stir in pecans.
3. Spoon over top of warm cake (still in pan).
4. Put pan several inches below oven broiler and remove when topping bubbles, about 1½ minutes.
5. Remove cake from pan and slice at time of serving.

Makes approximately twenty-nine 2″ squares. If not served warm, store in the refrigerator in an airtight container, where it will keep up to one week. Serve cold.

Coconut Fruit Cake

Orange and coconut are a delectable combination in this fine-textured tea cake.

1½ cups all-purpose flour	Baking pan, 9¼″ x 5¼″ x 2¾″,
¼ teaspoon salt	greased, the bottom lined
2 teaspoons double-acting baking powder	with wax paper
	Cake rack
½ cup corn-oil margarine, softened	Cake tester
	Egg separator
1 cup granulated sugar	Electric mixer, medium bowl,
¼ teaspoon vanilla extract	and small bowl
⅔ cup grated coconut	Food chopper, medium-
⅔ cup chopped blanched almonds	toothed
	Grater, medium-toothed, for
4 tablespoons chopped candied orange peel	coconut
	Measuring cups and spoons
⅔ cup low-fat milk	Sifter and medium bowl
3 egg whites	Spatula for folding

1. Preheat oven to 350° F.
2. Sift together flour, salt, and baking powder; set aside.
3. In medium bowl of mixer, cream margarine, sugar, and vanilla until fluffy, then add coconut, nuts, and peel.
4. In alternate thirds, add flour mixture and milk, beating continuously at low speed, then set aside.

5. Beat egg whites until stiff but not dry and fold gently into batter.
6. Pour in pan and bake until cake tester inserted in center comes out clean, 35–45 minutes. Let rest in pan for 10 minutes, then remove from pan to cool on rack before serving.

Makes one loaf, or approximately eighteen ½″ slices. Will hold one week in an airtight container.

COCONUT SUPREME CAKE

Soft, sweet, and for coconut fanciers.

2 cups sifted cake flour	Baking pan, 10″ round, greased
1 teaspoon double-acting	and floured, the bottom
baking powder	lined with wax paper
1 cup granulated sugar	Cake rack
½ cup sweet butter, softened	Cake tester
⅔ cup milk	Egg separator
4 egg whites	Electric mixer, medium bowl,
1 cup grated coconut	and small bowl
Cocoa Coconut Frosting	Grater for coconut
(recipe follows)	Measuring cups and spoons
	Sifter and medium bowl
	Spatula

1. Preheat oven to 350° F.
2. Sift flour and baking powder together; set aside.
3. Cream butter and sugar until fluffy.
4. Add half the milk, beating continuously, then half the flour, beating continuously. Repeat with remaining milk and flour.
5. Beat at medium speed for 2 minutes; set aside.
6. Beat whites until stiff but not dry and fold into dough.
7. Gently fold in coconut.
8. Bake until browned and cake tester inserted in center comes out clean.
9. Remove from heat and rest cake in pan for 10 minutes, then remove from pan and cool on rack.
10. When completely cool, cover top and sides with Cocoa Coconut Frosting.

Cocoa Coconut Frosting

½ cup sweet butter, softened	Electric mixer and small bowl
2 cups confectioners sugar	Grater for coconut
2 tablespoons cocoa	Measuring cups and spoons
½ teaspoon vanilla extract	Spreader
Hot water	
½ cup grated coconut	

1. Beat butter, sugar, and cocoa until fluffy.
2. Add vanilla, beating continuously until of spreading consistency.
3. If too thick, add a few drops of hot water.
4. Spread on top and sides of cake and sprinkle top with grated coconut.

Makes one 10" round cake. It will keep up to one week in an airtight container.

COFFEE SPICE CAKE

Especially nice when some of those at your "tea" will be drinking coffee or chocolate, but one of those rare cakes that almost everyone seems to enjoy.

¾ cup sifted all-purpose flour	Baking pan, 8" x 8" x 2",
¾ teaspoon double-acting	greased, the bottom lined
baking powder	with greased wax paper
½ teaspoon ground cinnamon	Cake rack
⅛ teaspoon ground ginger	Cake tester
⅛ teaspoon ground nutmeg	Electric mixer and medium
2 tablespoons cream	bowl
2 tablespoons strong coffee	Measuring cups and spoons
¼ cup lightly salted butter,	Sifter and small bowl
softened	
½ cup light-brown sugar,	
packed	
1 large egg	
¼ teaspoon vanilla extract	
¼ teaspoon lemon extract	
Coffee Frosting	
(recipe follows)	

1. Preheat oven to 350° F.
2. In one bowl combine the flour, baking powder, and spices; in another bowl the cream and coffee; set aside.
3. Cream butter and sugar until fluffy. Add egg, beating continuously, then vanilla and lemon extracts.
4. Alternately add flour mixture and coffee mixture to the creamed ingredients, beating continuously at low speed.
5. When thoroughly combined, pour into baking pan. Bake until light brown and a cake tester inserted in center comes out clean, about 25 minutes.
6. Remove from heat and let rest in pan for 5 minutes, then remove cake from pan to cake rack, and cool.
7. When completely cool, top with Coffee Frosting, cut into 2″ squares, and serve.

Coffee Frosting

3 tablespoons lightly salted butter, softened	Electric mixer and small bowl
¼ teaspoon vanilla extract	Measuring cups and spoons
1¼ cups confectioners sugar	Spreader
1¾ tablespoons strong coffee	

1. Cream butter until fluffy, then beat in vanilla.
2. Reduce beater speed to low and slowly add sugar, beating continuously.
3. When sugar is thoroughly blended, add coffee, return speed to high, and beat a few more seconds.

Makes sixteen 2″ squares. Will keep up to one week in an airtight container.

Currant Tea Cakes

The piquancy of currants is the keynote here.

1 cup all-purpose flour	Butter melter
1½ teaspoons double-acting	Cake tester
baking powder	Fork and medium bowl
⅓ teaspoon salt	Measuring cups and spoons
¼ cup granulated sugar	Muffin tin, 2″ cups, greased
1 egg, beaten	Sifter and small bowl
1 tablespoon corn-oil	Whisk and small bowl
margarine, melted	
½ cup low-fat milk	
¼ cup currants, dredged in 2	
tablespoons flour	

1. Preheat oven to 400° F.
2. Sift together flour, baking powder, salt, and sugar and set aside.
3. Stir together egg, margarine, and milk and add to flour mixture, combining thoroughly, then stir in currants.
4. Spoon into muffin cups to two-thirds full, and bake until cake tester inserted in center of the middle muffin comes out clean, 20–30 minutes.

Makes one dozen 2″ muffins. Serve hot with corn-oil margarine or butter. Will keep one week in an airtight container, but the muffins are best served at once.

DELICATE CAKE

An interesting cake with an unusual flavor and texture.

1 cup sifted all-purpose flour	Baking pan, 10″ round,
½ teaspoon cream of tartar	ungreased, the bottom lined
¼ cup cornstarch	with wax paper
½ cup grated coconut	Cake rack
½ cup ground hazelnuts	Cake tester
½ cup milk with ¼ teaspoon	Egg separator
teaspoon baking soda	Electric mixer, medium bowl,
dissolved in it	and small bowl
⅓ cup butter	Grater for coconut and
¾ cup granulated sugar	hazelnuts
3 egg whites	Measuring cups and spoons
Confectioners sugar for	Sifter and small bowl
topping	Spatula

1. Preheat oven to 350° F.
2. Combine flour, cream of tartar, cornstarch, coconut, and hazelnuts and set aside.
3. Cream butter and sugar until fluffy.
4. Add flour mixture and milk in thirds alternately, beating continuously until thoroughly combined. Set aside.
5. Beat egg whites until stiff but not dry, then fold into the batter by hand, using no more strokes than necessary.
6. Gently pour batter into baking pan. Bake until lightly browned and cake tester inserted into center comes out clean, about 50 minutes.
7. Let rest in pan away from heat for thirty minutes, then remove cake to rack and allow to cool thoroughly. When removing from pan, use spatula to loosen edges.
8. When thoroughly cool, sprinkle with confectioners sugar.

Makes one 10″ round cake. For a nice touch, put a stencil or lace doily over top of cake when cool and sift the confectioners sugar over the stencil to produce a pattern. Remove the stencil carefully. Slice at teatime after guests have had a chance to admire the result. Will keep up to two weeks in an airtight container.

DELICIOUS NO-CHOLESTEROL CAKE

A good cake in which the flavor of the fruit and spices compensates for the lack of richness.

1 cup all-purpose flour	Baking pan, 8″ x 8″ x 2″,
3 teaspoons double-acting baking powder	greased, the bottom lined with greased wax paper
½ cup light-brown sugar	Cake rack
1⅛ cups water	Cake tester
½ cup raisins	Measuring cups and spoons
2 tablespoons chopped candied citron	Saucepan, medium, heavy
	Sifter and small bowl
3 tablespoons corn-oil margarine	Spoon, stirring
¼ teaspoon salt	
½ teaspoon nutmeg	
½ teaspoon cinnamon	

1. Preheat oven to 350° F.
2. Sift together flour and baking powder; set aside.
3. In saucepan combine remaining ingredients and boil for 3 minutes.
4. When boiled combination cools, add flour mixture, and stir well.
5. Pour into baking pan and bake until cake tester inserted in center comes out clean, 30–40 minutes.
6. Let rest in pan away from heat for 10 minutes, then remove from pan to cake rack to cool before serving.

Makes sixteen 2″ slices. Will keep for two weeks in an airtight container.

DUNDEE CAKE

A pretty, traditional English tea cake with an interesting texture and fruity taste.

½ cup lightly salted butter, softened
½ cup granulated sugar
3 medium eggs
1¼ cups all-purpose flour
⅓ cup dried currants
⅓ cup seedless raisins
¼ cup chopped candied orange peel
¼ cup chopped candied lemon peel
¼ cup ground almonds
1½ tablespoons finely grated orange peel
½ teaspoon baking soda dissolved in ½ teaspoon milk
6 candied cherries, halved
¼ cup blanched, slivered almonds

Baking pan, 6″ round by 3½″ deep, greased and floured, the bottom lined with greased and floured wax paper
Cake rack
Cake tester
Cup and fork
Electric mixer and large bowl
Grater, fine-toothed, and small bowl
Knife, small, sharp
Measuring cups and spoons
Nut grinder

1. Preheat oven to 300° F.
2. Cream butter and sugar until fluffy. Add one egg, then one-third of flour. Repeat, beating continuously at slow speed until all of the eggs and flour have been thoroughly incorporated.
3. Continuing to beat slowly, add the currants, raisins, candied orange and lemon peel, ground almonds, and fresh orange peel.
4. Remove from mixer and stir in dissolved baking soda and cherries.
5. Pour into pan, top with slivered almonds, and bake until cake tester inserted in center comes out clean, 40–50 minutes.
6. Remove from heat and let rest in pan for a few minutes before removing cake to rack to cool completely.

Makes one 6″ round cake. Will keep up to two weeks in an airtight container.

ECCLES CAKES

An English bakery shop favorite that's as much pastry as a cake.

PASTRY:

7 tablespoons lightly salted butter, chilled and cut into small pieces

1½ cups all-purpose flour

1 tablespoon granulated sugar

4 tablespoons ice water

FILLING:

⅓ cup currants

Boiling water

⅓ cup granulated sugar

GLAZE:

3 teaspoons milk

2 teaspoons granulated sugar

Baking sheet, greased

Cake racks and metal spatula

Cookie cutter, 3" round

Fork, medium bowl, and small bowl

Kettle, small

Knife, small, sharp

Measuring cups and spoons

Pastry brush

Rolling pin

Spoon

Wax paper, three sheets, flour-dusted

PASTRY:

1. Put butter, flour, and sugar into bowl and work lightly with fingertips until just mealy.
2. Add ice water, stir, and gather dough into a ball. If too crumbly, add a few more drops of water. If too wet, add a spoonful or two of flour.
3. Wrap dough ball in a sheet of wax paper and refrigerate one to two hours.

FILLING:

1. Put currants into bowl and add just enough boiling water to cover. Let sit for 5 minutes.
2. Drain thoroughly, add sugar, and mix.

ASSEMBLY:

1. Preheat oven to 350° F.
2. Roll dough between floured wax paper to ¼" thickness. Cut into 3" circles.
3. Place 6 of the circles 2" apart on baking sheet. Put a teaspoon of filling

in middle of each circle, and carefully pull together outer edges to form small pastry bag with the currant mixture inside.
4. Turn over and flatten slightly. Brush with milk, sprinkle with sugar, barely pierce tops with three parallel cuts in center of each cake.
5. Bake until light brown, 10–12 minutes. Remove at once to cake racks to cool.

Makes fourteen 2" cakes. May be served warm or cold. Will keep four days in an airtight container.

ETHEL'S BROWN SUGAR CHEWS

A very easy recipe, this is one of the best-tasting cakes around for the minimal effort involved.

½ cup corn-oil margarine	Baking pan, 9¼" x 5¼" x 2¾", greased
2 cups dark-brown sugar, packed	Cake tester
2 eggs	Measuring cups and spoons
1 teaspoon vanilla extract	Nut chopper
1¾ cups all-purpose flour	Saucepan, large, heavy, and stirring spoon
1 teaspoon double-acting baking powder	
1 cup chopped pecans	

1. Preheat oven to 350° F.
2. Stirring constantly, cook margarine and sugar in saucepan over medium heat until melted, then remove from heat and let cool.
3. Beat in eggs and vanilla, then add remaining ingredients and mix thoroughly.
4. Pour into baking pan and bake until browned and a tester inserted in center comes out clean, about 30 minutes.

Makes sixteen 2" squares. To improve taste and chewiness, allow to rest one day in an airtight container before cutting into 2" squares and serving. Will keep approximately ten days in an airtight container.

FARMHOUSE CAKE

A light, sweet, nutty cake.

½ cup cake flour
⅔ cup granulated sugar
2 eggs, separated
¼ cup cream sherry
⅓ cup pecan pieces

Cake pan, 6" x 3½", the sides
   and bottom lined with
   baking parchment
Cake rack
Cake tester
Egg separator
Electric mixer, medium bowl,
   and small bowl
Measuring cups and spoons
Sifter and small bowl
Spatula

1. Preheat oven to 350° F.
2. Sift together flour and sugar, resift, then set aside.
3. In medium bowl beat egg yolks and sherry together until thick. Add flour mixture, beating continuously at low speed, and set aside.
4. Beat egg whites until stiff but not dry and quickly fold into dough along with pecan pieces.
5. Pour into cake pan. Bake until medium brown and cake tester inserted in center comes out clean, 35–45 minutes.
6. Let rest in pan for several minutes, then remove cake to rack to cool completely, carefully removing baking parchment from sides and bottom. Slice at time of serving.

Makes one 6" round cake. Will keep for one week in an airtight container.

GOLDENGLOW CAKE

A mouth-watering cake.

1¼ cups all-purpose flour	Baking pan, 10″ round,
2 teaspoons double-baking	greased, the bottom lined
baking powder	with greased wax paper
⅛ teaspoon salt	Butter melter
¼ cup corn-oil margarine,	Cake rack
softened	Cake tester
¾ cup granulated sugar	Egg separator
2 tablespoons grated orange	Electric mixer, medium bowl,
rind	and small bowl
1 egg, separated	Grater and small bowl
½ cup milk	Measuring cups and spoons
¾ square (¾ ounce) baking	Sifter and medium bowl
chocolate, melted	Spatula for folding
Orange Chocolate Icing	Whisk and small bowl
(recipe follows)	

1. Preheat oven to 350° F.
2. Sift together flour, baking powder, and salt; set aside.
3. Cream margarine and sugar until fluffy, then add orange rind and beaten egg yolk.
4. In alternate thirds, add flour mixture and milk, beating continuously at low speed; set aside.
5. Beat egg white until stiff but not dry and gently fold into batter.
6. Divide batter into two portions, then add chocolate to one portion.
7. Put into baking pan by tablespoons, alternating dark and light batter.
8. Bake until tester inserted in center comes out clean, 30–40 minutes.
9. Let rest away from heat for 10 minutes, then remove from pan to rack to cool completely before topping with Orange Chocolate Icing.

Orange Chocolate Icing

1½ tablespoons corn-oil margarine, melted

1½ cups confectioners sugar

1 tablespoon orange juice

2 tablespoons grated orange rind

½ cup orange pulp (seeds and membrane removed)

1 egg white

1 square (1 ounce) baking chocolate, grated

Egg separator

Electric mixer, medium bowl, and small bowl

Grater, fine-toothed

Juicer

Measuring cups and spoons

Spreader

1. In medium bowl of mixer, combine margarine, sugar, and orange juice, then add orange rind and pulp, beating at low speed until smooth, then set aside.
2. Beat egg white until stiff but not dry and fold into icing.
3. Spread thickly on top and sides of cooled cake, then sprinkle with grated chocolate.

Makes one 10" cake, or twelve generous slices. Will keep for four days in an airtight container.

HAZELNUT SQUARES

A dense cake popular in Europe. Very good and with a taste that is subtle yet completely unlike anything else.

¾ cup sifted all-purpose flour	Butter melter
1 teaspoon double-acting baking powder	Cake pan, 8″ x 8″ x 2″, greased and floured
½ cup whole hazelnuts, ground	Cake rack
1 egg	Cake tester
¼ teaspoon vanilla extract	Electric mixer and medium bowl
⅔ cup granulated sugar	
¼ cup milk	Fork
¼ cup lightly salted butter, melted	Measuring cups and spoons
	Nut grinder and small bowl
Confectioners sugar	Sifter and small bowl

1. Preheat oven to 325° F.
2. Sift flour and baking powder together, then mix with nuts; set aside.
3. Beat egg until frothy, then add vanilla and sugar gradually, beating continuously at high speed until mixture is thick and lemon colored.
4. Alternately add nut-flour mixture and milk, beating continuously at low speed until mixture is thoroughly combined.
5. Using fork, stir in melted butter, being sure to combine thoroughly.
6. Pour into cake pan and bake until tester inserted in center comes out clean, 40–50 minutes.
7. Remove from pan immediately, inverting onto cake rack. When cool, sprinkle with sifted confectioners sugar, cut into squares and serve.

Makes sixteen 2″ squares. For a really rich version, you may want to frost with a chocolate topping (see page 267). Will keep for one week in an airtight container.

HONEY DROP CAKES

Individual cakes for honey lovers.

¾ cup all-purpose flour	Egg separator
¾ teaspoon double-acting	Electric mixer and medium
baking powder	bowl
¹⁄₁₆ teaspoon salt	Juicer
3 tablespoons corn-oil	Measuring cups and spoons
margarine, softened	Muffin tin, 2″ cups, greased
2 tablespoons granulated sugar	Sifter and small bowl
¼ cup honey	Spatula for folding
1 egg, separated	
1 teaspoon lemon juice	

1. Preheat oven to 400° F.
2. Sift together flour, baking powder, and salt; set aside.
3. Cream margarine and sugar until fluffy.
4. Add beaten egg yolk and lemon juice, then the flour mixture, beating continuously at low speed. Set aside.
5. Beat egg white until stiff but not dry and fold gently into batter.
6. Fill muffin cups two-thirds full and bake until top springs back when lightly touched, 10–15 minutes.
7. Serve hot.

Makes twelve 2″ muffins. Will keep four days in an airtight container.

MADEIRA CAKE

This cake is traditionally served with Madeira wine. Mild but good.

¾ cup sifted all-purpose flour

1 teaspoon double-acting baking powder

¼ cup sweet butter, softened

½ cup confectioners sugar

2 eggs

⅛ cup milk

Thin slice of candied orange or lemon peel

Cake pan, 6" round x 3½" deep, bottom and sides lined with baking parchment

Cake rack

Cake tester

Electric mixer and medium bowl

Measuring cups and spoons

Sifter and small bowl

Spatula

Whisk and small bowl

1. Preheat oven to 350° F.
2. Sift together flour and baking powder and set aside.
3. Whisk eggs into milk and set aside.
4. Cream together the butter and sugar until fluffy, then add the egg mixture by the spoonful, beating continuously.
5. Using spatula, gently fold in flour. Put the mixture into the paper-lined pan, leveling and smoothing the top.
6. Lay the citrus peel across the center of the top and immediately put the pan into the oven.
7. Bake undisturbed until browned and a cake tester inserted in center comes out clean, about 50 minutes.
8. Remove from pan (paper will adhere to cake) to rack and carefully peel paper off the bottom and sides.
9. Cool completely before cutting.

Makes one 6" round cake. Will keep several days in an airtight container.

MADELEINES

A small, delicate cake from France with pretty, shell-like form and mild citron flavor. It should appeal to Proustians.

6 tablespoons sweet butter	Baking sheet and 20″ sheet
2 eggs	of aluminum foil
¼ cup granulated sugar	Butter melter
¼ teaspoon lemon extract	Cake rack
½ cup sifted all-purpose flour	Electric mixer and medium
	bowl
	Madeleine tin
	Measuring cups and spoons
	Pastry brush
	Sifter and medium bowl
	Spatula
	Tablespoon

1. Preheat oven to 375° F.
2. Melt butter and allow to stand until cool and the milky solids have settled to the bottom. The clear liquid remaining is clarified butter.
3. Use pastry brush to coat madeleine molds with 2 tablespoons of the clarified butter, then invert tin to drain excess butter from molds.
4. Beat eggs and sugar until lemon colored and the mixture forms ribbons off end of beaters, about 10 minutes at medium speed.
5. Fold in lemon extract.
6. Sift half of flour over egg mixture and fold in, then sift remaining flour over mixture and fold gently.
7. Thoroughly but gently fold in remaining clarified butter.
8. Spoon molds two-thirds full of batter.
9. Set tin on baking sheet and bake on bottom rack of oven until light gold, about 20 minutes. Check in 10 minutes and if cakes are browning too quickly, cover tin loosely with foil.
10. Remove cakes from molds at once and cool on cake rack.

Makes twenty-four 1¼″ by 2½″ cakes. Will keep three days in an airtight container.

MAPLE NUT CAKES

So reminiscent of maple sugar you'll think you're in Vermont in the spring.

1½ cups whole wheat pastry flour

¼ teaspoon salt

2 teaspoons double-acting baking powder

⅓ cup corn-oil margarine, softened

1 cup light-brown sugar

2 eggs, separated

1 teaspoon vanilla extract

½ cup milk

1 cup chopped pecans

Maple Icing

(recipe follows)

Cake rack

Egg separator

Electric mixer, medium bowl, and small bowl

Fork

Measuring cups and spoons

Muffin tins, 2″ cup, greased

Nut chopper

Sifter and medium bowl

Spatula for folding

1. Preheat oven to 375° F.
2. Sift together flour, salt, and baking powder; set aside.
3. Cream margarine and sugar until fluffy, then add egg yolks, vanilla, and milk.
4. Add flour mixture, beating continuously at low speed.
5. Stir in nuts and set aside.
6. Beat egg whites until stiff but not dry and fold gently into batter.
7. Fill muffin cups two-thirds full and bake until the center of a muffin springs back when lightly touched, about 25 minutes.
8. Let rest away from heat for 10 minutes, then remove from tin to cake rack to cool before topping with Maple Icing.

Maple Icing

2 cups granulated sugar	Candy thermometer
1 cup water	Egg separator
2 egg whites	Electric mixer and medium
1 teaspoon maple flavoring	bowl
½ cup chopped pecans	Nut chopper
	Saucepan, heavy, large
	Spreader

1. In saucepan boil sugar and water without stirring to 238° F., or until syrup spins a thread.
2. Meanwhile, beat egg whites until stiff but not dry.
3. Pour syrup over beaten whites, add flavoring, and beat until thick.
4. Let rest a few minutes before spreading thickly over cooled cakes.
5. Sprinkle tops of iced cakes with chopped nuts.

Makes approximately sixteen 2" cakes. Keeps four days in an airtight container.

MARBLE SPICE CAKE

This cake has an attractive visual effect.

LIGHT PORTION:

EQUIPMENT:

1 cup sifted all-purpose flour	Baking pan, 9¼" x 5¼" x 2¾",
½ teaspoon double-acting	greased and floured
baking powder	Cake rack
½ cup granulated sugar	Cake tester
¼ cup lightly salted butter,	Egg separator
softened	Electric mixer, small bowl,
⅓ cup milk	medium bowl
¼ teaspoon vanilla extract	Measuring cups and spoons
2 egg whites	Sifter, medium bowl, small
	bowl
	Spatula
	Teaspoon

LIGHT PORTION:

1. Preheat oven to 350° F.
2. Sift flour and baking powder together; set aside.
3. Cream sugar and butter until fluffy.
4. Add half the milk, beating continuously, then half the flour, beating continuously. Repeat with remaining flour and milk.
5. Add vanilla and beat at medium speed 2 minutes; set aside.
6. Beat egg whites until stiff but not dry and fold into dough.
7. Set dough aside.

DARK PORTION:

    2 cups sifted all-purpose flour

    1 teaspoon double-acting baking powder

    4 egg yolks

    1 cup granulated sugar

    ½ cup lightly salted butter, softened

    ⅔ cup milk

    ¼ teaspoon ground cloves

    1 teaspoon ground cinnamon

    1 teaspoon ground nutmeg

    1 teaspoon ground allspice

EQUIPMENT:

As above

DARK PORTION:

1. Sift flour and baking powder together; set aside.
2. Beat yolks and sugar together until lemon colored and thick.
3. Add butter and beat at high speed until light.
4. Add half the flour mixture and half the milk separately, beating continuously. Repeat with remaining flour and milk.
5. Add spices, beating continuously, and beat at medium speed for 2 minutes.

ASSEMBLY:

1. Pour thin layer of dark batter into baking pan.
2. Scatter four or five teaspoons of light batter on top of dark.
3. Cover with another thin layer of dark batter.

4. Repeat process until all batter is used.
5. Bake until browned and cake tester inserted in center comes out clean, 60–70 minutes.

Makes eighteen ½" slices. Do not slice until just before serving. Will keep in an airtight container for ten days.

ORANGE AND CASHEW CAKE

Here's a moist, fruity cake that's not very sweet.

1 cup sifted all-purpose flour	Baking pan, 8" x 8" x 2",
1 teaspoon double-acting	greased and floured
baking powder	Cake rack
½ cup granulated sugar	Cake tester
¼ cup corn-oil margarine	Egg separator
2 eggs, separated	Electric mixer, medium bowl,
2 teaspoons finely grated	and small bowl
orange rind	Fork
½ cup orange juice	Grater and small bowl
½ cup ground or finely	Measuring cups and spoons
chopped baked cashew nuts	Nut chopper or grinder
(may use salted, but will	Sifter and small bowl
alter flavor somewhat)	
¼ cup crushed shredded wheat	
Orange Glaze	
(recipe follows)	

1. Preheat oven to 350° F.
2. Sift flour and baking powder together; set aside.
3. Cream margarine and sugar together until fluffy. Add egg yolks, one at a time, beating continuously, then orange rind.
4. Slowly and in small, alternate portions, add flour mixture and orange juice to creamed ingredients, beating continuously. Remove from mixer, stir in nuts and shredded wheat, and set aside.
5. Beat egg whites until stiff but not dry, then fold gently into the batter, being careful not to overmix.

6. Pour batter into baking pan, and bake until lightly browned and cake tester inserted into center comes out clean, 20–30 minutes.
7. Remove from pan at once to rack to cool.
8. When completely cool, top with Orange Glaze. Cut into 2″ squares just before serving.

Orange Glaze

½ cup sifted confectioners sugar	Electric mixer and small bowl
	Measuring cups and spoons
2 tablespoons orange juice	Spreader

1. Combine both ingredients and beat at low speed until smooth and of spreading consistency.
2. Use to spread on Orange and Cashew Cake before it is cut into squares.

Makes sixteen 2″ squares. Will keep up to four days in an airtight container.

ORANGE SURPRISE MUFFINS

A tantalizing flavor combination.

1 cup all-purpose flour
¼ cup cocoa
⅛ teaspoon ground cloves
1 teaspoon double-acting
  baking powder
¼ cup corn-oil margarine,
  softened
½ cup granulated sugar
1 egg
½ teaspoon vanilla extract
½ cup low-fat milk
2 tablespoons chopped dried
  orange peel
¼ cup chopped pecans
2 tablespoons confectioners
  sugar, sifted

Cake rack
Electric mixer and medium
  bowl
Fork
Knife and chopping board
Measuring cups and spoons
Muffin tin, 2″ cups, greased
Nut chopper
Sifter and medium bowl

1. Preheat oven to 400° F.
2. Sift together flour, cocoa, cloves, and baking powder; set aside.
3. Cream margarine and granulated sugar until fluffy, then add egg and vanilla.
4. To creamed mixture, add flour mixture and milk in alternate thirds, beating continuously at low speed until thoroughly combined.
5. Stir in peel and nuts.
6. Fill muffin cups two-thirds full and bake until center of middle muffin springs back when lightly touched, 15–18 minutes.
7. Let rest in pan for 5 minutes, then remove from tin to cool on cake rack before dusting with confectioners sugar.

Makes twelve 2″ muffins. Will keep one week in an airtight container.

RAISIN BRANDY SQUARES

A finely grained cake appealing to those who prefer their sweets on the subtle side.

½ cup corn-oil margarine, softened

¾ cup granulated sugar

3 eggs, separated

1½ cups all-purpose flour, sifted twice

1 tablespoon brandy

⅓ cup milk

¼ teaspoon ground nutmeg

½ teaspoon baking soda dissolved in 1 teaspoon hot water

¾ cup raisins dredged in ½ cup all-purpose flour

Brandy Icing (recipe follows)

Baking pan, 8″ x 8″ x 2″, greased, the bottom lined with greased wax paper

Cake rack

Cake tester

Egg separator

Electric mixer, large bowl, and medium bowl

Measuring cups and spoons

Pastry fork

Sifter and small bowl

Spatula

Whisk and small bowl

1. Preheat oven to 350° F.
2. In medium bowl of mixer, cream margarine and sugar together until fluffy.
3. Beat egg yolks well and add to creamed mixture, beating continuously.
4. Add flour and milk alternately to the creamed mixture, blending thoroughly after each addition.
5. Add brandy, nutmeg, and dissolved baking soda, beating continuously.
6. Add raisins to dough and mix thoroughly with fork; set aside.
7. Beat egg whites at highest speed until stiff but not dry.
8. Fold whites carefully into dough.
9. Pour into baking pan. Bake until lightly browned and cake tester inserted in center comes out clean, about 35 minutes.
10. Remove at once from pan to cake rack and frost with Brandy Icing while still warm.

Brandy Icing

1 cup sifted confectioners sugar	Electric mixer and small bowl
1½ tablespoons sweet butter, softened	Measuring cups and spoons
⅛ teaspoon salt	Sifter and small bowl
1 teaspoon brandy	

1. Cream butter until fluffy.
2. Gradually add sugar, beating continuously until fluffy, then add salt and brandy, continuing to beat.
3. Spread atop warm raisin cake.
4. Cut cake into 2″ squares and serve either warm or cold.

Makes sixteen 2″ squares. Will keep up to one week in an airtight container.

RED CURRANT JELLY ROLL

Although other jellies may be used, red currant is especially good and a pretty color. This is an easy cake that gives a spectacular result and appeals to those who prefer a light cake.

1 cup sifted cake flour	Egg separator
1 teaspoon double-acting baking powder	Electric mixer, medium bowl, and small bowl
6 eggs, separated	Jelly roll pan, 12″ x 18″ x 1″, greased and floured, bottom lined with greased and floured wax paper
1 cup granulated sugar	
1 teaspoon vanilla extract	
¾ cup red currant jelly	
¼ cup granulated sugar, sifted	Measuring cups and spoons
	Sifter and two small bowls
	Spatula
	Spreader
	Tea towel, large

1. Preheat oven to 375° F.
2. Sift flour with baking powder, resift, then set aside.

3. Beat egg yolks until lemon colored and light.
4. Slowly add 1 cup granulated sugar and vanilla extract, beating continuously, then add flour mixture, beating continuously. Set aside.
5. At highest speed, beat egg whites until stiff but not dry and fold into egg yolk mixture.
6. Pour mixture into jelly roll pan, smooth until surface is level, then bake until uniformly light brown, 12–15 minutes.
7. While cake is baking, sprinkle ¼ cup sugar over tea towel.
8. As soon as pan is removed from oven, loosen edges of cake with sharp-edged metal spatula or knife, then invert pan on tea towel, peeling paper carefully from bottom.
9. When cake sheet has cooled completely, spread with the red currant jelly and roll. If jelly roll is not to be served immediately, leave it wrapped in tea towel, seam side down. When ready to serve, carefully · place the unsliced roll, seam side down, onto an oblong dish and slice as required.

Makes fifteen ¾" slices. You can also make the sponge a day or two ahead, roll it unfilled, then fill no more than three or four hours before serving. This cake does not keep well.

ROCK CAKES

A traditional English tea cake; tasty with a somewhat different flavor.

1 cup all-purpose flour, sifted	**Baking sheets, greased**
½ teaspoon double-acting baking powder	**Cake racks and metal spatula**
	Cookie dropper or spoon
½ cup corn-oil margarine, cut into small pieces	**Fork and medium bowl**
	Measuring cups and spoons
½ cup confectioners sugar, sifted	**Sifter**
	Whisk and small bowl
⅓ cup currants	
1 egg, beaten	
¼ teaspoon lemon extract	
1 tablespoon brandy	

1. Preheat oven to 350° F.
2. Using your fingertips, combine flour, baking powder, and margarine until meal-like.
3. Add sugar and currants, and toss lightly with fork until evenly mixed.
4. Into this mixture stir egg, lemon extract, and brandy. The resulting dough will be stiff.
5. Drop by spoonful onto baking sheet, 2" apart. Do not smooth or shape the dough, for the final product is supposed to look "rocky."
6. Bake until light brown, about 12 minutes.
7. Remove from baking sheet to racks and cool thoroughly before storing.

Makes fourteen 2" cakes. Will keep one week in an airtight container.

SALLY WHITE CAKE

A rich, smooth, well-nigh irresistible cake.

1⅔ cups cake flour	Baking pan, 8" x 8" x 2",
2 teaspoons double-acting	greased, the bottom lined
baking powder	with greased wax paper
¼ teaspoon salt	Cake tester
⅛ teaspoon ground mace	Electric mixer and medium
½ cup sweet butter	bowl
¾ cup granulated sugar	Grater, medium-toothed, for
3 eggs, to be added separately	coconut
¼ cup fresh coconut milk	Measuring cups and spoons
¾ cup grated coconut	Nut chopper
½ cup blanched chopped	Pastry fork
almonds	Sifter and two medium bowls
Almond Cream Icing	
(recipe follows)	

1. Preheat oven to 350° F.
2. Sift together flour, baking powder, salt, and mace; resift and set aside.
3. Cream butter and sugar until fluffy, then add the eggs, one at a time, combining each thoroughly with the creamed mixture before adding the next.

4. Gradually add the coconut milk, then the flour mixture, beating continuously at a slow speed until thoroughly combined.
5. Gently stir in the grated coconut and chopped nuts.
6. Pour into pan and bake until cake tester inserted in center comes out clean, 35–45 minutes.
7. Let cake cool in pan away from heat before removing to frost with Almond Cream Icing.

Almond Cream Icing

1 egg white	Egg separator
4 tablespoons cream	Electric mixer and small bowl
1 teaspoon sweet butter, softened	Measuring cups and spoons
1½ to 2 cups confectioners sugar	Nut chopper
1 teaspoon almond flavoring	Oven toaster
⅓ cup blanched, chopped almonds, lightly toasted	Spreader

1. Beat egg white, cream, and butter until thoroughly combined.
2. Beating continuously at low speed, gradually add enough confectioners sugar to make a mixture thick enough to spread (amount depends on size of egg).
3. Add flavoring, incorporating thoroughly.
4. Spread thickly on top and sides of cooled cake, then sprinkle with almonds.

Makes one 8" x 8" cake, or sixteen 2" squares. Will hold one week in an airtight container.

TENNESSEE BLACK CAKE

A luscious cake for the many people who can't resist the combination of coffee and chocolate.

1½ cups all-purpose flour
2 teaspoons double-acting baking powder
¼ teaspoon salt
¼ teaspoon ground cinnamon
¼ teaspoon ground mace
6 tablespoons corn-oil margarine, softened
1⅛ cups dark-brown sugar
1½ squares (1½ ounces) baking chocolate, melted
7 tablespoons cold strong coffee
2 eggs, to be added separately
½ cup chopped pecans
2 tablespoons sifted confectioners sugar

Baking pan, 9¼″ x 5¼″ x 2¾″, greased and floured, the bottom lined with greased wax paper
Butter melter
Cake tester
Electric mixer and medium bowl
Measuring cups and spoons
Nut chopper
Sifter and medium bowl

1. Preheat oven to 350° F.
2. Sift together flour, baking powder, salt, and spices and set aside.
3. Cream margarine and brown sugar until fluffy, then add the melted chocolate.
4. In alternate thirds, add the flour mixture and the coffee, beating continuously at low speed.
5. Add eggs, one at a time, incorporating the first before adding the second.
6. Pour into pan, sprinkle with nuts, and bake until cake tester inserted in center comes out clean, 35–45 minutes.
7. Let cool in pan away from heat, then remove and dust with confectioners sugar.

Makes one 9¼″ loaf, or approximately nineteen ½″ slices. Will hold one week in an airtight container.

· 11 ·

Confections

Apricot Treats

A nice, chewy, fruity confection.

½ pound dried apricots	Double boiler
1 small orange, with seeds	Food chopper
removed	Fork
½ cup granulated sugar	Measuring cups
½ cup chopped cashews	Nut chopper
Confectioners sugar	

1. Put apricots and orange through food chopper, then repeat.
2. Place resulting coarsely ground mixture into top of double boiler and add sugar.
3. Heat over boiling water, covered about 25 minutes.
4. Remove from heat, cool completely, then mix in nuts. By this point mixture should be malleable but stiff.
5. Shape into 1″ balls and roll in confectioners sugar.

Makes about thirty balls. If not to be served immediately, store in an airtight container, where they will keep indefinitely.

AROMATIC PECANS

Very good to nibble.

2 cups pecan halves	Baking pan, 8″ x 8″ x 2″
2 tablespoons corn-oil margarine	Measuring cups and spoons
	Paper towels
1 teaspoon Angostura bitters	Saucepan, small
½ teaspoon seasoned salt	

1. Preheat oven to 300° F.
2. Put nuts into baking pan and bake for 20 minutes, then remove and set aside.
3. Melt margarine, then add bitters and salt, stirring to combine thoroughly.
4. Pour margarine mix over nuts, return to oven, and bake 15 more minutes, stirring occasionally.
5. Before storing in airtight container, spread on paper towels to cool and dry thoroughly.

Makes two cups. Will keep several weeks in an airtight container.

CHOCOLATE CREAM DROPS

Tastes like the commercial variety, only fresher and free of preservatives.

1 cup granulated sugar	Baking sheet covered with wax paper
¼ cup water	Double boiler, small
1 teaspoon vanilla extract	Electric mixer and small bowl
4 squares (ounces) unsweetened baking chocolate	Measuring cups and spoons
	Melon ball scoop
	Saucepan, small, heavy, and stirring spoon
	Tongs

1. In saucepan over medium heat, bring sugar and water to boil.
2. Boil for 5 minutes exactly.
3. Remove from heat, add vanilla, and beat at highest speed until stiff enough to be shaped, 1–2 minutes.

4. Form mix into ¾″ balls (melon ball scoop is helpful).
5. Set balls 2″ apart on baking sheet and allow to harden. This may take up to 10–15 minutes, depending upon the humidity.
6. Meanwhile, melt chocolate in top of double boiler over boiling water.
7. Drop hard cream balls, one at a time, into the chocolate, coat thoroughly, then remove with tongs to baking sheet.
8. Repeat with succeeding balls.
9. When all balls have been coated with chocolate and replaced on the baking sheet, put sheet in refrigerator and give chocolate time to harden, about an hour.

Makes about twenty balls. If not eaten at once, store in an airtight container in the refrigerator. Will hold about ten days.

CHOCOLATE RAISIN DELIGHTS

A luscious and very easy recipe with a result that a candy shop might envy.

¼ cup honey	Measuring cups and spoons
4 squares (ounces) unsweetened baking chocolate	Nut chopper
	Pan, 8″ x 8″ x 2″, lined with wax paper
1½ cups raisins	
1 cup chopped English walnuts	Saucepan, small, heavy, and stirring spoon
1½ teaspoons vanilla extract	
2 tablespoons granulated sugar	

1. Heat honey in saucepan over medium heat; do not allow to boil.
2. Remove from heat and add chocolate; stir constantly until chocolate has melted and mixture is completely blended.
3. Stir in raisins, walnuts, and vanilla extract.
4. When thoroughly mixed, pour into paper-lined pan and pat mixture to ½″ thickness, then sprinkle with sugar.
5. Keep in refrigerator overnight. Before serving, cut in 1″ squares.

Makes about 1¼ pounds, or sixty-four 1″ squares. Will keep ten days in an airtight container in the refrigerator.

COCONUT BALLS

A rich but oh so tasty confection.

1 cup confectioners sugar	Electric mixer and small bowl
1 cup grated coconut	Grater, medium-toothed, for
⅓ cup sweet butter	coconut
⅛ teaspoon vanilla extract	Measuring cups and spoons
(½ teaspoon cream)	Melon scoop, small

1. Beat butter and sugar until creamy, then add vanilla, beating continuously.
2. Add coconut and, if mixture is too stiff, the cream. Otherwise, omit the cream.
3. Form into small balls (melon scoop is helpful), place on plate, and refrigerate until firm, about half an hour.

Makes twenty-four ¾" balls. May be served as soon as firm, or will hold for several days in an airtight container in the refrigerator, and for as long as a month in the freezer without appreciably losing quality.

COFFEE CREAMS

For coffee-lovers with a sweet tooth.

1 cup strong coffee	Candy thermometer
2 cups granulated sugar	Electric mixer
⅛ teaspoon salt	Measuring cups and spoons
¼ teaspoon cream of tartar	Nut chopper
1 tablespoon cream	Platter, buttered
1 tablespoon sweet butter	Saucepan, large, heavy, with
½ teaspoon almond extract	cover
1 cup chopped pecans	Stirring spoon

1. In saucepan bring coffee to a boil and remove at once from heat.
2. Add sugar, salt, cream of tartar, cream, and butter, stirring until dissolved.
3. Return saucepan to medium-high heat and stir mixture continuously until it boils.
4. Cover saucepan and let cook approximately 3 minutes.

5. Remove cover and cook over medium heat until mixture reaches the hard ball stage, a temperature of 238° F.
6. Remove saucepan from heat and let mixture cool to 110° F.
7. Add the extract and beat until mixture begins to harden, then stir in the nuts.
8. Pour onto platter and cool until hard, then cut into pieces.

Makes about one pound. Will hold two weeks in an airtight container.

CURRIED CASHEWS

These are good as a balance against the sweets served.

¼ cup corn-oil margarine	Measuring cups and spoons
2 cups lightly roasted cashews	Paper towels
1 tablespoon curry powder	Skillet, heavy, medium-sized,
½ teaspoon salt	and stirring fork

1. Melt butter in skillet over low heat.
2. Add nuts and cook until brown, stirring occasionally to be sure all nuts are thoroughly coated.
3. Spread on paper towels to drain.
4. Sprinkle with curry powder and salt and leave on towels until thoroughly cool and dry.

Makes two cups. Stored in an airtight container, these will keep several weeks.

GREAT-AUNT MINNIE'S CANDIED GRAPEFRUIT PEEL

A sweet citrus tang and absolutely delicious.

2 grapefruit with unblemished skins	Cake racks
	Knife, small and sharp
Cold water	Saucepan, heavy, large, and
2 cups granulated sugar	stirring spoon
	Sifter
Granulated sugar for coating	Wax paper

1. Remove peel from grapefruit in quarters, then cut lengthwise into thin, uniform strips.
2. Place strips in saucepan and cover with cold water. Quickly bring to a boil, then pour off water.
3. Repeat the entire Step 2 seven times. This will remove the bitter oil of the rinds.
4. After last boiling, drain grapefruit strips well, leaving in saucepan, and add 2 cups sugar to the hot, damp peel.
5. Return to low heat and cook very slowly while the sugar forms a syrup.
6. Stirring occasionally, cook until the strips are transparent and most of the syrup is absorbed.
7. Remove the strips and arrange in one layer on cake racks with wax paper underneath to catch the drips.
8. Let dry for several hours or until strips are only slightly sticky.
9. Sift granulated sugar onto a clean piece of wax paper, then roll each strip in sugar until completely coated.
10. Let dry in one layer for several hours, then store in airtight container between sheets of wax paper.

Makes sixty to eighty strips. Will keep indefinitely in an airtight container.

NO-COOK DIVINITY DROPS

A very sweet, nutty candy with a crusty exterior, softer interior, and smooth texture.

2¾ cups confectioners sugar	Cake racks
1 egg white	Cookie dropper or teaspoon
1 tablespoon cold water	Electric mixer and small bowl
¾ teaspoon of your favorite	Fork
flavoring (apricot extract is	Measuring cups and spoons
good)	Wax paper
1 cup English walnut pieces	

1. Blend egg white, water, flavoring, and one-half of sugar at low speed until thoroughly blended, then gradually add remaining sugar, beating continuously.

2. Turn mixer to highest speed and beat until mixture is fluffy and beginning to thicken.
3. Quickly stir nuts into mixture and drop by spoonfuls onto wax paper. When light crust begins to form, transfer candy drops to cake racks and let dry completely before transferring to airtight container. (The time required will vary with humidity and temperature.)

Makes thirty 1½" drops. Don't make this on very humid days, as the mixture may not harden properly. Will keep four days in an airtight container, but is at its best one day after making.

ORANGE CREAMS

A strong orange flavor combines well with the crunchiness of the walnuts.

½ cup evaporated milk	Aluminum foil and dropping
½ cup granulated sugar	spoon
2 tablespoons boiling orange	Butter melter for heating juice
juice	Candy thermometer
1 cup granulated sugar	Double boiler
⅛ teaspoon salt	Electric mixer
4 tablespoons grated orange	Grater, fine-toothed
rind	Measuring cups and spoons
½ cup chopped English	Nut chopper
walnuts	Saucepan, medium, heavy, and
	stirring spoon

1. Heat milk in top of double boiler.
2. In saucepan melt ½ cup sugar until a rich brown, then slowly stir in boiling orange juice and hot milk.
3. Add 1 cup sugar and salt, stirring until dissolved.
4. Bring to a boil, cover saucepan, and cook for 3 minutes.
5. Remove cover and cook over low heat until mixture reaches temperature of 238° F. (hard ball stage).
6. Stir in orange rind and let mixture cool to 110° F.
7. Beat until creamy, then stir in walnuts.
8. Drop by teaspoonfuls onto foil sheet.

Makes about one pound. Will hold two weeks in an airtight container.

PEANUT BUTTER BITS

A fun-to-eat, protein-rich confection.

½ cup crunchy peanut butter	Fork and medium bowl
2 tablespoons honey	Measuring cups and spoons
2½ to 4 tablespoons nonfat dry milk	Wax paper
½ cup raisins	

1. Blend peanut butter and honey, then add enough powdered milk to make a stiff but easy-to-handle mixture. (Quantity will depend on oiliness of peanut butter.)
2. Using your hands, knead the raisins into the mixture, distributing them throughout.
3. Form into 8″–10″ long log, wrap in wax paper, and chill.
4. To serve, slice or tear into bits.

Makes one 8″–10″ log. Will hold two weeks in an airtight container in the refrigerator.

PEPPERMINT DROPS

A minty candy that pleases almost everyone.

½ cup water	Candy thermometer
1 cup granulated sugar	Measuring cups and spoons
6 tablespoons light corn syrup	Platter, buttered
1½ tablespoons sweet butter	Saucepan, large, heavy, with
⅛ teaspoon oil of peppermint	cover
(Green food coloring)	Stirring spoon

1. Boil water in saucepan.
2. Remove from heat and add sugar, syrup, and butter, stirring until dissolved.
3. Return to heat and bring to boil, then cover and cook 3 minutes.
4. Remove cover and cook over high heat until mixture reaches temperature of 310° F.
5. Reduce heat to low and stir in flavoring and—if desired for effect—food coloring.

6. Drop by half-teaspoonfuls onto buttered surface and allow to harden.

Makes about three-quarters of a pound. Will hold indefinitely in an airtight container.

POPPY SEED TOFFEE

An unusual looking candy that is especially appealing to nut lovers.

½ cup dark molasses	Candy thermometer
¾ cup poppy seeds	Knife, small, sharp
4 tablespoons blanched, slivered almonds	Measuring cups and spoons
	Platter, buttered
¾ teaspoon corn oil margarine	Saucepan, small, heavy, and wooden stirring spoon

1. Put molasses into saucepan and bring almost to a boil.
2. Add other ingredients, stirring continuously.
3. Cook until temperature of 285° F. is reached, then pour candy onto platter. If thicker than 1", flatten it out.
4. Cut or break into bite-sized pieces.

Makes approximately twenty-five pieces. Will keep two weeks between layers of wax paper in an airtight container.

SESAME BALLS

A tasty, crunchy confection.

⅓ cup dark brown sugar	Cookie dropper or spoon
¼ cup corn oil margarine	Measuring cups and spoons
1 tablespoon milk	Saucepan, heavy, medium, and stirring spoon
¼ cup raisins	Wax paper
⅔ cup rolled oats	
½ cup sesame seed	
½ cup slivered, blanched almonds	

1. Over medium heat melt sugar, margarine, and milk together. Boil 1 minute.
2. Add the other ingredients in order given, stirring constantly.
3. Drop by spoonful onto wax paper and allow to harden before storing in airtight container. Hardening time depends on humidity.

Makes about twenty-eight 1½" pieces. Will keep five days in an airtight container.

SUGARED ALMONDS

If you don't like your nuts straight, this is one of the best-tasting ways to dress them up.

1½ cups blanched, whole almonds

¼ cup corn oil

2 cups confectioners sugar

2 teaspoons rum extract

⅛ teaspoon ground cinnamon

⅛ teaspoon ground ginger

1/16 teaspoon ground nutmeg

Baking sheet, ungreased

Measuring cups and spoons

Spoon and bowl

1. Preheat oven to 350° F.
2. Place almonds one layer deep on a baking sheet, and bake in oven for 10 minutes.
3. Combine remaining ingredients.
4. Mix almonds with sugar mixture, coating each nut thoroughly.
5. Spread nuts on baking sheet, one layer deep, and allow to cool.

Makes 1½ cups. If not to be served immediately, store these in an airtight container, where they will keep indefinitely.

· 12 ·

Cookies

Apricot Snaps

The richness of the topping sets off and enhances the crisp cookie.

½ cup lightly salted butter,
   softened
½ cup granulated sugar
¼ teaspoon baking soda,
   dissolved in 2 teaspoons
   warm water
¾ teaspoon apricot flavoring
1 cup sifted all-purpose flour
Apricot Brandy Topping
(recipe follows)

Baking sheet, greased
Cake racks, metal spatula
Cookie or canape cutter,
   1″ square
Electric mixer and small bowl
Measuring cups and spoons
Rolling pin
Sifter and small bowl
Wax paper, 2 sheets, flour-
   dusted

1. Preheat oven to 375° F.
2. Cream butter and sugar until fluffy.
3. Add soda water and apricot flavoring then, gradually, the flour, beating continuously at low speed. Dough will be very stiff.
4. Put dough between floured sides of wax paper and roll to ⅛″ thickness.

257

5. Cut into 1″ squares, place 1½″ apart on baking sheet, and bake until pale gold, 6–8 minutes.
6. Remove from oven, let rest on baking sheet for 1 or 2 minutes, then remove at once to cake racks.
7. When completely cool, frost with Apricot Brandy Topping.

Apricot Brandy Topping

¾ cup semi-sweet bits
1 teaspoon apricot flavoring
½ teaspoon brandy

Double boiler, small, and
   stirring spoon
Measuring cups and spoons
Spreader

1. Melt semi-sweet bits in top part of double boiler over boiling water.
2. Stir in apricot flavoring and brandy.
3. Spread atop each 1″ square apricot snap.

Makes fifty to sixty bite-sized snaps. Will keep one week between layers of wax paper in an airtight container.

BRANDY BITES

These are pretty cookies with an interesting granular texture that's unexpected with this flavor.

½ cup all-purpose flour
½ teaspoon double-acting
   baking powder
¼ cup lightly salted butter,
   softened
⅛ cup granulated sugar
1½ teaspoons brandy
1½ teaspoons strong coffee
½ teaspoon heavy cream
1 cup quick oats
Brandy Butter Topping
(recipe follows)

Baking sheet, greased
Cake racks, metal spatula
Cookie cutter, 1″ round
Electric mixer and medium
   bowl
Measuring cups and spoons
Pastry fork
Rolling pin
Sifter and small bowl
Wax paper, two sheets, flour-
   dusted

1. Preheat oven to 350° F.
2. Sift flour with baking powder; set aside.
3. Cream butter and sugar until fluffy.
4. Add brandy, coffee, and cream, beating continuously.
5. Using fork, add flour mixture and oats to butter mixture.
6. Roll dough between floured sides of wax paper to ⅛″ thickness.
7. Cut into rounds and place 1″ apart on baking sheet.
8. Bake until firmly set, 10–12 minutes.
9. Remove cookies to cake racks and cool completely.
10. When cool, frost with Brandy Butter Topping.

Brandy Butter Topping

1½ teaspoons brandy	Electric mixer and small bowl
1½ teaspoons strong coffee	Measuring cups and spoons
½ teaspoon heavy cream	Spoon
½ cup confectioners sugar, sifted	Spreader
(Boiling water)	

1. Mix brandy, coffee, and cream.
2. Add sugar and beat at highest speed until smooth and of spreading consistency. If too stiff, add a few drops of boiling water.
3. Spread topping over top of cookies.

Makes thirty 1″ rounds. Will keep in an airtight container one week.

CARRIE'S MOLASSES BARS

This is a very old recipe for a plump, gingery cookie that smells wonderful cooking.

½ cup granulated sugar	Baking sheet, greased
½ cup corn oil margarine	Cake racks, metal spatula
1 egg	Electric mixer and medium
½ cup dark molasses	bowl
½ teaspoon salt	Kettle
¼ cup boiling water with	Knife, small, sharp
2 teaspoons baking soda	Measuring cups and spoons
dissolved in it	Refrigerator bowl, covered
½ teaspoon ground cinnamon	Rolling pin
½ teaspoon ground ginger	Wax paper, two sheets, flour-
2⅛ cups all-purpose flour	dusted
White Ornamental Frosting	
(recipe follows)	

1. Cream sugar and margarine until fluffy.
2. Add egg and beat thoroughly, then blend in molasses, salt, and water, beating continuously.
3. Gradually add flour at low speed and beat until completely blended. Dough will be stiff.
4. Store dough overnight in covered bowl in refrigerator.
5. Before removing dough from refrigerator, preheat oven to 350° F.
6. Roll dough to ¼" thickness, and cut into 3" x 1" bars.
7. Arrange 2" apart on baking sheet and bake until brown and firm to the touch, about 15 minutes.
8. Remove from baking sheet to racks and allow to cool completely.
9. When cool, top with White Ornamental Frosting.

White Ornamental Frosting

2 egg whites	Egg separator
¼ teaspoon cream of tartar	Electric mixer and small bowl
¼ teaspoon vanilla extract	Measuring cups and spoons
3½ cups sifted confectioners	Sifter and bowl
sugar	Spreader

1. Beat egg whites, cream of tartar, and vanilla at highest speed until they foam.
2. Slowly add sugar, beating continuously at low speed.
3. When all sugar has been added, resume highest speed and beat until frosting is stiff.
4. Spread over tops of Molasses Bars.

Makes about thirty bars. Will keep approximately one week in an airtight container.

CHOCOLATE DABS

An interesting cake-like texture and very strongly chocolate in flavor.

½ cup cocoa	Baking sheet, greased
½ cup granulated sugar	Cake rack
3 egg whites	Cookie dropper or spoon
	Egg separator
	Electric mixer and small bowl
	Fork
	Measuring cups
	Sifter and small bowl
	Spatula, metal

1. Preheat oven to 325° F.
2. Sift together cocoa and sugar; set aside.
3. Beat egg whites until stiff but not dry.
4. Using a fork, lightly stir beaten whites into cocoa mix until just blended. Do not overstir.
5. Drop by teaspoonful onto baking sheet, 2″ apart.
6. Bake until set, about 10 minutes.

7. Remove at once from baking sheet and cool on cake rack.

Makes about fifteen cookies. Will keep up to ten days in an airtight container.

COCONUT SUGAR DROPS

A very delicate cookie that often appeals even to those who are not particularly fond of coconut. In fact, everyone seems to like this cookie.

⅓ cup lightly salted butter, softened

⅓ cup granulated sugar

1 large egg

½ teaspoon vanilla extract

1 cup sifted all-purpose flour, resifted

½ cup grated coconut

Vanilla Coconut Frosting (recipe follows)

Baking sheet, ungreased

Cake racks, metal spatula

Cookie dropper or teaspoon

Electric mixer and small bowl

Grater, medium-toothed, for coconut

Measuring cups and spoons

Pastry fork

Sifter and small bowl

1. Preheat oven to 375° F.
2. Cream butter and sugar until fluffy, then add egg and vanilla, beating continuously.
3. Gradually add flour, beating continuously at low speed and being careful to combine thoroughly.
4. Stir in coconut.
5. Drop by teaspoonfuls onto baking sheet, 1½″ apart.
6. Bake until very light brown, about 8 minutes.
7. Remove from baking sheet and place on cake racks to cool.
8. When cool, frost with Vanilla Coconut Frosting.

Vanilla Coconut Frosting

¾ cup sifted confectioners sugar

1 tablespoon heavy cream

1 teaspoon vanilla extract

½ cup grated coconut, lightly
   toasted

Electric mixer and small bowl

Grater, medium-toothed, for
   coconut

Measuring cups and spoons

Sifter and small bowl

Spreader

Toaster oven

1. Toast one layer of grated coconut under broiler until light brown.
2. Beat sugar, cream, and vanilla at highest speed until smooth.
3. Spread over cookies.
4. Sprinkle with coconut.

Makes about twenty-four 1½" cookies. Will keep in an airtight container for one week.

FLORENTINES

A traditional European cookie with a distinctively fruity flavor that is nicely complemented by the chocolate topping. An English tea favorite.

½ cup plus 1 tablespoon heavy
   cream

3 tablespoons granulated
   sugar

⅓ cup blanched, slivered
   almonds

¼ cup diced candied orange
   peel

¼ cup diced candied lemon
   peel

4 candied cherries, diced

¼ cup all-purpose flour

½ cup semi-sweet bits

(Hot water)

Baking sheet, coated with
   sweet butter

Butter melter

Cake rack and small metal
   spatula

Fork and medium bowl

Kettle

Knife, small, sharp

Measuring cups and spoons

Spreader

Teaspoon

1. Preheat oven to 350° F.
2. Combine cream and sugar, mixing well, then add almonds, fruit peel, cherries, and flour.
3. Drop by spoonfuls onto baking sheet 2″ apart (they spread in cooking), and bake until golden brown, about 10 minutes. They burn easily, so keep a careful watch.
4. Remove at once from baking sheet to cake rack and cool completely.
5. Melt semi-sweet bits and spread melted chocolate (diluted with a few drops of boiling water if too thick to spread) on flat bottom of cooled cookies. Store bottom-side-up in airtight container.

Makes about twenty-eight 2″–3″ cookies. Will keep one week in an airtight container.

GRANDMA'S OATMEAL COOKIES

A hearty cookie that's a toothsome variation on an old favorite.

½ cup raisins	Baking sheet, greased
¼ cup water	Cake racks
1¼ cups whole wheat flour	Electric mixer and small bowl
½ teaspoon baking soda	Measuring cups and spoons
¼ teaspoon salt	Saucepan, medium, with cover
¾ teaspoon ground cinnamon	Sifter and large bowl
¼ teaspoon ground nutmeg	Spatula, metal
¼ teaspoon ground cloves	
1½ cups rolled oats	
½ cup blanched, slivered almonds	
⅓ cup plus 1 tablespoon safflower oil	
1 egg, unbeaten	
¾ cup light-brown sugar, packed	

1. Put raisins and water into saucepan over medium heat. When it boils, turn off heat, cover saucepan, and let raisins stand.
2. Sift together flour, soda, salt, cinnamon, nutmeg, and cloves.

3. Drain liquid from raisins and mix it into flour mixture; set aside.
4. Add the oats and almonds to the drained raisins; set aside.
5. Beat oil, egg, and sugar at high speed until fluffy.
6. Add raisin mixture and oil mixture to flour mixture and combine thoroughly.
7. Refrigerate two hours or more.
8. Preheat oven to 375° F.
9. Remove dough from refrigerator and form into 1½″ diameter balls and place 2″ apart on baking sheet. Flatten balls.
10. Bake until set, about 10 minutes.
11. Remove from baking sheet to cake racks immediately and cool before serving.

Makes about thirty 2″ cookies. Will keep one week in an airtight container.

HURON CAKE DROPS

An English tea favorite.

½ cup corn oil margarine, softened	Baking sheets, greased
	Cake racks and metal spatula
¾ cup granulated sugar	Cookie dropper or spoon
1¼ cups sifted all-purpose flour	Electric mixer and medium
1 egg, beaten with 1	bowl
tablespoon yogurt	Measuring cups and spoons
Apricot jam	Spoon

1. Preheat oven to 375° F.
2. Cream margarine and sugar until fluffy, then add flour, beating continuously at low speed.
3. Add egg-yogurt mixture, continuing to beat until thoroughly combined.
4. Drop by spoonfuls 2″ apart on baking sheet and bake until palest brown, 5–7 minutes.
5. Remove at once from sheet to racks and allow to cool thoroughly before placing a dollop of jam in center of each cookie.

Makes about thirty 2″–3″ cookies. Although very susceptible to humidity, these will keep two to three days in an airtight container.

ISCHELER TORTELETTES

These very fragile cookies have a good flavor.

1 cup sifted all-purpose flour	Baking sheets, greased and
¼ teaspoon double-acting	floured
baking powder	Cake racks
½ cup lightly salted butter	Cookie cutter, 2″ round
½ cup blanched, ground	Grater, fine-toothed
almonds	Knife
⅓ cup plus 1 tablespoon	Measuring cups and spoons
granulated sugar	Nut grinder
2 tablespoons lemon juice	Plastic wrap
1 tablespoon grated lemon	Rolling pin
rind	Sifter and small bowl
⅓ cup apricot jam	Spatula, metal
Chocolate Topping	Wax paper, two sheets, floured
(recipe follows)	

1. Resift flour with baking powder; set aside.
2. Cut butter into small pieces.
3. Add butter, almonds, sugar, lemon juice, and lemon rind to flour, then knead lightly with fingertips until dough is smooth and elastic.
4. Wrap dough in plastic wrap and refrigerate at least 3 hours.
5. Preheat oven to 350° F.
6. Remove one quarter of the dough, roll between wax paper to ¼″ thickness, and cut into rounds.
7. Place rounds 2″ apart on baking sheet and bake until pale gold, 8–10 minutes.
8. Remove cookies from sheets at once, using spatula (these cookies are very fragile), and place on cake racks.
9. When completely cool, make cookie sandwiches by coating one half of the cookies on one side with jam and covering with the remaining cookies. Frost with Chocolate Topping.

Chocolate Topping

¾ tablespoon lightly salted
  butter
1 cup semi-sweet chocolate bits
1 tablespoon hot water, if
  needed
3 tablespoons ground almonds

Double boiler, small
Electric mixer and small bowl
Measuring cups and spoons
Nut grinder

1. Melt chocolate and butter over hot water in double boiler.
2. Put into bowl of mixer and beat until smooth. If too thick to spread, gradually add up to 1 tablespoon hot water.
3. Frost top of cookie sandwiches, then sprinkle ground almonds over the top of each sandwich.

Makes about sixteen cookie sandwiches. Will keep four days in an airtight container.

ORANGE-ALMOND ROUNDS

A favorite with almost everybody.

½ cup corn-oil margarine
¼ cup granulated sugar
1 large egg
2½ tablespoons orange juice
1½ cups all-purpose flour
¼ teaspoon salt
¼ teaspoon soda
½ tablespoon grated orange
  rind
¼ cup blanched, chopped
  almonds

Baking sheet, greased
Cake rack and knife
Electric mixer and small bowl
Fork
Grater, fine-toothed
Knife, small, sharp
Measuring cups and spoons
Nut chopper
Wax paper

1. Cream margarine and sugar until fluffy, then add egg and orange juice and blend well.
2. Add flour, salt, and soda, beating at slow speed until thoroughly combined.
3. Using fork, stir in orange rind and almonds, mixing well.

4. Form roll about 3" in diameter and wrap in wax paper.
5. Put into refrigerator and chill four hours or overnight.
6. Preheat oven to 400° F.
7. Remove dough from refrigerator and cut into rounds ⅛" thick.
8. Place on baking sheet 2" apart and bake until lightly browned, 8–10 minutes.
9. Remove from baking sheet at once and cool on rack.

Makes about thirty 1½" cookies. Will keep up to ten days in an airtight container.

ORANGE LACE CRISPS

A subtle citrus flavor with an unexpected crunch.

½ cup lightly salted butter, softened	Baking sheet, greased
	Cake racks
⅓ cup granulated sugar	Cookie dropper or teaspoon
1 large egg	Electric mixer and small bowl
2 teaspoons finely grated orange rind	Grater, fine-toothed, and small bowl
¼ teaspoon vanilla extract	Grater, medium-toothed, for
¼ cup sifted all-purpose flour, resifted	coconut
	Measuring cups and spoons
½ cup rolled oats	Sifter and small bowl
⅓ cup grated coconut	Spatula, small, metal
Cold water	

1. Preheat oven to 350° F.
2. Cream butter at high speed, slowly adding sugar, beating continuously, then add egg, orange rind, and vanilla, continuing to beat.
3. Blend in flour at low speed, then add oats and coconut.
4. Drop small amount of dough (approximately ½ teaspoonful) 2" apart on baking sheet. Dip spatula in cold water and gently level each ball.
5. Cookies will spread somewhat while baking, thinning out at edges, creating the lace effect. Bake until edges are palest brown, about 6 minutes.

6. Remove from heat at once, using spatula to lift cookies from baking sheet to cake racks for cooling.

Makes about fifty 1½" crisp cookies. Best if served right away.

PAT'S SPICE COOKIES

Unbelievably crisp and gingery. These are good served with Mascarpone, a cream cheese spread (recipe following).

¼ cup brown sugar	Baking sheets, greased
½ cup dark molasses	Bowl, medium, and spoon
3 tablespoons lightly salted	Butter melter
butter	Cake racks and metal spatula
½ tablespoon ground	Cookie cutters
cinnamon	Measuring cups and spoons
½ teaspoon ground cloves	Plastic wrap
½ teaspoon ground ginger	Rolling pin
¼ teaspoon ground mace	Sifter
1 teaspoon baking soda	Wax paper, four sheets,
2 cups all-purpose flour	flour-dusted

1. Add sugar to molasses and mix well.
2. Melt butter, cool slightly, and stir into molasses.
3. Sift into this mixture the spices, soda, and ¼ cup of the flour. Stir well.
4. Add remaining flour and knead until thoroughly blended. (This will be a very stiff dough—you might hold back ¼ cup of the flour until it begins to stick together.)
5. Form into a log, wrap in plastic, and let ripen in refrigerator for at least two days. The dough will keep for several weeks, so cookies may be baked as needed once dough is ripened.
6. When ready to bake, preheat oven to 375° F.
7. Pinch off small piece of dough, roll out no more than $\frac{1}{16}$" thick (the thinner the better) on a well-floured surface. Cut with cookie cutters, place ½" apart on baking sheet, and bake until done, 6 to 8 minutes. Tops must not be allowed to brown perceptibly, or they will taste burnt.

8. Cool on cake racks and store in airtight container.

Makes about three dozen 1½" cookies. Will keep ten days in an airtight container.

MASCARPONE

May be topped with slivered, toasted almonds for garnish.

3 oz. cream cheese, room temperature	Spoon and small bowl
	Grater, fine-toothed
1 tablespoon confectioners sugar	Measuring cups and spoons
	Plastic wrap
1 teaspoon grated lemon peel	
1½ teaspoon lemon juice	

1. Combine all ingredients and beat until thoroughly blended.
2. Form into a ball, wrap loosely in plastic wrap, and refrigerate until ready to serve.
3. Unwrap and serve with Spice Cookies.

Makes four ounces of spread. Will keep several days in an airtight container.

PECAN PATS

A delicious, crunchy bite. Vanilla Sugar may be bought commercially, but if home-made is preferred, the recipe follows.

½ cup corn-oil margarine, softened	Baking sheet, ungreased
	Electric mixer and small bowl
¼ cup granulated sugar	Measuring cups and spoons
½ teaspoon water	Sifter and small bowl
1 teaspoon vanilla extract	
1¼ cups sifted all-purpose flour	
20–30 pecan halves	
Vanilla Sugar	
(recipe follows)	

1. Preheat oven to 350° F.
2. Cream margarine, sugar, water, and vanilla until fluffy.
3. Blend in flour and mix well.
4. Take ½ teaspoon dough and pat it round and flat.
5. Position a nut in center and fold dough over nut from all sides. Repeat until dough runs out.
6. Place 1″ apart on baking sheet and bake until light gold, about 15 minutes.
7. Remove from oven and roll immediately in Vanilla Sugar.

Makes twenty to thirty pats. Will keep ten days in an airtight container.

Vanilla Sugar

Although not cheap to prepare, it is more economical than buying commercial Vanilla Sugar.

1 pound confectioners sugar	Container, airtight
3 vanilla beans	Knife, small, sharp
	Sifter and medium bowl

1. Sift sugar.
2. Chop beans into ½″ pieces and add to sugar, distributing pieces throughout.
3. Leave undisturbed in container for at least three days, after which sugar is ready to use.

Makes one pound. Will keep indefinitely and improve with age.

PEPPER PRETTIES

An elusive flavor that will tantalize guests.

3 cups sifted all-purpose flour
1 teaspoon salt
1 teaspoon ground cinnamon
1 teaspoon ground cloves
⅛ teaspoon white pepper
½ teaspoon ground ginger
½ teaspoon ground cardamom
¾ cup corn-oil margarine, softened
½ cup granulated sugar
½ cup dark corn syrup
1 tablespoon brandy
½ cup blanched, ground almonds
½ tablespoon finely grated lemon rind
Vanilla Frosting
(recipe follows)

Baking sheet, ungreased
Cake racks
Cookie cutters
Electric mixer and medium bowl
Grater, fine-toothed
Measuring cups and spoons
Nut grinder
Rolling pin
Sifter and two medium bowls
Wax paper, two sheets, flour-dusted

1. Sift flour, salt, cinnamon, cloves, pepper, ginger, and cardamom, then resift and set aside.
2. Cream margarine and sugar until fluffy; add syrup and brandy, beating continuously at low speed.
3. Add flour mixture, almonds, and lemon rind to creamed mixture, in small increments, beating slowly and constantly, until thoroughly combined. Dough will be stiff.
4. Place dough in airtight container and chill overnight.
5. Just before removing from refrigerator, preheat oven to 350° F.
6. Roll a small portion of dough between floured sides of wax paper to ⅛″ thickness or less.
7. Using sharp cookie cutters, cut into desired shapes.
8. Arrange 1″ apart on baking sheet and bake until lightly browned, about 8 minutes.
9. Remove from baking sheet and set onto racks to cool thoroughly then frost with thin topping of Vanilla Frosting.

Vanilla Frosting

¾ cup sifted confectioners sugar	Electric mixer and small bowl
	Measuring cups and spoons
1 tablespoon cream	Sifter and small bowl
¾ teaspoon vanilla extract	Spreader

1. Combine ingredients and beat at medium-high speed until smooth.
2. Spread thinly on pepper cookies.

Makes about forty 2" cookies. The cookies may also be frozen, then thawed and frosted just before serving. Unfrozen will keep several weeks in an airtight container.

RUTH'S CRUNCHY CHOCOLATE MOUNDS

A delicious, chunky cookie that is very fast and easy once mastered.

¼ cup granulated sugar	Cookie dropper or teaspoon
1 tablespoon cocoa	Measuring cups and spoons
⅛ cup milk	Nut chopper
2 tablespoons corn-oil margarine	Saucepan, heavy, medium, and stirring spoon
⅛ cup peanut butter, crunchy	Wax paper
⅔ cup rolled oats	
½ cup chopped pecans	
½ teaspoon vanilla extract	

1. In saucepan over medium heat, mix together sugar, cocoa, milk, and margarine and bring to a complete boil, stirring all the time.
2. Boil for 1 minute.
3. Add remaining ingredients.
4. Drop by teaspoonfuls onto wax paper.
5. Let set, uncovered, until firm, anywhere from 15 to 60 minutes, depending on humidity.

Makes sixteen cookies. For best results, do not make on very humid days. Will keep approximately one week in an airtight container.

SAVORY CRISPS

These cookies are paper-thin, old-fashioned looking, and very good, but mild.

1 cup all-purpose flour	Baking sheet, greased
2 teaspoons coriander seed, ground	Cake racks and metal spatula
	Cookie dropper or teaspoon
4 eggs, separated	Egg separator and two small bowls
1 cup sifted confectioners sugar	Electric mixer and two medium bowls
1 tablespoon grated lemon rind	Grater, fine-toothed, and small bowl
1 tablespoon lemon juice	Measuring cups and spoons
	Mortar and pestle
	Pastry fork
	Sifter and small bowl

1. Preheat oven to 350° F.
2. Sift flour and combine with coriander seed; set aside.
3. Beat egg yolks until frothy; set aside.
4. Beat egg whites until frothy.
5. Combine egg yolks and whites, stirring constantly.
6. Sprinkle sugar over eggs, beating continuously.
7. Beat sugar and egg mixture at medium speed for 5 minutes.
8. Using pastry fork, gently stir lemon rind and juice and flour mixture into eggs.
9. Drop mixture onto baking sheet by teaspoonful 2″ apart and bake until edges are just beginning to color, 5–6 minutes.
10. Using sharp-edged spatula, immediately remove from baking sheet to cake racks to cool.

Makes thirty-six 2″ cookies. Will keep three days in an airtight container.

SHERRY DROPS

A sophisticated chocolate chip cookie.

1½ cups all-purpose flour	Baking sheet, ungreased
1 teaspoon double-acting baking powder	Cake racks and metal spatula
	Cookie dropper or teaspoon
¼ teaspoon ground nutmeg	Electric mixer and medium
¼ teaspoon salt	bowl
⅓ cup sweet butter, softened	Fork
½ cup granulated sugar	Measuring cups and spoons
1 medium egg	Sifter and small bowl
¼ cup cream sherry	
½ cup semi-sweet chocolate bits	

1. Preheat oven to 375° F.
2. Sift together flour, baking powder, nutmeg, and salt. Set aside.
3. Cream butter and sugar until fluffy and add egg, beating continuously.
4. Add flour mixture and sherry in alternate thirds, beating continuously at low speed. Stir in chocolate bits with the fork.
5. Drop by rounded spoonfuls 2″ apart on baking sheet and bake until set and lightly browned, 10–12 minutes.
6. Remove cookies at once to cake racks to cool.

Makes twenty-four 2″ cookies. Will keep ten days in an airtight container.

SUGAR COOKIES

A delicious, cake-like cookie made with a Victorian recipe.

1⅔ cups all-purpose flour	Baking sheet, greased
½ cup sweet butter, chilled and cut into bits	Cake racks and metal spatula
	Cookie cutter, 3″ round
2 teaspoons grated lemon rind	Fork and medium bowl
¼ cup granulated sugar	Grater, fine-toothed, and small bowl
1 medium egg, beaten with ¼ teaspoon lemon extract	Measuring cups and spoons
1 tablespoon granulated sugar	Rolling pin
	Wax paper, two sheets, flour-dusted
	Whisk and small bowl

1. Preheat oven to 350° F.
2. Put flour, butter, and lemon rind into medium bowl and combine with fingertips until meal-like in texture.
3. Add ¼ cup sugar, combining thoroughly.
4. Add egg and lemon extract mixture, mix thoroughly, and gather into ball. (If dough is too sticky, work in a little more flour. If crumbly, add a few drops of ice water.)
5. Roll to ¼″ thickness between sheets of floured wax paper, cut into rounds, and sprinkle with 1 tablespoon sugar.
6. Place 1″ apart on baking sheet, and bake until set and a pale brown around edges, 12–14 minutes.
7. Remove at once to cake racks to cool.

Makes twelve 3″ cookies. Will keep one week in an airtight container.

SWEDISH SPRITS

This is a good basic cookie. Using a cookie press is a quick way to achieve interesting shapes.

2 cups all-purpose flour	**Baking sheet, greased**
½ teaspoon double-acting baking powder	**Cake racks**
	Cookie press and discs
¾ cup lightly salted butter	**Electric mixer and small bowl**
½ cup granulated sugar	**Measuring cups and spoons**
1 large egg, well beaten	**Sifter and small bowl**
1 teaspoon vanilla extract	**Whisk and small bowl**
Cake decors or colored sugar	

1. Preheat oven to 400° F.
2. Sift together flour and baking powder; set aside.
3. Cream butter and sugar until fluffy, then add egg and vanilla, continuing to beat.
4. Add flour mixture, beating at low speed until of smooth consistency.
5. Put through cookie press onto baking sheet, 2″ apart, using various discs.
6. Decorate with cake decors or colored sugar.
7. Bake until lightly browned, 8 to 10 minutes.
8. Remove at once from baking sheet and cool on racks.

The yield depends on the size of disc used, but it is usually forty to fifty.
Will keep ten days in an airtight container.

VIENNESE CRESCENTS

Mouth-watering. You'll find the Vanilla Sugar recipe following that for Pecan Pats.

⅔ cup ground English walnuts | Baking sheet, greased
½ cup sweet butter, cut into bits | Bowl, small
 | Cake racks and metal spatula
⅓ cup granulated sugar | Knife
1¼ cups sifted all-purpose flour | Measuring cups and spoons
 | Nut grinder
¾ teaspoon vanilla extract | Sifter and small bowl
Vanilla Sugar |

1. Preheat oven to 350° F.
2. Combine all ingredients except Vanilla Sugar, and knead to a smooth consistency.
3. Take 1 teaspoon of dough at a time and shape into 1½"-long crescents.
4. Arrange 1" apart on baking sheet and bake until very lightly browned, about 15 minutes.
5. Remove from oven, cool 1 minute, then roll in Vanilla Sugar.
6. Allow to cool completely on the cake racks, then roll again in Vanilla Sugar.

Makes about thirty-five 1½" crescents. Will keep two weeks in an airtight container.

· 13 ·

Sandwiches

To Store Preassembled Sandwiches

Butter one side of both slices of the bread before filling, then spread the filling between the buttered sides. Arrange the sandwiches one-layer deep between sheets of paper, then enclose the whole in another sheet of wax paper and wrap in a dampened cloth and store in the refrigerator, not the freezer. To serve, remove from wrappings and take immediately to tea table.

Bread Crusts

It is traditional in England to remove the crusts from bread for tea sandwiches and to cut the sandwiches in small sections. This lends a more festive air to the tea and differentiates them from "regular" sandwiches served at other times of the day. Also, the crusts are more vulnerable both to the drying influence of air and, especially, to the moistening influence of humidity in refrigerated sandwiches. There is no need to waste the crusts—crumb them for toppings, casseroles, and other uses.

BASIL AND ONION SANDWICH

Good, but with a strong onion flavor that may not appeal to everyone.

4 tablespoons cream cheese, softened	Chopping board and small, sharp knife
1 tablespoon heavy cream	Fork and small bowl
1 tablespoon finely grated onion	Grater, fine-toothed, and small bowl
1 teaspoon chopped dried basil	Measuring spoons
8 slices thin white sandwich bread, with crusts removed	Spreader

1. Combine all ingredients, except bread, mixing thoroughly.
2. Spread mixture on one side of four bread slices, top with remaining slices, then cut each sandwich into equal halves.
3. Arrange on a plate and serve immediately, if possible. If not and pre-assembly is necessary, follow directions for storing assembled sandwiches in refrigerator (page 279).

Makes eight rectangular sandwiches.

BREAD AND BUTTER SANDWICH

The basic tea sandwich and the best, if really good butter and bread are used. These are a wonderful foil for richer tea treats and something almost everyone will eat.

½ cup butter, softened	Cutting board and small, sharp knife
8 slices thin bread (preferably whole wheat), with crusts removed	Measuring cup
	Spreader

1. Spread one side of four bread slices with butter, top with remaining slices, and cut each sandwich into equal triangles.
2. Arrange on a plate and serve at once, if possible. If not and pre-assembly is necessary, follow directions for storing assembled sandwiches in refrigerator (page 279).

Makes eight triangular sandwiches.

CARROT CREAM SANDWICH

This sandwich has a marvelous sweet-and-sour flavor which is tempered by the creaminess of the cheese.

2 teaspoons cornstarch	Chopping board and small,
1 tablespoon brown sugar	sharp knife
1 teaspoon vinegar	Fork and small bowl
1 tablespoon chili sauce	Grater, fine-toothed
1 teaspoon cognac	Measuring cups and spoons
½ cup cold water	Skillet and stirring fork
1 tablespoon corn oil	Toaster or toaster oven
3 tablespoons chopped dill pickle	
¼ teaspoon ground ginger	
1½ cups grated raw carrot	
4 tablespoons cream cheese, softened	
8 slices whole wheat bread, toasted and with crusts removed	

1. Mix together cornstarch, brown sugar, vinegar, chili sauce, and cognac. When well combined, add water to thin the paste and set aside.
2. Heat corn oil to bubble stage, add pickles and ginger and stir for one minute.
3. Add cornstarch paste mixture to pickle mixture in skillet and cook until combined mixture thickens, stirring continuously.
4. Add carrots and cook for one minute.
5. Remove from heat and, when cool, add carrots and enough of the sauce to the cream cheese to make a good spreading consistency, being careful to combine thoroughly.
6. Spread on one side of four bread slices, top with remaining slices, and cut into halves.
7. Arrange on plate and serve immediately.

Makes eight rectangular sandwiches.

CRAB AND OLIVE SANDWICH

The predominating taste of this sandwich is the olive, with crab as a tantalizing undertone.

4 tablespoons shredded crab meat	Chopping board and small, sharp knife
4 tablespoons cream cheese, softened	Fork and small bowl
2 tablespoons mayonnaise	Measuring spoon
6 tablespoons sliced, pimento-stuffed Spanish (green) olives	Spreader
	Toaster or toaster oven
8 slices thin white sandwich bread, toasted and with crusts removed	

1. Combine all ingredients, except bread.
2. Spread mixture on one side of four toast slices, top with remaining slices, and cut into halves.
3. Arrange on a plate and serve immediately.

Makes eight rectangular sandwiches.

CUCUMBER AND BUTTER SANDWICH

A traditional English tea sandwich.

Large cucumber, peeled and cut into paper-thin slices	Cutting board and small, sharp knife
6 tablespoons sweet butter, softened	Measuring spoons
8 slices thin white bread, with crusts removed	Spreader

1. Spread one side of each bread slice with softened butter.
2. On four of the slices arrange in overlapping rows a layer of sliced cucumber, then top with remaining bread slices, and cut each sandwich into equal triangles.
3. Arrange on plate and serve at once.

Makes eight triangular sandwiches.

CURRY-BUTTER SANDWICH

This has a distinctive flavor that people seem either to like or dislike, with not much middle ground.

4 tablespoons lightly salted butter, softened	Chopping board and small, sharp knife
¾ teaspoon curry powder	Fork and small bowl
8 slices thin white sandwich bread, with crusts removed	Measuring spoons
	Spreader

1. Combine butter and curry thoroughly.
2. Spread mixture on one side of four bread slices, top with remaining slices, and cut each sandwich into halves.
3. Arrange on a plate and serve immediately, if possible. If pre-assembly is necessary, follow directions for storing assembled sandwiches in refrigerator (page 279).

Makes eight rectangular sandwiches.

EGGY OLIVE SANDWICH

A satisfying light sandwich for egg lovers.

2 eggs	Chopping board and small, sharp knife
4 tablespoons sliced, pimento-stuffed, Spanish (green) olives	Fork and small bowl
4 tablespoons sour cream	Measuring spoons
8 slices pumpernickel bread, with crusts removed	Saucepan, small, enamel
	Spreader

1. Put eggs in saucepan and cover with water. Bring to a boil over medium-high heat, then reduce heat to medium and let boil for approximately 18 minutes.
2. Plunge eggs at once into cool water, remove, and discard shells.
3. Using fork, gently mash eggs, then add olives and sour cream.
4. Spread mixture on one side of four slices of bread, top with remaining slices, then cut into halves.
5. Arrange on plate and serve at once if possible. If not and pre-

assembly is necessary, follow directions for storing assembled sandwiches in refrigerator (page 279).

Makes eight rectangular sandwiches.

Jam and Butter Sandwich

Apart from plain bread and butter, this is the easiest tea sandwich and one of the most popular.

6 tablespoons sweet butter, softened	Cutting board and small sharp knife
6 tablespoons of your favorite jam	Measuring spoons Spreader
8 slices thin white sandwich bread, with crusts removed	

1. Spread one side of each bread slice with butter.
2. On four of the buttered slices spread jam, then top with remaining slices, buttered side down, and cut each sandwich into halves.
3. Arrange on plate and serve at once if possible. If pre-assembly is necessary, follow directions for storing assembled sandwiches in refrigerator (page 279).

Makes eight rectangular sandwiches.

Lemon Crab Sandwich

The lemon rind provides an unexpected flavor.

3 tablespoons shredded crab meat	Chopping board and small, sharp knife
4 tablespoons lemon juice	Fork and small bowl
1 tablespoon grated lemon rind	Grater, fine-toothed, and small bowl
2 tablespoons kosher-style dill pickles, diced	Measuring spoons
2 tablespoons mayonnaise	Spreader
8 slices rye bread, toasted, with crusts removed	Toaster or toaster oven

1. Marinate crab in lemon juice for at least two hours in covered container in refrigerator.
2. Add other ingredients, except bread, and mix well.
3. Spread mixture on one side of four toast slices, top with remaining slices, and cut each sandwich into halves.
4. Arrange on plate and serve immediately.

Makes eight rectangular sandwiches.

Mrs. Witherspoon's Raisin and Nut Sandwich

An unusual and very good sandwich filling.

1 cup raisins	Chopping board and small,
1 cup nuts (pecans or hazel-	sharp knife
nuts are best)	Food grinder and small bowl
(2 tablespoons mayonnaise)	Measuring cups and spoons
8 slices whole wheat bread,	Spreader
thinly sliced, with crusts	
removed	

1. Put raisins and nuts through grinder together. This will produce a thick mixture.
2. For easier spreading, you may add the mayonnaise unless you prefer the flavor of the pure fruit and nuts.
3. Spread mixture on one side of four slices of bread, top with the remaining four slices, cut each sandwich into four squares.
4. Arrange on plate and serve at once, if possible. If pre-assembly is necessary, follow directions for storing assembled sandwiches (page 279).

Makes sixteen small sandwich squares. The filling keeps well for days in the refrigerator before spreading.

MUSHROOM SANDWICHES

A zippy mushroom spread.

¼ cup bottled horseradish, drained	Bowl
½ cup sour cream	Knife, small, sharp
¼ teaspoon hot mustard	Measuring cups and spoons
½ teaspoon salt	Spreader
½ teaspoon white pepper	
1 cup diced fresh, mushrooms	
10 thin slices of good white sandwich bread, with crusts removed	

1. Combine all ingredients except mushrooms and bread, then add mushrooms and adjust seasoning.
2. Spread on one side of five bread slices, top with remaining slices, and cut sandwich into halves.
3. Arrange on plate and serve at once, if possible. If pre-assembly is necessary, follow directions for storing assembled sandwiches (page 279).

Makes ten rectangular sandwiches. The filling may be made ahead of time and refrigerated until use.

OLIVE AND CREAM CHEESE SANDWICH

One of the simplest and tastiest of tea sandwiches.

6 tablespoons sliced, pimento-stuffed, Spanish (green) olives	Chopping board and small, sharp knife
6 tablespoons cream cheese, softened	Fork and small bowl
1 tablespoon heavy cream	Measuring spoons
8 slices thin white sandwich bread, with crusts removed	Spreader

1. Combine all ingredients except bread.

2. Spread mixture on one side of four slices of bread, top with remaining slices, then cut each sandwich into two equal triangles.
3. Arrange on plate and serve at once, if possible. If pre-assembly is necessary, follow directions for storing assembled sandwiches in refrigerator (page 279).

Makes eight triangular sandwiches.

PARMESAN EGG SANDWICH

The freshly grated Parmesan gives the special flavor.

2 eggs	Chopping board and small,
¼ cup freshly grated Parmesan	sharp knife
cheese	Fork and small bowl
¼ teaspoon paprika	Grater for hard cheese and
1 tablespoon prepared horse-	small bowl
radish	Saucepan, small, enamel
2 tablespoons mayonnaise	Spreader
8 slices pumpernickel bread,	
with crusts removed	

1. Put eggs into saucepan and cover with water. Bring to a boil over medium-high heat, then reduce heat to medium and let boil for approximately 18 minutes.
2. Plunge eggs at once into cool water, then remove. Peel and discard the shells.
3. Using fork, gently mash eggs, and then add all the other ingredients, except bread.
4. Spread mixture on one side of four slices of bread, top with remaining slices, then cut into halves.
5. Arrange on plate and serve at once, if possible. If pre-assembly is necessary, follow directions for storing assembled sandwiches in refrigerator (page 279).

Makes eight rectangular sandwiches. If you prefer a creamier spread, you may adjust the amount of mayonnaise.

PECAN AND CREAM CHEESE SANDWICH

An easy, delicious sandwich.

5 tablespoons chopped pecans	Chopping board and small,
6 tablespoons cream cheese, softened	sharp knife
	Fork and small bowl
2 tablespoons diced Maraschino cherries	Spreader
2 tablespoons heavy cream	
8 slices thin white sandwich bread, with crusts removed	

1. Combine all ingredients except bread.
2. Spread on one side of four slices of bread, top with remaining slices, then cut each sandwich into two equal triangles.
3. Arrange on plate and serve at once.

Makes eight triangular sandwiches. If available, chocolate bread makes a good substitute for the white bread for a sweeter sandwich. (See index for Chocolate Muffins.)

PIMENTO PECAN SANDWICH

An old American favorite, slightly modified, that works well for tea.

4 tablespoons chopped pimento	Chopping board and small, sharp knife
6 tablespoons grated, extra-sharp Cheddar cheese	Grater, fine-toothed, and small bowl
2 tablespoons chopped pecans	Measuring spoons
4 tablespoons mayonnaise	Spreader
8 slices very thin white sandwich bread, with crusts removed	

1. Combine all ingredients except bread.
2. Spread on one side of four bread slices, top with remaining slices, and cut each sandwich into equal triangles.
3. Arrange on plate and serve immediately.

Makes eight triangular sandwiches.

PINEAPPLE CREAM SANDWICH

A mouth-watering combination for pineapple lovers, or for anyone who likes a sweet sandwich.

6 tablespoons cream cheese, softened

3 tablespoons undrained, crushed pineapple

9 3"-4" square slices of sweet bread or cake (either Chocolate Muffin Bread* or Chocolate Citron Cake* is especially good) or 9 slices white sandwich bread with crusts removed

Chopping board and sharp knife

Fork and small bowl

Measuring spoons

Spreader

1. Combine cheese and pineapple, mixing well.
2. Spread mixture on one side of six slices of sweet bread or cake.
3. Assemble sandwich by topping one cream-covered slice with another cream-covered slice, then topping the whole with a plain slice—that is, make a triple layer.
4. Cut each of the three, triple-layer sandwiches into quarters and serve at once.

Makes twelve 1½"-2" square sandwiches.

*See Index.

POTTED SHRIMP SANDWICH

An unusual spread with a mildly pungent flavor.

⅔ cup lightly salted butter
¼ teaspoon ground mace
¼ teaspoon ground nutmeg
⅛ teaspoon cayenne powder
½ teaspoon salt
1 cup canned tiny shrimp, drained
8 slices thin white sandwich bread, toasted, with crusts removed

Butter melter and spoon for skimming
Chopping board and small, sharp knife
Cup
Measuring cups and spoons
Refrigerator dish, 6" x 8"
Saucepan, medium, heavy, and stirring spoon
Spreader
Toaster or toaster oven

1. Over low heat, melt ⅛ cup of butter slowly. Skim surface foam and remove saucepan from heat to rest for 3 minutes.
2. Pour the top layer of clear butter into a cup, discarding milky solids that have settled to bottom of melter. Set aside the cup of clarified butter.
3. Melt remaining butter over medium heat in saucepan and remove from stove; then, when foam subsides, add remaining ingredients, except bread, in order given, being sure to coat shrimp well with butter mixture.
4. Put shrimp mixture into refrigerator dish in thin layer and seal by coating with the clarified butter from Step 2.
5. Cover and refrigerate at least 8 hours.
6. Spread mixture on one side of four toast slices, top with remaining slices, then cut each sandwich into equal triangles.
7. Arrange on plate and serve at once.

Makes eight triangular sandwiches (or more, if you spread the mixture thinly over extra bread).

SALMON WITH CAPERS SANDWICH

A tantalizing combination of flavors.

2 tablespoons mayonnaise

2 tablespoons sour cream

2 tablespoons capers, drained
and minced

2 tablespoons sweet onion,
grated

¼ teaspoon lemon juice

7 ounces canned salmon,
drained and flaked

14 slices thin white sandwich
bread, toasted, with crusts
removed

Fresh parsley

Chopping board and small,
sharp knife

Fork and small bowl

Grater, fine-toothed, and small
bowl

Measuring spoons

Toaster or toaster oven

1. Combine all ingredients except bread and parsley, and mix thoroughly.
2. Spread mixture on one side of seven bread slices, top with remaining slices, and cut each sandwich into equal triangles.
3. Arrange in a pinwheel pattern on a round platter, garnish with parsley and serve at once.

Makes fourteen triangular sandwiches. Be certain that the capers are fresh, or have been properly refrigerated, as they can mold very quickly once the jar has been opened.

Salmon Mayonnaise Pinwheels

An attractive, unusual sandwich that doesn't take nearly as long to prepare as it might seem at first glance.

BREAD:

1 cup sifted cake flour	Baking pan, 12″ x 12″ x 1″,
½ teaspoon double-acting	greased and floured, the
baking powder	bottom lined with greased
¼ teaspoon salt	and floured paper
3 eggs, separated	Egg separator
2 tablespoons dried,	Electric mixer, medium bowl,
chopped basil	and small bowl
½ cup milk	Herb chopper
	Knife, small
	Measuring cups and spoons
	Sifter and small bowl
	Spatula
	Tea towel

1. Preheat oven to 375° F.
2. Sift together flour, baking powder, and salt. Resift, then add basil and set aside.
3. Beat egg yolks until thick and lemon colored. In alternate thirds, beating continuously, add flour mixture and milk. Set aside.
4. Beat egg whites until stiff but not dry and fold into dough.
5. Spread evenly in baking pan and bake until set and light brown, 5–8 minutes.
6. Loosen edges with knife and lay face down on tea towel, carefully peeling paper from bottom. Make the filling while it cools.

FILLING:

1 egg yolk, room temperature	Egg separator
1 teaspoon white wine vinegar	Electric mixer and small bowl
½ teaspoon mustard	Fork
¼ teaspoon salt	Herb chopper
⅛ teaspoon white pepper	Knife, small, sharp
½ cup olive oil	Measuring cups and spoons
½ cup lemon juice	Spreader
¼ cup dried, chopped basil	
¾ teaspoon garlic salt	
6 ounces canned salmon, drained and flaked	
2 tablespoons diced onion	

1. Put egg yolk in warm, dry mixing bowl. Add ½ teaspoon of wine vinegar, the mustard, the salt, and the pepper.
2. Beat at high speed and very slowly add ¼ cup of the oil, beating continuously, then the remaining ½ teaspoon of the wine vinegar. The mixture will begin to thicken.
3. Still beating continuously, add the remaining ¼ cup of oil, then the lemon juice, basil, and garlic salt. The mixture will be thick.
4. Stir in salmon and onion, and taste. If desired, adjust seasoning by adding more salt, pepper, or lemon juice.
5. Spread mixture evenly over bottom of bread, then roll, jelly-roll fashion. Leave wrapped in tea towel for several minutes, seam side down, before cutting into ¾″ slices.

Makes twelve to fifteen pinwheel sandwiches. The bread and the filling may each be made in advance and assembled at the last minute.

THUNDER AND LIGHTNING SANDWICHES

A delicious sweet sandwich.

8 ¼"-thick slices of good white cake or pound cake	Cookie cutter, 3" round
2 tablespoons sweet butter, softened	Electric mixer and small bowl
¼ cup heavy cream, whipped very thick	Knife, small, sharp
¼ cup lemon, maple, or golden syrup	Measuring cups and spoons
	Spreader

1. Spread one side of each cake slice with softened butter.
2. On four of the slices, spread syrup over butter, cover with a layer of cream, then top with remaining cake slices, buttered side down.
3. Serve at once.

Makes four 3" round sandwiches. They do not keep well and should be eaten soon after they are made.

TOMATO BUTTER SANDWICHES

These are especially good when fresh tomatoes are plentiful.

½ cup lightly salted butter, softened	Knife, small, sharp
2 tablespoons diced, peeled tomatoes	Measuring cups and spoons
2 tablespoons chili-sauce	Spreader
Salt to taste	
8 thin slices good, white sandwich bread, with crusts removed	

1. Combine butter, tomatoes, and chili sauce, and add salt to taste.
2. Spread on one side of four bread slices, top with remaining slices, and cut each sandwich into two equal triangles.

Makes eight triangular sandwiches. The filling may be made ahead of time.

TOMATO CHEDDAR SANDWICH

A traditional tea sandwich.

1 cup grated, extra-sharp Cheddar cheese	Chopping board and small, sharp knife
½ cup diced fresh tomato	Fork and small bowl
Enough mayonnaise to moisten mixture thoroughly (amount will depend on moisture content of tomato)	Grater, fine-toothed, and small bowl
	Measuring cups
	Spreader
8 thin slices white sandwich bread, with crusts removed	

1. Combine all ingredients, except bread, until thoroughly mixed.
2. Spread mixture on one side of four slices of bread, top with remaining slices, and cut each sandwich into two equal triangles.
3. Arrange on plate and serve at once.

Makes eight triangular sandwiches.

TUNA ALMOND SANDWICH

The nuts add an unexpected crunchiness.

7 ounces solid white tuna (spring water pack), drained and broken into small pieces	Chopping board and small, sharp knife
3 tablespoons diced onion	Fork and small bowl
5 tablespoons diced kosher pickles	Measuring spoons
5 tablespoons mayonnaise	Spreader
4 tablespoons slivered almonds, toasted	Toaster oven and shallow pan
½ teaspoon salt	
8 thin slices white sandwich bread, toasted, with crusts removed	

1. Combine all ingredients except bread.
2. Spread mixture on one side of four slices of toast, top with remaining slices, and cut each sandwich into halves.
3. Arrange on plate and serve immediately, preferably on a warm plate.

Makes eight rectangular sandwiches.

WATERCRESS AND BUTTER SANDWICH

Another of the traditional English tea sandwiches. Worth the trouble of looking for good, fresh watercress.

6 tablespoons chopped watercress	Cutting board and small, sharp knife
6 tablespoons butter, softened	Fork and small bowl
8 slices thin white bread, with crusts removed	Measuring spoon Spreader

1. Combine watercress and butter and mix thoroughly.
2. Spread one side of four bread slices with mixture, top with remaining slices, and cut each sandwich into equal triangles.
3. Arrange on plate and serve at once if possible. If not and preassembly is necessary, follow directions for storing assembled sandwiches in refrigerator (page 279).

Makes eight triangular sandwiches.

· 14 ·

Tarts, Tartlets, and Pastries

APPLE DUMPLING TURNOVERS

Especially good fresh from the oven on cold days, but may also be served cold.

PASTRY:

7 tablespoons lightly salted butter, chilled, and cut into small pieces

1½ cups all-purpose flour

1 tablespoon granulated sugar

4 tablespoons ice water

Fork and medium bowl

Measuring cups and spoons

Wax paper, one sheet, flour-dusted

1. Put butter, flour, and sugar into bowl and work lightly with fingertips until just mealy.
2. Add ice water, stir, and gather dough into a ball. If too crumbly, add a few more drops of water. If too wet, add a spoonful or two of flour.
3. Wrap dough ball in a sheet of wax paper and refrigerate one to two hours.

FILLING:

¼ cup lemon juice	Fork and medium bowl
1 teaspoon grated lemon peel	Grater, fine-toothed, and small
3 tablespoons dark-brown	bowl
sugar	Knife, small, sharp
¼ teaspoon ground cinnamon	Measuring cups and spoons
1 cup peeled and diced apples	

1. Combine all ingredients except apples and mix completely.
2. Marinate apples in mixture at least 30 minutes.

TOPPING:

1 teaspoon water	Bowl, small
2 tablespoons granulated sugar	Measuring spoons
	Pastry brush

ASSEMBLY:

Baking sheet, greased
Cookie cutter, 3″ round
Fork
Rolling pin
Wax paper, two sheets,
   flour-dusted

1. Preheat oven to 350° F.
2. Roll dough between floured wax paper to ¼″ thickness.
3. Cut into circles with cutter. Place six of the circles 2″ apart on baking sheet. Put generous spoonful of undrained apples in middle of each round, top with remaining six rounds of pastry. Crimp edges together with fork and pierce tops of turnovers with fork tines.
4. Bake for 15 minutes. Remove from oven, brush tops with water, sprinkle with granulated sugar, put baking sheet back in oven, and bake another 10 minutes, or until dough is lightly browned.

Makes six 2¾″ turnovers. Will keep two days in an airtight container.

GRAPEFRUIT TARTLETS

A delicious citrus tart.

PASTRY:

1 cup all-purpose flour	Fork
⅟₁₆ teaspoon salt	Grater and small bowl
¼ cup granulated sugar	Measuring cups and spoons
2 tablespoons corn-oil	Muffin tins, 1″ cup, greased
margarine, chilled and cut	Sifter and small bowl
into bits	
1 teaspoon grated lemon rind	
1 egg, beaten	

1. Preheat oven to 350° F.
2. Sift together flour, salt, and sugar.
3. Using your fingertips, work in margarine until mixture is mealy.
4. Add lemon rind and egg, stirring until thoroughly incorporated. Dough should be stiff. If too sticky, add another teaspoon or two of sifted all-purpose flour; if too crumbly, a few drops of water.
5. Line each muffin cup—bottom and sides—with thin layer of dough and fill two-thirds full with grapefruit mixture, as below.

FILLING:

1 cup chopped grapefruit pulp	Knife, small, sharp, and
(with juice but without seeds	chopping board
and membrane)	Measuring cups and spoons
¼ cup granulated sugar	Spoon and small bowl
¼ cup chopped English walnuts	
(½ cup whipped cream)	

1. Combine grapefruit, sugar, and nuts and mix well.
2. Put 1 tablespoon into each dough-lined muffin cup and bake until pastry is done, about 15 minutes.
3. Serve either hot or cold. If served cold, a dollop of whipped cream atop each tartlet is a nice touch.

Makes about fifteen 1″ tartlets. Should be served as soon after baking as possible, but pastry and filling may be prepared separately ahead of time, then combined and baked on the day of serving.

LEMON CURD TARTS

These tarts have a lovely piquant flavor.

PASTRY:

7 tablespoons lightly salted butter, chilled and cut into small pieces	Fork and medium bowl
	Measuring cups and spoons
	Wax paper, one sheet, flour-dusted
1½ cups all-purpose flour	
1 tablespoon granulated sugar	
4 tablespoons ice water	

1. Put butter, flour, and sugar into bowl and work lightly with finger-tips until just mealy.
2. Add ice water, stir, and gather dough into a ball. If too crumbly, add a few more drops of water. If too wet, add a spoonful or two of flour.
3. Wrap dough ball in a sheet of wax paper and refrigerate one to two hours.

FILLING:

4 lemons, peeled and juiced	Juicer
2½ cups water	Knife, small, sharp
2½ cups granulated sugar	Measuring cups and spoons
2 tablespoons cornstarch	Saucepan, medium, heavy, stirring spoon

1. Put the thin peel of four lemons, water, and sugar in saucepan over medium heat and stir continuously until sugar is dissolved. Allow to simmer until quantity is reduced by about a fourth. Remove lemon rinds and discard.
2. Dissolve cornstarch in lemon juice and stir into the saucepan.
3. Bring to a boil and cook until thick, stirring occasionally.

ASSEMBLY:

Cookie cutter, 3″ round
Rolling pin
Spoon
Tart tins, 1½″, greased
Wax paper, two sheets, flour-dusted

1. Preheat oven to 375° F.
2. Roll dough between floured wax paper to ¼" thickness. Cut into 3" circles. (Will make 12 rounds.)
3. Press rounds into tart tins, then fill each tin two-thirds full of the lemon curd. Bake until tart edges are lightly browned, about 15 minutes.

Makes twelve 1½" tarts. To enjoy them at their best in taste and texture, serve as soon as cool.

LINZER TART

Easy but time-consuming, this very fruity tart is especially appealing to apricot lovers.

FILLING:

6 ounces dried apricots, chopped	Chopping board and small, sharp knife
¼ cup orange juice	Grater, fine-toothed, and small bowl
2 teaspoons grated orange rind	
⅛ cup light molasses	Measuring cups and spoons
½ cup water	Saucepan, heavy, medium, and stirring spoon
½ cup granulated sugar	
¼ cup finely chopped English walnuts	

1. Combine apricots, orange juice, orange rind, molasses, water, and sugar in saucepan over medium-high heat. Bring to a boil, stirring constantly.
2. Reduce heat to medium-low and continue to boil until mixture thickens and looks like jam.
3. Let cool and fold in nuts.

CRUST:

1 cup all-purpose flour	Cake pan, 8" x 8" x 2",
½ teaspoon double-acting	ungreased
baking powder	Fork and medium bowl
¼ teaspoon salt	Grater, fine-toothed, and small
⅓ cup granulated sugar	bowl
⅓ cup corn-oil margarine, cut	Knife, small, sharp
into small pieces	Measuring cups and spoons
2 teaspoons grated lemon rind	Rolling pin
1 egg, lightly beaten	Wax paper, two sheets 14"
	long, flour-dusted
	Whisk and small bowl

1. Preheat oven to 350° F.
2. Mix together flour, baking powder, salt, and sugar.
3. Add margarine and knead with fingertips until particles look like fine cornmeal.
4. Add lemon rind and egg and combine thoroughly.

ASSEMBLY:

1. Put three-quarters of dough in pan.
2. Using your fingers, press dough against bottom and up 1" of sides of pan, covering evenly.
3. Spread filling over dough.
4. Put remaining dough between floured sides of wax paper and roll into 8" x 4" rectangle, ⅛" thick.
5. Cut into ½"-wide strips.
6. Lay strips in lattice fashion on top of filling.
7. Bake until golden brown, about 30 minutes.
8. Cool and cut into small squares.

Makes sixteen 2" squares. Will keep approximately four days in an airtight container.

MERINGUES

A nice crispy shell that can be made ahead, then filled at the last minute.

½ cup confectioners sugar,
sifted
2 egg whites

Baking sheet, covered with
baking parchment
Cake rack, metal spatula
Electric mixer and small bowl
Measuring cups and spoons
Sifter and small bowl
Spatula for folding
Tablespoon

1. Preheat oven to 350° F.
2. Beat egg whites until stiff but not dry.
3. Carefully fold in sugar and at once drop by spoonfuls 2″ apart on baking sheet.
4. Bake until pale brown, 4 or 5 minutes. Remove from heat. Carefully lift meringues from paper, turn over, and scoop out soft insides.
5. Put clean parchment on baking sheet, and lay meringues, bottom side up, on sheet, return to oven and allow to remain until just browned, 2-3 minutes.
6. Remove from oven, cool on rack, and store in airtight container.
7. Just before serving, fill with jam, custard, sweetened whipped cream, or applesauce mixed with nuts.

Makes about fourteen 2″ confections.

Mocha Tartlets

An unusual tartlet because of the coffee flavor. Good.

PASTRY:

1¼ cups all-purpose flour	Cookie cutter, 3″ round
1½ tablespoons ground almonds	Measuring cups and spoons
	Muffin tins, 1″ cup, greased
⅓ teaspoon salt	Nut grinder
¼ cup granulated sugar	Sifter and medium bowl
6 tablespoons corn-oil margarine, chilled and cut into bits	Wax paper, two sheets, flour-dusted
1 egg, beaten	Whisk and small bowl
Water	

1. Preheat oven to 350° F.
2. Sift together flour, ground nuts, salt, and sugar.
3. Using your fingertips work in margarine until mixture is mealy.
4. Stir in egg, then add just enough water to make a stiff paste.
5. Let rest in a cool place for two hours, then roll between sheets of wax paper to ¼″ thickness and cut into 3″ rounds.
6. Line each muffin cup with a round of dough pressed firmly on bottom and sides, trimming any excess, and bake until lightly browned, 10–12 minutes. Cool and fill.

FILLING:

1 teaspoon cornstarch	Double boiler and stirring spoon
1 tablespoon cold coffee	
1 square (1 ounce) baking chocolate	Electric mixer and small bowl
	Fork and small bowl
⅓ cup cream	Grater and small bowl
⅔ cup strong coffee	Measuring cups and spoons
1 egg yolk	
1 egg	
⅛ teaspoon salt	
¾ cup plus 2 tablespoons granulated sugar	
(½ cup whipped cream)	
(2 tablespoons grated chocolate)	

1. Make a smooth paste of cornstarch and 1 tablespoon coffee; set aside.
2. In top half of double boiler, over hot water, combine chocolate, cream and ⅔ cup coffee, stirring until melted.
3. Stir in the cornstarch paste and continue stirring and cooking for 8 minutes, then cover and cook an additional 10 minutes.
4. Meanwhile, beat eggs and salt, then gradually add sugar, beating continuously at low speed.
5. Add 3 tablespoons of the hot cornstarch/chocolate mixture to the egg mixture, then stir back into remaining cornstarch/chocolate mixture in double boiler.
6. Cook an additional 2 to 3 minutes, stirring gently the while.
7. Remove from heat and continue stirring lightly until cool.
8. Fill each cooled tartlet shell three-quarters full and—if desired—top with dollop of whipped cream and sprinkle with grated chocolate.

Makes about sixteen tartlets. They should be served as soon after assembly as possible, but pastry and filling may be made separately ahead of time, then combined on day of serving.

PALMIERS

The name is French for "palm tree," and you'll see why with the shape of the finished pastries.

1 cup sifted all-purpose flour	Baking foil, aluminum
1 cup sweet butter, softened	Baking sheet, greased
Juice of 1 lemon and enough	Bowl, medium
cold water to make 1 cup	Juicer
¾ cup granulated sugar	Knife, small, sharp
	Measuring cups and spoons
	Rolling pin
	Sifter and medium bowl
	Wax paper, several sheets,
	floured

1. Sift the flour into one of the medium bowls and set aside.
2. Put butter into second medium bowl and knead about ⅙ cup of the flour into it to absorb the moisture in the butter. If still wet, add another spoonful or two of flour and work in.
3. Add enough of the lemon-water mixture to the sifted flour to make a

smooth dough of the same consistency as the butter mixture. This is very important. If the butter mixture is firm, so must the dough be and vice versa.

4. Knead the dough until it begins to feel elastic, then roll it into a square shape approximately ¼" thick.
5. Lightly mark an inner square about half the size of the whole square, then roll the outer edges so that they form relatively thin flaps.
6. Mold the floured butter into a square approximately the size of the inner square.
7. Place butter atop inner square and fold flaps over it, covering it completely. Cover with cloth and let rest for fifteen minutes.
8. Turn dough envelope over (flaps will now be underneath) and very carefully roll it to an oblong ¼" thick. Roll very slowly as butter must not break through the dough envelope.
9. Fold dough in three to form a rough square, turn it at a right angle.
10. Roll again into a ¼" thick oblong, fold in three, and turn again.
11. Wrap in foil and let rest for two hours.
12. Repeat steps 9 and 10, then let dough rest two more hours. Repeat and rest one final hour before using.
13. Preheat oven to 425° F.
14. Roll dough out carefully, ¼" thick, and trim the sheet to an 8" square. Mark a line across the middle to divide the dough into two equal rectangles.
15. Sprinkle generously with sugar, then fold sheet in from each side so that the edges meet on the middle line.
16. Sprinkle again with sugar and fold in half along middle line. You now have a flat dough roll.
17. Cut into ¾"-thick slices and place 1½" apart on baking sheets. Sprinkle with sugar.
18. Bake until golden brown, 12–15 minutes.

Makes twelve pastries. Will keep several days in an airtight container.

PETTICOAT TAILS

An old English pastry. Very light and good.

1¾ cups all-purpose flour, sifted	Baking sheet, greased
½ cup corn-oil margarine, cut into small pieces	Cake racks and metal spatula
	Cookie cutter, 1″–1½″ round
½ cup confectioners sugar, sifted	Fork and medium bowl
	Knife, small, sharp
1 egg, beaten	Measuring cups and spoons
	Plate, 6″ round
	Rolling pin
	Sifter
	Wax paper, flour-dusted

1. Preheat oven to 350° F.
2. Using fingertips, combine flour with margarine until mixture is mealy.
3. Lightly stir in sugar until evenly combined, then add egg to make a stiff dough.
4. Work firmly with hands until elastic ball is formed. Divide into three equal portions. Roll each portion to ⅛″ thickness.
5. To form Petticoat Tail shape, put 6″-round plate face down on dough and cut circle of dough. Remove plate, cut circle from center of larger circle using cookie cutter. Divide outer part into eight equal sections.
6. Place 1″ apart on baking sheet and bake until set, about 7 minutes. Petticoat Tails remain white, so do not wait for them to brown.
7. Remove at once from baking sheet to cake racks to cool.

Makes thirty-six 3″ Petticoat Tails. Will keep one week in an airtight container.

Book Jacket Recipes

Courtesy Thomas J. Lipton, Inc.

Sweet 'n Spicy Party Sandwiches

7 ounces water-packed tuna, drained and flaked	Bowl, medium, with cover
	Fork
¼ cup English walnuts, coarsely chopped	Herb mincer
	Knife, small, sharp, and cutting board
¼ cup sweet, spicy French dressing	Measuring cups and spoons
½ tablespoon chopped parsley	Nut chopper
4 (or 8) slices white sandwich bread, lightly toasted, with crusts removed	Spreader
	Toaster

1. Combine all ingredients except bread and chill in covered bowl.
2. Just before serving, toast bread and spread mixture on one side of 4 slices. If open-faced sandwiches are desired, simply quarter and serve. For regular tea sandwiches, top each sandwich with another piece of toast and cut into halves.
3. Serve at once.

Makes sixteen small, open-faced sandwiches or eight regular tea sandwiches.

TROPICAL TUNA CUPS

6 large oranges	Bowls, small and medium
7 ounces water-packed tuna, drained and flaked	Herb mincer
	Kitchen foil
1 cup finely chopped zucchini	Knife, small, sharp, and cutting board
½ cup Italian dressing	
2 tablespoons chopped parsley	Measuring cups and spoons

1. Cut off top one-third of each orange.
2. Remove pulp and chop enough of the pulp to equal 2 cups.
3. Combine pulp with tuna, zucchini, and Italian dressing, then fill each orange cup with mixture.
4. If not to be served at once, wrap in foil and place in refrigerator.
5. Just before serving, garnish with parsley.

Makes six Tuna Cups.

STRAWBERRY SUPREME

1½ pints fresh strawberries, hulled and sliced	Blender or food processor
	Bowl, large
1 envelope unflavored gelatin	Egg separator
¼ cup granulated sugar	Electric mixer, large bowl, and small bowl
2 eggs, separated	
⅔ cup milk	Measuring cups and spoons
½ cup heavy cream	Nut chopper
¼ cup blanched, slivered almonds	Saucepan, medium, and stirring spoon
6 ladyfingers	Springform pan, 6″ round

1. In blender or food processor, purée 1½ cups of the sliced strawberries; set aside.
2. In saucepan, combine gelatin with ⅛ cup sugar.
3. Meanwhile, add egg yolks to milk, then add to gelatin mixture.
4. Let stand one minute, then stir over low heat until gelatin is completely dissolved, about five minutes.
5. Stir in puréed strawberries, then pour into large bowl and chill, stirring occasionally, until mixture mounds slightly when dropped from a spoon.

6. In large bowl of electric mixer, beat egg whites until soft peaks form, then gradually add remaining sugar and beat until stiff. Set aside.
7. Beat cream until fluffy; set aside.
8. Fold egg whites into the gelatin, then fold in whipped cream, remaining sliced strawberries, and almonds.
9. Place ladyfingers, rounded side out, against sides of springform pan. Turn gelatin mixture into pan and chill until firm.
10. Serve as soon as removed from refrigerator.

Makes six servings.

PEACHY TEA PUNCH

Nice in summer or winter.

1 cup boiling water	Juicer
3 teaspoons black tea	Kettle
2⅞ cups peach nectar	Measuring cups and spoons
2 cups unsweetened pineapple juice	Saucepan, large, and stirring spoon
1½ cups orange juice	Tea strainer
¼ cup brown sugar, firmly packed	Teapot
3 whole cloves	
1½ cinnamon sticks, broken	
(Pineapple spears)	

1. In teapot pour boiling water over tea and brew 3 to 5 minutes. Strain tea leaves and discard, then set tea aside.
2. In saucepan, combine fruit juices, sugar, and spices, and cook over medium heat, stirring constantly, until sugar dissolves. Then reduce heat and simmer 10 minutes. Remove spices.
3. Add tea to juice mixture and heat thoroughly. If it is to be served in a punch powl, float pineapple spears in the liquid. If it is to be served in a warmed teapot, omit the spears.

Makes ten medium or six generous servings.

Marmalade Tea Treat

5 cups boiling water	Kettle
6 teaspoons black tea in tea ball	Measuring cups and spoons
or 6 regular-sized tea bags	Stirring spoon
½ cup orange marmalade	Teapot
2 tablespoons lemon juice	
2 tablespoons granulated sugar	
(Lemon or orange slices)	

1. In teapot, pour boiling water over tea and stir in orange marmalade.
2. Cover and brew 5 minutes, then remove tea ball or bags.
3. Stir in lemon juice and sugar.
4. Serve in warm teapot with a side dish of orange or lemon slices, if desired.

Makes eight medium servings.

Honey Spiced Tea

Good for a cold day.

4 cups boiling water	Measuring cups and spoons
6 teaspoons black tea	Stirring spoon
⅓ cup honey	Tea strainer
1 tablespoon lemon juice	Teapot
⅛ teaspoon ground allspice	
⅛ teaspoon ground nutmeg	
(Lemon slices)	

1. In teapot, pour boiling water over tea, cover, and brew 5 minutes. Strain out tea leaves.
2. Stir in remaining ingredients save for lemon slices and serve hot in teapot or in individual cups or mugs garnished with lemon slices.

Makes about six medium servings.

Mail-Order Sources for Tea and Coffee

Some of the following companies offer catalogues, some will provide price lists. For further information write directly to the supplier, enclosing a first-class stamp (International Reply Coupon in the case of the foreign concerns).

Anzen Pacific Corporation
P.O. Box 11407
Portland, Oregon 97211

Not a very descriptive price list, but an interesting and reasonably priced assortment of teas in loose and bag form, including some from Japan.

Bon Appetit
213 South 17th Street
Philadelphia, Pennsylvania 19103

Nice selection of coffees, including a Dutch Chocolate Almond bean that would be delicious for a winter tea.

313

J. Bradbury & Company, Inc.
P.O. Box 2366
Grand Central Station
New York, New York 10163

Good loose-tea selection, including Japanese Gyokuro. Also herb and flavored teas. A truly international coffee selection in whole-bean form. A most attractive catalogue.

Cheese Coffee Center
2115 Allston Way
Berkeley, California 94704

Over fifty teas, true and herb, including the intriguing Dragon's Well, Hibiscus Flowers, Lover's Leap, and Russian Caravan. Over forty-five coffees, with decaffeinated as well as straights and blends.

O. H. Clapp & Company, Inc.
47 Riverside Avenue
Westport, Connecticut 06880

A small number of high-priced, premium-quality vintage teas, including Rose Congou, a delicious rose-petal tea.

Conte Di Savoia
555 W. Roosevelt Road
Jeffro Plaza, Store #7
Chicago, Illinois 60607

Teas, loose and bag, as well as a variety of coffees in both bean and grind, including an Italian Aromatic with Cardamom (bean) and Kona (grind). Some cakes and candies that would be good for the emergency tea larder, including Panettone, Torrone, Panforte, and Amaretti.

The Daily Grind
P. O. Box 607C
Nashville, Indiana 47448

Bulk teas, also Fox Mountain herbal teas. Straight, blended, and decaffeinated coffee, including their own EKG blend of Colombian and Kilimanjara.

Egertons
Lyme Street
Axminster
Devon
England EX13 5DB

Quality teas from Kenya, China, India, and Ceylon, as well as several coffees. Interesting assortment of commercially prepared English tea treats, including Scottish Shortbread, Petticoat Tails, Ashbourne Gingerbread, "White Horse" Whisky Cake, Oatcakes, Dundee Cake, Madeira Cake, and Genoa Cake, as well as British candies. In the condiment line, the famous Elsenham preserves and Devon and Cornwall honey.

Fortnum & Mason Ltd.
Piccadilly
London
England W1A 1ER

A wide range of teas, of which their own Royal Blend is perhaps the best-known. Commercially prepared English tea treats—cakes, shortbreads, etc.—along with candies and preserves. When you're in London, this is *the* place to have tea.

Lekvar-by-the-Barrel
H. Roth & Son
1577 First Avenue
New York, New York 10028

Marvelous selection of spices, herbs, and herb teas. Also some true teas and cocoa. Imported marmalades and preserves, as well as dried and candied fruit.

Nichols Garden Nursery
1190 North Pacific Highway
Albany, Oregon 97321

From this wonderfully descriptive and informative catalogue you can buy herb seeds and plants, dried herbs, and a wide selection of fine herb teas.

Old North Church Gift Shop
193 Salem Street
Boston, Massachusetts 02113

Stage your own Boston Tea Party with tea from Davison Newman of London, "England's oldest teamen," ordered from the city of the original do. Best of all, the price list assures us that there is "NO TAX ON TEA!"

Paprikas Weiss Importer
1546 Second Avenue
New York, New York 10028

Teas, herb teas, fine cocoa, and a good coffee selection, including a winy Guatamela Antigua. A variety of goodies, including preserves, baked goods, and baking aids. Especially nice—Chinese cinnamon sticks for coffee and chocolate.

Schapira Coffee Company
117 West 10th Street
New York, New York 10011

Many fine teas, including their own special blend of rare India and China teas called Flavor Cup. Also especially interesting are Russian Blossom and Imperial Mandarin. Some herb teas. Both blended and unblended coffees, including their own Colombian blend: Flavor Cup. Interesting sidelight—these are the Schapiras who wrote the authoritative, eminently readable survey of tea and coffee, *The Book of Coffee and Tea* (New York: St. Martin's Press, 1975, paperback and hardback).

The Sensuous Bean
228 Columbus Avenue
New York, New York 10023

Some well-known tea brands, also more than a dozen loose teas, including their own Sensuous Blend. Reasonably priced loose coffees, including Kona, and will custom-blend at no extra charge.

Specialty Spice Shop
2757 152nd Avenue, N.E. #4
Redmond, Washington 98052

Known for Ruby Kutelonis's famous Market Spice Tea.

Simpson & Vail, Inc.
53 Park Place
New York, New York 10007

Nice assortment of blacks, greens, oolongs, as well as an interesting line of flavored teas, including Apple, Black Currant, Rum, Almond, and Chocolate Mint. Tea and coffee in attractive metal canisters, also tea bricks. A novel idea—Tea-of-the-Month and Coffee-of-the-Month, in which the participant is automatically sent a different tea or coffee each month. People with an evocative way of describing tea in their very informative material.

Uwajimaya
Sixth Avenue South and South King Street
Seattle, Washington 98104

Japanese and Chinese teas, as well as some interesting oriental confections.

The Vermont Country Store
Weston, Vermont 05161

Indian, Chinese, and Japanese teas, also several coffees ground to order. Nice assortment of jams, jellies, and marmalades. An unusual catalogue full of high-quality, old-fashioned merchandise.

Walnut Acres
Penns Creek, Pennsylvania 17862

A well-known supplier of fine organic and natural foods that offers an interesting assortment of herb teas in loose and bag form, as well as some intriguing coffee substitutes, including Malted Carob, Celestial Roasta-roma, and Instant Bambu.

Young & Saunders Ltd.
5 Queensferry Street
Edinburgh
Scotland EH2 4PD

Quality teas, including a Darjeeling De Luxe and Assam "Creamy Cup" No. 5. Straight and blended coffees from Africa, Central America, Ethiopia, Java, and India. Also traditional English and Scottish tea treats and preserves.

Metric Measure Conversion Table
(Approximations)

When You Know (U.S.)	Multiply by	To Find (Metric)
WEIGHT		
ounces	28	grams
pounds	0.45	kilograms
VOLUME		
teaspoons	5	milliliters
tablespoons	15	milliliters
fluid ounces	30	milliliters
cups	0.24	liters
pints	0.47	liters
quarts	0.95	liters
TEMPERATURE		
degrees Fahrenheit (°) F	subtract 32° and multiply the remainder by 5/9 or .556	degrees Celsius or Centigrade (°) C

Recipe Index

Index

Page numbers for illustrations are in bold face.
See also Recipe Index

Win-haus, 60
Worcester porcelain, 74, **93**

Yosai. *See* Eisai Myō-an
Young Hyson tea, 124

Zen Buddhism
 aesthetic concerns of, 22
 and Ashikaga shogunate, 29
 and Bodhidharma, 27
 and *cha-no-yu,* 22, 25–27, 29–30, 41,
  45, 53
 Eisai and, 25–26
 and introduction of tea to Japan,
  25–27
 and Kamakura shogunate, 25–27
 political position of, 26–27, 32, 34
 precepts of, 22, 26, 27, 45
 tea cultivation by monks of, 24, 26
 and tea drinking, 18, 22, 25–27, 58
 and Tokigawa shogunate, 41